The Sunday Telegraph

Guide to
Looking After Your Property

WHO IS JEFF HOWELL?

I first worked on building sites during summer vacations from university. I graduated in 1975 with a degree in Nuclear Engineering and the Philosophy of Science, which made me unemployable, so I carried on with the building site work. I did a bricklaying course at a government training centre, and spent most of the next twelve years as a full-time brickie. With my engineering and philosophy education, though, it was clear to me that a lot of what goes on in the construction industry is based more on witchcraft than science.

In 1989 I started teaching part-time at a building college in London, and I was in the right place at the right time when a lecturing job came up at South Bank Polytechnic. And when, shortly afterwards, the polytechnics were rebranded as universities, I was able to boast that I had gone from being a brickie to a university lecturer in two years.

In 1997 I got the chance to write a weekly column in the *Independent on Sunday*. Two years later the column moved to *The Sunday Telegraph*, and the 'Ask Jeff' readers' questions and answers section has made me aware of the many problems that householders have in getting building work done on their homes.

The Sunday Telegraph

Guide to
Looking After
Your Property

JEFF HOWELL

EBURY
PRESS

ACKNOWLEDGEMENTS

Many building colleagues have helped me to answer these questions. My special thanks go to Tony Poole and George Bennett of Mercury Plumbing and Heating, Dave Sims of DSE Electrical, Jay Webb of Fenestration Associates, Steve Bradford, Mike O'Leary, Peter O'Shea, Brian Cathcart, David Hewett, Paul Morris, Stephen Boniface and Eddie Bennett.

Thanks also to all the staff on *The Sunday Telegraph* Home & Living section who have helped make the Ask Jeff feature such a success, and to Jack Scott, former editor of *Building Engineer*, who was the first person to pay me for writing anything.

1 3 5 7 9 10 8 6 4 2

Original edition published by Macmillan in 2002
This edition published in 2008 by Ebury Press, an imprint of Ebury Publishing

A Random House Group Company

The Random House Group Limited Reg. No. 954009

Addresses for companies within the Random House Group can be found at www.rbooks.co.uk

A CIP catalogue record for this book is available from the British Library

The Random House Group Limited makes every effort to ensure that the papers used in our books are made from trees that have been legally sourced from well-managed and credibly certified forests. Our paper procurement policy can be found on www.randomhouse.co.uk

To buy books by your favourite authors and register for offers visit www.rbooks.co.uk

Printed and bound in Singapore by Tien Wah Press

ISBN 9780091922832

CONTENTS

ILLUSTRATION ACKNOWLEDGEMENTS

p14 © Andy Hall

p18 © Society for the Protection of Ancient Buildings

p23 © Dennis Gilbert/View

p36 © BonaKemi Limited

p43 courtesy of www.chimneycare.co.uk

p47 © ARUP

p51 © Everest Ltd

pp58, 59 *Double-glazing units: a BRE guide to improved durability* © BRE

p69 Pictures courtesy of *Professional Electrician and Installer Magazine*

p73 courtesy of F L Patents

pp120, 125 © Strippers Paint Removers

pp124, 174 © David Hoffman Photo Library

pp133, 175 © Abbey Independent Surveys

pp151, 183, 190, 192 courtesy of BRE

p153 *Thermal Insulation: avoiding risks* © BRE

p155 © Kingspan Insulation

p157 © Annette Everett

p162 courtesy of Selectaglaze Ltd. of St Albans, www.selectaglaze.co.uk

p.163 *Improving Sound Insulation in Homes* © BRE

p168 © Garden Matters

p179 © Ellen Rooney/the Garden Picture Library

p186 © Paul Bennett

p202 © Artex-Rawlplug, www.artex-rawlplug.co.uk

p211 © Bat Protection Trust

p213 © RSPB

All line drawings © Jim Robbins

All other pictures © Jeff Howell

A NOTE ON MEASUREMENTS

The British construction industry has officially used the metric system of measurement since 1970. This puts it in line with engineering and farming, but at odds with estate agents and euro-sceptic politicians. The only comment I would make on this is that the metric system is not a fiendish plot by the European Union, but the official system in most Commonwealth and former Eastern Bloc countries and much of the developing world. The metric system is an attempt to harmonize a worldwide system of measurement. Although it is not without its faults, it is simpler and less prone to error than the old imperial system. To avoid ambiguity, the British construction industry uses millimetres, rather than metres and centimetres, and on construction drawings you will often find that the comma after thousands and the 'mm' after all measurements are omitted. So a town house is 5500 wide, a door opening is 2100 high, and a kitchen worktop is 600 deep. The style used in this book is that where a reader's letter uses imperial measurements, these are left as written, and the metric equivalents added in brackets. My answers are written using metric. Readers who feel a need to translate metric into imperial are advised to forget about complicated conversion formulae and instead to compare the figures on either side of a tape measure. You'll soon get the hang of it. For easy reference, the nearest equivalents are:

> 25mm = 1 inch
> 50mm = 2 inches
> 75mm = 3 inches
> 100mm = 4 inches
> 150mm = 6 inches
> 300mm = 12 inches
> and 1 metre = 39 inches, or 3 feet 3 inches.

For weights, a kilogram is just over two pounds and 50 kilograms is roughly a hundredweight. A metric tonne (1000 kilograms) is about the same as an imperial ton.

For temperatures, I have been thinking in degrees Celsius (or Centigrade) for so long that I find Fahrenheit (which is not an English system, but a Prussian one) confusing. In Celsius, water freezes at 0 and boils at 100, 20 is a comfortable temperature indoors, 30 is too hot to go out in the sun without a hat, 37 is blood temperature, and 60 is the recommended British Standard temperature for hot water.

INTRODUCTION

Buying and maintaining a home is the greatest single item of expenditure in most people's lives, but the average person embarks upon home ownership with surprisingly little idea about how to look after their prize investment.

Within living memory, most British people lived in rented accommodation, with repairs and maintenance being the responsibility of the landlord – whether private or local authority. Those who did buy their own homes usually managed it only after first saving up for years with a building society, so that when they did finally become homeowners, they had already rented for years and had some idea of the dos and don'ts of property care.

But since the deregulation of the financial sector in the 1980s, it has become easier for anyone with an income to buy a home rather than rent one and many people now buy houses and flats having never really thought about the responsibility this carries. And whilst the estate agents and mortgage lenders are keen to tell first-time buyers how much money they can borrow as a multiple of their earnings, they rarely mention that an additional sum of between 1 and 5 per cent of the value of the property they are buying will need to be spent every year to keep it in good order.

In an ideal world, homeowners would engage the professionals – chartered surveyors – to advise them and to arrange and supervise building work. But most people are unwilling to pay the fees involved. Quite often this is because they are so unimpressed by the performance of surveyors during the first and only contact they have with them, which is during the home-buying process itself. The average surveyor doing a mortgage valuation or Homebuyer Survey gives a passable impression of someone who doesn't want to get the knees of his suit dirty, doesn't want to commit himself on anything about the property and simply issues a list of things that should be looked at by other 'experts'.

Into this breach leap the companies and individuals offering 'free' surveys. Homeowners never seem to realize that this is nothing more than a crude marketing trick. And whilst people complain about the difficulty of finding a decent builder, there is never any shortage of advertisements for 'quick-fix' solutions for leaky roofs, draughty windows and damp walls. In fact, the first experience that most homeowners have of this end of the building industry is when their mortgage-valuation survey report instructs them to invite estimates for 'treatment' from damp-proofing and timber-treatment companies. In reality, rising damp only occurs in pre-1877 houses standing in swamps, most woodworm holes date from before the First World War, and dry rot is cured by mending the gutters. But once given the green light by the surveyor's report, these companies are quick to find 'evidence' of rising damp, woodworm and dry rot and to specify remedial chemical treatment available from themselves.

There is a clear conflict of interests in having these so-called problems diagnosed and treated by the same companies, but the Royal Institution of Chartered Surveyors (RICS) will do nothing to stop its members from directing their unsuspecting clients down this route.

There are many other unnecessary, damaging or bogus building treatments and gadgets that are mis-sold to the public, ranging from foam roof undercoatings to external wall coverings. Many of them are sold on the promise of 'zero maintenance' by companies whose only interest is in a quick profit. Some of these businesses are even 'phoenix' companies, who offer twenty-year guarantees for their useless products and then liquidate every year to avoid responsibility for failed work, setting up again with slightly altered company names. And because consumer-protection legislation is practically non-existent in the UK, there is nothing at all illegal about any of this.

Even if you do know a trained, competent, conscientious builder, always remember that all building problems are liable to be mis-diagnosed if you turn to the wrong tradesman. After all, a carpenter will usually seek a solution that involves timber; a plasterer will suggest plaster, and a decorator will want to cover it up and paint it.

A recurrent theme in readers' letters is, 'I have been told that my x, y or z needs replacing – what do you think?' The missing information in these questions is: told by *whom*? Because if it was by somebody who was trying to sell you the replacement, the chances are that their opinion was not objective.

Of particular concern in this respect is the role of the privatized utilities, such as British Gas Services. Many people still refer to British Gas as the 'Gas Board', and assume that if the British Gas Three Star Service engineer tells them that their boiler needs replacing, he is doing so out of a sense of public duty. But British Gas Services is now a private company, owned by the Centrica Corporation, and it is in business to make a profit.

The most common question that I get asked is, 'How can I find a decent builder?' But in many cases this is the wrong question. What the homeowner should really be asking is, 'What building work does my home need, and what is the best way of getting it done?' This book is for anybody seeking the answers. Over the past eight years I have received over 11,000 readers' questions, and what follows is a selection of answers to the most common ones.

STRUCTURES & MATERIALS

Most readers' queries about structural matters concern the removal of internal walls, and the difference between a load-bearing wall and a non-load-bearing wall. There is no mystery to this; if an internal wall has something resting on top of it – floor joists, ceiling joists or another wall – then it is load-bearing, and it would be unwise to remove or cut holes in it. However, the vogue for open-plan living means that some people will always be determined to buy old houses and rip the guts out of them. Many thousands of Victorian terraced houses have had the central spine wall knocked through at ground-floor level; this used to be done by leaving two nibs or piers of brickwork at the sides and sliding in an RSJ (Rolled Steel Joist) to pick up the floor joists above. Rather belatedly it became clear that by concentrating the load on the two nibs, there was a chance of settlement, causing cracking damage right up the house, and possibly to neighbouring properties as well. So the preferred method now is to insert a rigid steel frame, which spreads the load right across the original span. There are plenty of cowboy builders around who still prefer to use the old RSJ trick, though.

But it should not be assumed that because a wall is non-load-bearing it can be knocked through or removed with impunity. Internal partition walls provide soundproofing, thermal insulation, can prevent fire from spreading and, in older houses, they may also have a bracing or stabilizing effect on the side walls (see also CHIMNEYS, chimney breast removal).

Also remember that if you turn two rooms into one, then you lose the wall space for bookshelves and furniture. And, because of the strange way in which British estate agents value property, a house with fewer rooms might even be worth less.

A rolled-steel joist (RSJ) is often used to support floor joists when a wall is removed.

LOAD-BEARING WALLS 1

Q My flat is the top two floors of a Victorian terraced house, and I would like to knock out the separating wall between two lower rooms to form a through lounge/diner. The partition wall is only timber and plaster, but my builder says it is a load-bearing wall. Can this be true?

A Yes. The wall between the front and back rooms in these types of houses is called the 'spine wall', and, although it is of timber construction, it supports the weight of the floors and the roof above and contains internal diagonal bracing which strengthens the whole building. If the bracing is cut through or removed then there could be serious structural movement. This type of wall should only be removed or altered under supervision from a qualified structural engineer.

LOAD-BEARING WALLS 2

Q Is there a simple way of identifying a load-bearing wall? I want to remove part of the internal wall between my kitchen and dining room. There is no wall directly above and the joists run parallel to the one I want to remove, which is made of concrete aggregate blocks. Two builders have told me it isn't load-bearing but I just want to make sure.

A If you are confident that there is no load on it, then, by definition, it isn't load-bearing. However, depending on the age of the house, there is a possibility that this wall may be providing a bracing or tying effect on the outside walls, so you really should seek professional confirmation before undertaking any work. Also, this wall will be performing other functions, such as fire-stopping, soundproofing and thermal insulation. You may wish to consider what effect these changes might have on the rest of the house before you knock through.

LOADS ON FLOORS

Q We have a large collection of books spread through most rooms of our house and anyone who has tried to lift a pile of books will know how heavy they are. In addition, our grandchildren, staying overnight, have recently found that jumping off their beds makes the floor bounce most satisfactorily! What are the normal weight limits for bedroom floors? Our house was built in 1973 with brick-and-block walls.

A Your 1973 house will have been built to the Building Regulations of the day, and the floors should be able to support at least 150kg per square metre. So a 4m x 5m room will be able to carry a load of 3000kg or 3 tonnes. If the books are spread across the floor, though, they may cause bending of the joists, and cracking of the plaster ceiling below. It would be preferable to concentrate the load near the ends of the joists – i.e. bookcases against the front and back walls. The same principle applies to the grandchildren.

CHANGING ROOM LAYOUTS

Q In 1930s semi-detached houses such as ours the kitchens are too small for all mod cons and there is no room under the stairs for a toilet. The house itself is big enough for our needs and we do not want to build an extension. Is it possible to alter the layout of the ground floor/staircase to provide the areas we need?

A It is always possible to change rooms around, but you need to take care. Non-load-bearing partitions are easy to remove; with load-bearing walls it is much more difficult – and expensive. Moving a staircase is also usually a fairly complicated procedure and I would have thought that there is an easier way to install a downstairs WC than moving the staircase. A good architect – preferably one with engineering skills – will be able to advise you on what is possible [ARCHITECTS, SURVEYORS & ENGINEERS].

STRENGTH OF JOISTS

Q I would like to make a storage area in my loft. The ceiling joists are 3in x 2in (75mm x 50mm). Would I need to strengthen them or not?

A Many older houses were built with 75mm x 50mm ceiling joists over the upper rooms, and whilst these are capable of supporting the weight of the ceiling and a few suitcases and boxes of Christmas decorations, they should not be loaded with too much else. (Having said that, many homes have 250-litre water storage tanks resting across two 75mm x 50mm ceiling joists!) Current Building Regulations require much more substantial timbers; 75mm x 50mm ceiling joists would only be allowed to span 1.4m, and if you wanted to use the loft as a habitable room then you would need to add at least 150mm x 50mm joists, which would allow you to span 3.5m. So the short answer is, it depends how much weight you want to store up there. The Loft Shop [LOFT CONVERSIONS] supply a free guide to loft conversions and the Building Regulations, and a leaflet answering frequently asked questions.

LOFT CONVERSIONS

Q My house has an open-plan living/dining area containing the staircase – i.e. there is no hallway. Is it true that if I have a loft conversion done I will need to reinstate the hallway for Building and Fire Regulations approval? Would it not be OK as long as the loft window is easy to get out of?

A If you turn a two-storey dwelling into a three-storey one by adding a loft conversion, you must provide a protected fire escape route from the loft down to the front door. This means having the staircase and hallway encased in a one-hour fire-protected enclosure (either masonry or plasterboard), with all doors adjoining this enclosure being self-closing.

Deeper joists must be added to turn a ceiling into a floor.

LOFT CONVERSION RULES

Q What are the possibilities of doing a conversion, with flooring, lighting, wall cladding, window, safety ladder etc., without obtaining planning permission, as 'storage plus study room' but actually using it as a spare bedroom for my three sons, age thirteen, eleven and nine?

A Most loft conversions do not need planning permission. The exceptions are houses in conservation areas, those that involve raising the height of the existing roof, those that have dormer windows facing the road, or if the house has already been extended to the limit of its permitted development (usually 15 per cent of its original size). There is no regulation governing minimum headroom. However, it would be very foolish to allow children to sleep in a loft conversion which did not comply with the fire and access requirements of the Building Regulations.

LOFT CONVERSION IN MODERN HOUSE

Q I own a six-year-old detached villa. It is timber-frame construction with brick outer walls. I need another bedroom but the roof is of modern construction with a 'lattice' of timbers joined together. Am I correct in thinking that this makes it virtually impossible to convert the roof space into a bedroom?

A Doing a loft conversion in a modern roof is by no means impossible, although it is clearly more complicated than in an older house with traditional rafters. Modern roof trusses are designed to make construction cheap and simple for builders, by using thin sections of timber, prefabricated in factories. In order to make space for a bedroom, the criss-crossing struts and ties will have to be cut out and replaced with an alternative load-bearing structure. One method is to strengthen the floor by spanning between the end walls with steel beams, and to use vertical timber studwork to pick up the weight of the rafters. This may sound complicated, but it is a fairly standard procedure and a loft conversion is usually the most cost-effective way of creating space in a house.

CONCRETE CORROSION

Q My 1960s cavity-wall bungalow has a reinforced concrete surround to the kitchen window. Some years ago there was water penetration above the window, and the reinforcement has rusted, causing the concrete to split. I regularly scrape out the splits and refill them with several different types of filler, none of which lasts for more than a season. Is there any combination of treatment of the reinforcement and filler that would be longer lasting or permanent? I naturally wish to avoid having the window and surround removed and replaced.

A When reinforced concrete is new, the alkalinity of the cement prevents the steel from rusting. But over the years it absorbs carbon dioxide from the atmosphere and becomes acidic. The steel inevitably rusts, expands and splits the concrete. This phenomenon can be seen all over the place on old concrete lamp posts, fence posts, bollards and park benches. Repair is a specialist job (see 'Concrete Repairs' in the Yellow Pages) involving re-alkalizing the concrete, coating the steel reinforcement with resin and bonding new concrete to the surface. It is unlikely to be economically viable in the case of one window surround.

SHALLOW FOUNDATIONS

Q My late 1920s semi-detached house has been well maintained and has no dampness or cracking. My worry is that it is built directly on to the soil, and that if a surveyor stated there was trouble with the foundations this would be off-putting to a potential buyer. Would I have to add a concrete raft or underpinning before I sell the property and what would this entail?

A Modern houses are routinely built on deep concrete foundations, but this is because they are built using brittle cement mortar which cracks at the slightest movement. Older houses such as yours were built with softer lime mortar and are able to withstand slight ground movement without cracking. There is no reason to apply modern construction practices retrospectively to well-built older properties and no surveyor worth his salt will suggest that the foundations of your house are inadequate.

BRICKWORK & MASONRY

Brick walls are one of the mainstays of building construction down the ages. The historical principle is simple. If you lived in a part of the world where there were a lot of trees (which included most of Britain until the sixteenth century) then you built your walls with wood. If there was no wood but you had access to broken stone, then you built your walls with stone. If you had neither of those, then it was probably because you lived on clay, as is the case in most of Central and Southern England and the Low Countries. These areas have a history of building with raw earth, and many examples survive, such as the cob houses of the West Country and the clay lump buildings of East Anglia.

But it had been known since Greek and Roman times that if you fired the clay in a kiln then you got a more hard-wearing material. At first this was used only to make clay roof tiles, but as kiln techniques got more sophisticated it became possible to produce large quantities of burnt clay bricks. Following the Great Fire of 1666, the London Building Acts required all new buildings to have brick walls – something that continued, throughout the country, until the re-introduction of timber-framed buildings in the 1980s.

plaster

flemish bond brickwork

skirting

joist

air brick

slate DPC

sleeper walls

stepped footing

SOLID BRICK WALL

Brick construction reached its peak in the eighteenth and nineteenth centuries, and many of the surviving brick terraced houses that still make up around 50 per cent of our housing stock were built with a skill and attention to detail that we may never see again. The twentieth century saw the introduction of the cavity wall, first built with two leaves of brickwork connected by wrought-iron ties, and later with an inner leaf of various types of lightweight concrete blocks. These are referred to by lay-people as 'breeze blocks' but are actually made from lightweight expanded clay aggregates (LECA) or aerated pulverized fuel ash (PFA).

Since the 1980s we have seen the introduction of insulation materials into the cavity. This has made the building of brick walls ever more difficult, and, coinciding with a drastic reduction in the availability of skilled bricklayers, means that modern brick houses are often built very badly. So, whilst a Victorian brick-built house remains a sound investment, one built since the Second World War may be hosting many problems.

Older brick houses are often spoilt by having the surface of the mortar joints (the 'pointing') replaced with sand-and-cement. This is harder than the original sand-and-lime mortar and can cause many problems. If there is any movement in the brickwork then the new pointing will be unable to move with it and this can result in cracking damage to the bricks; and because sand-and-cement is impermeable to moisture, the mortar will be unable to breathe, concentrating moisture evaporation in the bricks, which may then lose their faces through frost damage or salt crystallization. Damaging repointing is a classic example of misunderstanding the nature of traditional building materials. Our forebears understood that the pointing between the bricks was a sacrificial material, which served its purpose by being gradually worn away, to be replaced every half century or so. But today, when surveyors or builders see weathered pointing, they see it as a defect and think it would be better to replace it with a more hard-wearing material.

Lime mortar is easy to make and use. The only problem is trying to find a bricklayer prepared to use it. There is a common myth amongst builders that lime-and-sand mortar will not harden unless cement is mixed into it. This is simply not true, and once you get a brickie to try using sand-and-lime, you will probably have a convert on your hands.

MORTAR FOR POINTING STONE WALLS

Q What is the best mortar mix for pointing old stone walls? A quarrying firm says they find the best mix for the area is 1 part hydrated lime/1 part cement/1 part sand (theirs). This seems much too strong to us. Some pointing on our old stone house has been done with a strong cement mix, which appears to have affected some stones, causing a sponge-like appearance full of small holes.

A You are right – strong cement mixes can be very damaging to old stonework. Because the mortar is impermeable, it means that any evaporation must take place at the surface of the stone, causing salt efflorescence and frost damage. A more suitable mix would be 1 part hydrated lime: 4 parts washed coarse sharp sand – and absolutely no cement at all.

WRONG COLOUR MORTAR

Q We have put a deposit on a new house and visited the site to check progress. On one of the outside walls there is a strip of approximately twelve courses of bricks where the mortar is a different colour from the rest. The site foreman says that it will weather in time and blend in with the rest. Is he right?

A Different-coloured mortar indicates a different mix, and therefore a lack of quality control by the main contractor. On most newbuild sites the mortar arrives ready-mixed from a specialist supplier. A different colour usually indicates a batch knocked-up on site by the brickies' labourer. This may or may not have structural implications, but is not the quality that most people would expect from a new house.

MORTAR PLASTICIZER

Q The plans for our new extension, currently under construction, specify that the mortar is to be '6:1:1 building sand/hydrated lime/ordinary Portland cement, incorporating a suitable plasticizing additive'. I have seen 5-litre containers of 'mortar plasticizer' at the local builders' merchants, but the bricklayer insists on using my washing-up liquid instead. He says it is the same as plasticizer, only cheaper. Is this true?

A Mortar plasticizer works by lowering the surface tension of the water, so that the mortar will 'flow' without it being too wet and dribbling down the brickwork. Proper plasticizers are based on lignin, an organic substance extracted from wood. Washing-up detergent will certainly make the mortar flow, but it can also contain other undesirable ingredients, such as salt, which will corrode metal wall ties and may emerge as efflorescence on the surface of the finished wall.

NEED FOR REPOINTING?

Q Our semi-detached bungalow is thirty-four years old. Three neighbours have had their brickwork repointed although there seemed to be nothing wrong with it. When is repointing needed, and should it be an all-over job or done in patches?

A It seems unlikely that a thirty-four-year-old property would need repointing, and your neighbours may have been victims of over-enthusiastic builders or surveyors, who often specify repointing in survey reports. Odd patches of brickwork may sometimes be exposed to extreme weather conditions or water leaks which erode the mortar, and these areas should be repointed, but under normal conditions a house should not need repointing for sixty to 100 years. The pointing should be considered as a sacrificial medium which gradually erodes away, leaving the bricks intact, and over-enthusiastic repointing with strong mortars is responsible for a lot of damage.

REPOINTING: MODERN MORTAR

Q Most ready-mixed mortars sold in DIY stores dry to a grey colour. Most houses have beige mortar. Which mix (with or without cement) would match this colour? Would builders' merchants sell this mix in small amounts – of 10kg (or less) for instance?

A The grey colour comes from a high proportion of cement, which is probably mixed with a washed sharp sand. This mix is intended for patch repairs to renders and floor screeds, and is not generally suitable for brickwork repairs or repointing. The colour of the 'beige' mortar used in most post-war housing comes from the impurities (mostly clay) in soft 'building' sand, which is used in a 6:1:1 sand/cement/lime mix. You are unlikely to be able to buy this ready-mixed from a builders' merchants, although you may be able to persuade a builder to give you a bucketful.

POINTING OLD BRICKWORK

Q The previous owners of our property stripped the plaster off the chimney breast to expose the bricks. The brickwork is generally in very good condition and pleasant to the eye. But there are two problems: firstly, the lime mortar tends to crumble, giving off a continuous film of dust; and secondly, the previous owners had some repairs carried out with cement mortar which is completely different in colour and texture from the original and looks ghastly. We want to cut out the new mortar (we have tried a hammer and chisel to no avail so now intend to resort to an angle grinder) and would like to replace it with something as similar as possible to the remainder of the hearth and chimney breast.

Would you please advise what materials we need for the mortar and whether they are obtainable from builders' merchants or another source. Also, is it possible to seal the lime mortar pointing so that it retains its appearance but is less dusty?

A You should understand that your chimney breast was never meant to be exposed like this. It is not face brickwork, and the reason why the mortar is crumbling is that it was not finished off with a proper tooled joint, as it was always intended that it would be plastered. If you really want to keep the brickwork exposed, then you should rake out the mortar and repoint it with a 4:1 sand/lime mix, using washed, coarse sharp sand and hydrated lime, both available from most builders' merchants. Put the wet mortar in buckets, or cover with a plastic sheet, and leave to mature for at least 24 hours before using it. You can use this to replace the sections built with cement mortar as well.

To stop the exposed brickwork giving off dust, there are several types of resin- or polymer-based sealants sold in builders' merchants. Note that you want a masonry sealant and not an exterior water repellent [e.g. Watco Wallseal – BRICKWORK]. Any type of sealant is likely to darken the colour of the bricks and mortar, so try a small area first to see what it looks like.

REMOVING CEMENT POINTING

Q Having read around about pointing I am still confused about what to use. I have a 1930s semi built from Leamington brick. Previously repointed with cement mortar, some weaker bricks are spalling. The old mortar feels crumbly and is light brown, unlike modern cement mortar. Should I repoint the damaged bits with 1:1:6 (lime/cement/sharp sand)? If I remove the spalled material from the brick face will the brickwork be OK or has it been irreparably damaged?

A Old brickwork damaged by hard cement pointing is a real problem. There seems to be hardly a house left in the country that has not already been repointed using this damaging material, and

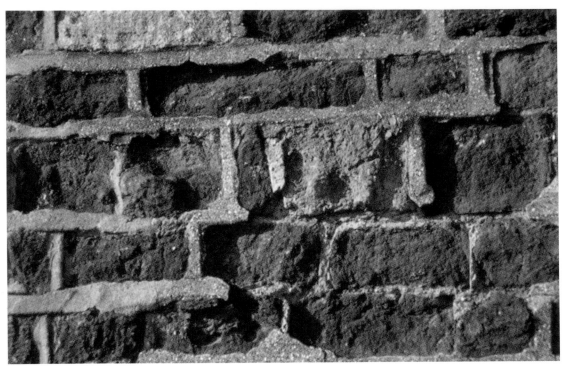

Hard cement pointing can hasten the deterioration of old brickwork.

surveyors and builders continue to specify and use it. Since some of your bricks have already spalled, it is likely that others will spall in the future, so the best thing would be to remove all the cement mortar and repoint with lime. Cement mortar can be removed cleanly using a diamond-covered 'Easy Raker' [BRICKWORK]. Bricks that are already damaged will have to be cut out and replaced since, having lost the fire skin from their faces, they will suffer from further weathering.

Lime mortar can be made using bagged hydrated lime and sharp sand, both available from builders' merchants. Try a mix of 4:1 sand/lime and do a small area first, to check for colour and consistency. Mix it dry, then add the water, cover it over with plastic sheeting (or in buckets) and leave it for at least 24 hours before remixing and using.

HYDRATED LIME OR HYDRAULIC LIME?

Q My local builders' merchants has told me that I should use hydraulic lime and not hydrated lime for pointing mortar. My house is 130 years old.

A Hydraulic lime is a kind of natural cement. It sets quickly by reacting with water and, like cement, it is too hard and too impermeable for repointing old brickwork. Hydrated lime, on the other hand, is a semi-slaked version of traditional lime putty. It sets slowly, by absorbing carbon dioxide from the atmosphere, and makes a softer, more breathable mortar, the same as that used to build your nineteenth-century walls. Hydrated lime is the correct material.

BRICK MATCHING

Q My neighbour is having a rear extension built. The houses are terraced, but staggered, so that part of the neighbour's side wall protrudes into my garden. I did not object to the planning application, because it said that the bricks used for the extension would match those in the existing house wall. But now the building has started, and the builders are using totally different coloured bricks. They have told me that since the houses are twenty years old, 'You can't get these bricks any more.' I have got to look at these different coloured sections of wall from my garden, and I am afraid it may affect the value of my property. Do I have any rights over this?

A   If the Planning Consent was granted on the condition that matching bricks were to be used, then they must be used. You should contact the local-authority Planning Department immediately and tell them that the building is in breach of the Planning Consent. All bricks can be matched, whether they are twenty years old or 120 years old, either from existing stock or specially made to match. The Brick Information Service [BRICKWORK] can provide details of brick merchants who provide a brick-matching service.

SPALLED BRICKS

Q   We have a north-facing end wall on our Victorian semi. Numerous bricks have lost their faces and previous owners have repaired some of these with cement. We have had a visit from a company who would use a fibreglass render and protective top coat. They give a twenty-year guarantee but have quoted £4,500. Someone else has said that ordinary rendering or pebbledash holds the wet in and is likely to break off, so shouldn't be used. What should we do?

A   All external renderings and coatings trap moisture behind them and stop walls from breathing. The modern versions are more expensive and more damaging, and the twenty-year 'guarantees' are meaningless. Spend your money on repairing the wall properly, by having the damaged bricks cut out and replaced, using lime mortar to match the original. It is likely that recent cement pointing has probably caused most of the spalling damage in the first place.

FROST-DAMAGED BRICKS

Q   After a period of wet weather followed by frost, some of the brickwork on my three-year-old house is flaking. This applies particularly to the bricks with smoother faces, those in brick-on-edge sills, and those near ground level, where the rain is splashing up off concrete paving. Is there some way of waterproofing the brickwork with a clear liquid during a warm, dry spell to prevent this flaking in frost?

A   No. Whatever the manufacturers' claims, external waterproofing compounds are at best ineffective and at worst can exacerbate the problem by trapping water in the brickwork. The spalling you describe is really a design problem, because the bricks used clearly are not of suitable quality to cope with the exposure conditions. Badly damaged bricks should be cut out and replaced, using frost-resistant new bricks (they should have an 'F' classification under British Standard BS3921, which means they can withstand freezing even when saturated).

EFFLORESCENCE

Q   The boundary wall of my house is thirty years old but in good condition. However, over the years unsightly white powdery patches have appeared. I have tried removing these – by scrubbing with water, vigorous application of a wire brush and attack with a high-pressure water jet – but all to no avail. Have you any suggestions please?

A   The photographs you have sent me show that your boundary wall is affected by efflorescence. This is caused by salts migrating to the surface of the brickwork in moisture and being deposited there when the moisture evaporates. Efflorescence is usually harmless and is nothing more than lime (calcium carbonate) being leached out of the mortar. It is an indication of the passage of moisture, and if it were in a wall of the house it might be something to get worried about, but since it is in a boundary wall, constantly wetted by rainwater, it is really not a problem. Paradoxically, your attempts to clean the efflorescence off by scrubbing and pressure-washing might be making the situation worse, because by introducing extra water into the wall, you are hastening the migration of salts to the surface of the brickwork. The best solution is to wait for a spell of dry weather and gently brush off the efflorescence with a soft brush.

CLEANING BRICKWORK

Q Have you any suggestions for removing ivy roots from brickwork? Once the ivy is stripped the root tendrils stay put.

A You are right to remove ivy from your brickwork, as it can cause serious damage. The tendrils cling to the surface, but ivy can also form secondary roots in the mortar joints, which will push the bricks apart. The remains of the tendrils will weather off naturally after a few years, but if you are impatient, try brick cleaning acid from any builders' merchants.

STONE REPAIRS

Q We have recently moved into an 1890s sandstone Edinburgh house. Below a bay window there are a couple of areas where the sandstone has started to spall and created a route for moisture ingress. There are signs of previous small cement repairs and I'm keen to do something to prevent further spalling when the winter freezes start. I am resisting the temptation for an (almost) sandstone-coloured coating that some neighbours are vandalizing their houses with!

A Once sandstone has started to delaminate, there is really nothing that can be done to repair it. Covering the damaged areas with cement-based mortar is at best a short-term cosmetic solution, which might actually hasten decay and cause dampness problems by trapping moisture behind it. The best course of action would be to have the damaged sections cut out and replaced by an experienced stonemason, which is a fairly common procedure in Edinburgh. Your local-authority Building Conservation Officer should be able to advise.

STONE CLEANING

Q We live in a limestone terrace, built 1899, and the stonework is very dirty after 100-plus years of soot, pollution, etc. Various of our neighbours have had the fronts of their properties sand-blasted and, since the process also scours out large amounts of crumbling mortar, have also had them repointed. It all looks very nice and we would like to do the same. However, I would like to know if this method of cleaning is good for the stonework and whether special mortar should be used for the repointing.

A Sand-blasting is a very destructive process, and should never be used to clean stone or brick buildings. It 'cleans' by removing the top surface of the material, equivalent to maybe fifty or 100 years' worth of natural weathering. It is analogous to cleaning the human body by stripping off the skin. The repointing that your neighbours have had done is likely to be equally destructive, as it will no doubt be done with hard cement mortar, rather than lime-and-sand to match the existing mortar. The process your neighbours have paid for is likely to have reduced the life-expectancy of their properties.

There are various sympathetic techniques for cleaning old stone and brick buildings, using solvents, steam or simply washing. These are likely to leave the original pointing largely intact, and any damaged areas should be made good with lime mortar. For further advice contact Stonehealth [BRICKWORK].

BRICKWORK & MASONRY

DECAYING SANDSTONE

Q The sandstone of my 120-year-old terraced house is now very friable. Would painting on a silicone water sealant delay further deterioration?

A No. If anything, it might make things worse by trapping moisture in the stonework and stopping it from breathing. Unfortunately, soft sandstone starts to deteriorate from the moment it is quarried, and exposure to the prevailing weather and traffic pollution speeds up the process. The traditional way of stabilizing sandstone (used successfully on churches up until the 1900s) was to apply an annual coat of limewater – the water that separates out on top of a bucket of limewash. This soaks in and binds the stone, but still allows it to breathe.

RETAINING WALLS

Q I have a path around the back of my bungalow, edged with a brick wall about 20 inches (500mm) high holding back the lawn. During heavy rainfall, water ponds near the wall and presumably adds to the pressure on it. There are cracks between the bricks and I'm sure that some water seeps out through them, relieving the pressure. Should I leave things as they are, or have the cracks pointed, which would presumably strengthen the wall but increase the pressure of the water and earth behind it?

A A retaining wall should really have weep-holes along the bottom edge to allow water to drain out on to the path. You could form these by cutting out a few joints with a chisel, or drilling some big holes with a masonry bit. However, these will only be really effective if a full-depth trench behind the wall is back-filled with gravel, to allow the ground to drain. And if you are going to go to the trouble of digging out the earth, then instead of weep-holes, you may as well install a length of perforated land drain, wrapped in geotextile, bedded on and back-filled with pea shingle, and extended off to drain to a lower level at one or both sides. This should take the pressure off the retaining wall and remove the puddles of water from the lawn as well. Land drain pipes and geotextiles can be bought from drainage contractors, agricultural merchants and garden centres.

REPLACING WALL TIES

Q I have bought a 1930s house and my mortgage survey has recommended cavity wall-tie replacement. I understand this is commonplace on any house purchase without an up-to-date guarantee against it, whether there is any sign of deterioration or not. I was told this would cost around £1000 but have had a survey done by the only local company and have been quoted nearer £3000. Do I need to get this work done, would it affect my insurance if I don't, and how can I source any companies that may operate in my area?

A Your mortgage-valuation surveyor has not inspected the state of your wall ties, so he has done you a disservice by recommending their replacement. He would have been entitled to recommend that you have the wall ties properly inspected, but he is not qualified to recommend that you undertake the considerable expense – and possible structural risks – of wall-tie replacement.

Cavity walls were first introduced in the early nineteenth century, with the inner and outer leaves of brickwork tied together using cast-iron ties. In dry conditions, these have good corrosion resistance and there is no need to assume that because the ties are old, they will necessarily be rusty. Wrought iron was then introduced, and used between 1850 and 1920. This has also performed well and is showing little corrosion. It is estimated that wall-tie failure will be found in only 15 per cent of buildings constructed in this way. Mild steel came into use between 1920 and 1950 and some of these ties are now showing signs of failure, particularly in more exposed areas, but it is still probable that corrosion will be found in only 35 per cent of the buildings so constructed. Galvanized thin wire 'butterfly' ties came into use between 1950 and 1981, and some types had less zinc protection because of variations in the requirements of the British Standard. (The required thickness of the zinc coating was actually reduced in 1964, before being revised upwards again in 1978 and again in 1981.) These ties are now vulnerable, and it is probable that tie failure will be found in 40 per cent of these buildings. Since 1981, galvanized ties have been designed to have an effective life of sixty years, and it is possible that tie failure will be found in 3 per cent of buildings that use them. Stainless steel and plastics have been used to an increasing extent since this date and are unlikely to corrode, except in extreme conditions.

The most obvious tell-tale sign of wall-tie failure occurs because metal corrosion results in expansion – iron oxides can occupy up to seven to fourteen times the volume of the original iron or steel. In the case of thin wire 'butterfly' ties the force of the expansion may be insufficient to overcome the weight of the brickwork above, and there will be no damage evident from outside the building. The corrosion of the thicker vertical-twist 'fishtail' ties, however, can cause distinctive cracking patterns, especially noticeable on rendered walls. Characteristic horizontal crack lines usually occur every five or six brick courses. This type of damage happens only in extreme cases, however. Some 15 million homes in the UK have cavity walls, and only a few will be affected by wall-tie corrosion sufficient to justify remedial action. If you suspect you have a problem then it is important to have the walls inspected by a Chartered Building Surveyor, using the method described in Building Research Establishment Digest 401, 'Replacing Wall Ties' [CONSTRUCTION LITERATURE]. This specifies that two bricks should be removed on each elevation, and individual wall ties tested for corrosion. Some firms advertising themselves as wall-tie 'specialists' (and who might also 'specialize' in damp-proofing and chemical timber treatment), will only drill a hole in the wall, and use a visual inspection through a boroscope to justify replacement.

If there are no clear external signs of wall-tie failure in the property, then there should be no need to alert your insurers.

CAVITY BRICK-AND-BLOCK WALL

ROOFS

The roof is your home's first line of defence against the rain, and leaks can seem very dramatic – although the total amount of moisture entering the house may be insignificant compared with a leaking gutter dripping against an outside wall, or the condensation introduced into the house by daily showers. It's that drip, drip into the saucepan that makes it seem like a desperate situation.

The roofing trade is notorious as a refuge for cowboys, which is a shame for the many skilled, conscientious roofers who get tarred with the same brush. So, although I am always loath to recommend trade associations, I do suggest that readers with roofing problems should always use members of the National Federation of Roofing Contractors or the Flat Roofing Alliance [ROOFING]. Membership of these bodies does not mean that a roofing company is 100 per cent wonderful, but it does mean that if something goes wrong, then you will at least have a point of reference to start chasing them. The main things to beware of are:

- Victorian houses where original slate roof coverings have been replaced with interlocking concrete tiles. These are heavier than the original slate and the extra weight can cause deflection of the rafters.
- Cement fillets around the edges of upstands instead of proper lead flashing.
- Anything sprayed or painted on top of a roof (usually black bituminous stuff, but sometimes red paint).
- Anything sprayed underneath a roof – e.g. insulating foam.

SPRAY-ON FOAM TREATMENT

Q Every year gusts of wind dislodge one or two of my roof slates. The roof is in its original 1920s condition with no underfelt. There are adverts in the papers for a 'foam spray solution' for old roofs. These are guaranteed for twenty or so years. Is this the easiest way forward, or should we look to get the whole roof redone?

A The fact that slates are slipping every year probably indicates that the nails holding them to the timber battens are rusted through. Roofers refer to this as nail fatigue or nail sickness, and it is definitely time to have the roof stripped off and re-covered. Having foam sprayed on to the undersides of the slates may sound like a wonderful high-tech solution but it is actually a bad idea. It is at odds with the recommendations of the Building Regulations, which require a clear 50mm ventilated gap between insulation and roof covering. The foam sets hard and removes the two vital attributes that allow a traditional roof to last and perform so well for so long – the ability to breathe and the ability to move. The foam completely encloses the timber battens and the top surfaces of the rafters, which might cause them to rot. It also sticks tight to the slates and makes it almost impossible for them to ever be re-used. You will also probably find that the cost of the spray-on foam solution will be three or four times that of having the roof re-covered in the traditional way. Try to find a roofer who will remove the existing slates carefully, and reuse as many as possible. Also make sure that the roofer uses a breathable sarking felt, and allows it to sag between the rafters. The ridge tiles and any hip tiles should be rebedded using lime-and-sand mortar to match the original; do not allow the roofer to use sand-and-cement.

FOAM FIRM'S CLAIMS

Q My son and his partner live in a 1930s ex-council property. It has a tiled roof and although it appears to be perfectly weatherproof, he is thinking about having the interior of the roof sprayed with foam, which is claimed to overcome almost all roofing problems (slipping tiles or slates, lack of underfelt, leaks and condensation, freezing pipes and tanks, nail fatigue). The company he is considering using have BBA approval, are members of the British Urethane Foam Contractors Association and are BSI registered.

A The firm itself does not 'have BBA (British Board of Agrément) approval'; BBA testing is paid for by the company, and only tests what they are asked to test – in this case that the foam sticks to tiles and slates. It does not mean that this is a good thing to do to a roof, and it does not prevent possible condensation and rot problems in the enclosed timbers. The British Urethane Foam Contractors Association is a trade association, and again, membership of this does not prove that it is a good thing to spray foam on roofs. Neither is the company 'BSI registered', although their paperwork may have conformed to BS5750 – which became obsolete in 1996, and was replaced by ISO9001. This same firm used to claim in their advertising that this made them 'government approved', which was not true, and was stopped following a ruling by the Advertising Standards Authority.

The National Federation of Roofing Contractors (another trade association, but one whose members repair roofs using traditional methods [ROOFING]) publish a technical bulletin on spray-on coatings of this nature, and a spokesman told me that they would only recommend it as a stop-gap measure to extend the life of an old building – a farmer's barn, for example – for another few years. They do not recommend it for use in houses.

FLAT-ROOF COVERINGS

Q The felted flat roof of my rear extension is leaking, and a number of firms are offering apparently foolproof solutions, such as fibreglass, rubber membranes, and jointless glassfibre-reinforced plastic coverings. These systems are all promoted with a variety of impressive-looking glossy brochures and promises of twenty-five-year guarantees.

A Flat roofs in Britain are notorious for leaking, and the problem does not usually lie with the roof covering material, but with poor workmanship. 'Flat' roofs actually need a fall of at least four degrees, a requirement that is often neglected. And if the timber roof joists are not thick enough, they can sag in the middle, allowing water to pond and find its way through any minor defect.

The problem with most of the 'instant fix' flat roof repairs on the market is that they simply cover the existing leaking flat roof with a new waterproof coating, which will not remedy the underlying causes of the leak. This is throwing good money after bad. The GRP (glassfibre-reinforced polyester) and glassfibre flat roofing systems are often advertised as having 'no joints', as if this was an advantage, but in fact a large flat roof area exposed to sunlight should always have movement joints to cope with thermal expansion. If there are no joints then there may be expansion damage later on. And the twenty-five-year 'guarantees' are usually meaningless. Also, the prices charged by these companies are often greater than the cost of getting the roof re-covered properly using tried and tested traditional methods. Modern high-tensile roofing felts should last for fifty years if they are installed properly.

FLAT-ROOF REPAIRS

Q Where can I obtain information on DIY flat roof repairs? I am an accomplished DIY enthusiast and am confident that I can carry out the necessary work properly but would like some tips on the correct method to adopt.

A Try the Flat Roofing Alliance which publishes a free booklet, 'The Householder's Guide to Flat Roofing', and a more detailed handbook for £17.50 [ROOFING].

REPLACING OLD SLATES

Q My roof needs attention because of slipping/cracked slates. Builders have said that, although it would be possible to reuse a lot of the slates and buy in replacements for the damaged ones, it would be very expensive. They have suggested using concrete 'slates', but I have been warned about the increased weight and consequent stress on the supporting timbers. Is there a cheaper product that would not be too heavy?

A Slate roofs should not be re-covered with interlocking concrete tiles, as they are heavier than the original slates, and may cause the rafters to sag, and the walls to be pushed outwards. Artificial slates are an acceptable substitute, although they do not look as good as real slate.

ARTIFICIAL SLATES

Q We have a 1924 semi with small-sized slates on the roof. Repairs or re-roofing is becoming necessary, and our neighbours who are building an extension want to roof this and the main house with fibre cement 'slates'. We think these look cheap but do not want to upset the neighbours. Is it possible to re-roof one half of a semi with different materials? Also what is your opinion of these imitation slates please?

A Slate roofs fail when the nails holding the slates to the timber battens rust through (known as nail sickness). If one or two slates slip out of place, they can be pushed back up and secured with slate clips – strips of lead or copper nailed to the batten and folded up under the bottom edges. This is accepted good building practice, but can look unsightly, and unfortunately many surveyors seem to believe it is only a temporary measure. Nevertheless, it may be worth getting an experienced RICS Building Surveyor to inspect the roof and give you a second opinion as to its real condition.

If you do decide to go ahead with re-roofing, then you and your neighbours would be well advised to have the job done properly using real slate, which will preserve the architectural integrity of the houses (and hence their value), and will last much longer than artificial slates.

Depending on the size of the roof and the number of original slates that can be saved and re-used, a complete re-roof on a pair of semis should cost from around £10,000, and the roof will then be good for another sixty years. It is not good practice to re-roof one half of a pair of semis using a different material. No matter how professionally it is done, it will look like a bodged job, and possibly affect the value of the properties.

Try to find a roofer who will strip the roof carefully, saving as many slates as possible, and make up for breakages by buying in second-hand slates of the same quality or new slates of a matching colour (National Federation of Roofing Contractors [ROOFING]).

If your neighbours insist on using artificial slates, then be warned that the cheaper ones are made from fibre-reinforced cement coloured with black pigment, and they can curl up, fade or fall to bits after only a few years. Better-quality ones are reconstituted from real slate dust, bonded with resin, but they cost almost as much as genuine new slates. Better to use the real thing.

USING FOREIGN SLATES

Q **We are proposing to renew the roof of our Victorian house, built in 1873. It has a slate roof which has been 'Turnerized' we think – it has had a covering of fibre matting with bitumen, which has largely worn off, and slates are beginning to slip. We have had three quotes, two of which have specified Spanish slates, the other Welsh ones. The latter is substantially more expensive, but the builder says he wouldn't use Spanish, as they only last ten years, if that. Could you advise or point the way to more information, please?**

A The first valuable point to take from your question is the danger of any kind of 'quick fix' solution in roofing. Applying reinforced bitumen coatings on top of old slate roofs was common in the 1960s and '70s, and unfortunately you have inherited the consequences in that you will not be able to re-use any of the slates.

I take it from your precise dating of your Victorian house that you are probably interested in its history and keen to restore it using traditional materials, which is admirable. Slate roofs have performed well for hundreds of years in the British climate, and a good-quality slate roof should easily last for another seventy to eighty years. However, slate is a natural geological material and its quality depends on a number of factors, including which quarry it comes from, its thickness, strength and chemical make-up. The millions of dwellings built during the Victorian housing boom were mostly roofed with slate from north Wales, and much of this has performed very well, but it is the quality of the slate that is important, not its Welshness. A large amount of slate is also imported from Spain, Brazil and China – some of this will be of good quality, and some less so.

British Standard BS680 has been used since 1942, and this has now been incorporated into the new European Standard EN12362-2. The problem seems to be that this combines standards from all the European countries, and whilst a slate product might perform well in one European climate, it might not necessarily last as long in the British climate. This is perhaps how some imported Spanish slate has given the whole Spanish slate industry a bad reputation. According to the Building Conservation Directory [CONSERVATION] the important point is to use a manufacturer with a management system based on the BSEN29000 series of quality assurance standards, which should ensure continuing testing of a good sample of supplied products.

SLATE REPAIRS

Q **I have a traditional turn-of-the-century (1900) house with a slate roof, which was recently repaired by a local contractor. He replaced missing slates and re-fixed loose ones using mastic. I believe this to be bad practice, but can I prove it? Does it contravene any**

BS Codes of Practice, and are there likely to be any detrimental effects? I would appreciate any advice.

A This is an interesting question. British Standards generally apply to new work, rather than repairs, and in any case it seems unlikely that you had a contract with this contractor specifying that his work had to comply with British Standards – or any other standards, for that matter. In the absence of any such contract or method statement detailing what method of repair you required, it would be difficult to prove that he has done anything wrong.

The correct method of replacing missing slates on an existing roof, or re-fixing slipped ones, is to use lead or copper clips, sometimes called tingles. The nails that secure each slate to its timber batten are hidden beneath the slates in the course above, and it is not possible to lift these in order to hammer in fresh nails. So a narrow lead or copper strip is nailed to the batten, the slate is slid into place, and the end of the strip is bent up under the bottom edge of the slate to hold it in place. This is a perfectly acceptable practice but, unfortunately, when some Building Surveyors see a roof that has been repaired using lead or copper clips, they are quite likely to decide that the roof is in a state of disrepair, and specify that it should be stripped off and re-covered.

So it is quite likely that your roofer has done you a favour by using mastic which, whilst not being the textbook method, at least has the advantage of leaving your roof looking clean and tidy, and avoiding possible future condemnation by an ignorant Building Surveyor. And as long as he used a good quality mastic, applied according to the manufacturers' instructions, there is no reason why the repairs should not last as long as those carried out using more traditional methods.

For readers considering similar repairs to slate roofs, there are some other alternatives to traditional lead or copper clips. Ubbink makes an adjustable nylon fixing strap which works in the same way, but which is claimed to be virtually invisible once fixed in position. For a truly 'secret' fixing, Owens Slate Services make their Jenny Twin slate fixings. These are steel clips that fit into the nail holes in the centre of a slate, which is then slid up into position, when the fixing engages over the batten. They cost around £1.50 per pair [ROOFING].

CRUMBLING VERGES

Q **The gable end of my house faces into the prevailing wind and nearly every year the high winds loosen the mortar which retains the end roof tiles. There is a danger of the loose mortar and tiles coming down through the conservatory roof. Could you advise a more secure way for my builder to retain the end roof tiles?**

A The mortar is not there to 'retain' the tiles – it just fills the gaps. The tiles along the verge should be held in place by being nailed every course (on the rest of the roof they should be nailed every fourth course). Lime-and-sand mortar will work better than cement-and-sand, which becomes hard and brittle, causing it to shrink and fall out. But most tile manufacturers also supply a 'dry verge' system, consisting of specially shaped plastic sections. Ask at your local specialist roofing suppliers.

ROOF CLEANING & SEALING – MOSS

Q **We live in a mid-1950s house and we have seen a couple of houses on the estate having their roof tiles cleaned with pressure hoses. This appears to clear the roof of moss and other stains. We certainly have a build-up of moss on our roof and we would appreciate your comments and advice about the process. Whilst it may clean the tiles up, does the pressure washing cause damage to the tiles or the roof in general?**

A I have been getting a large number of readers' letters about this practice recently and I assume it is because of the increasing numbers of firms who advertise roof cleaning and sealing services, sometimes at extortionate prices of £3000 or more. Some of the leaflets that they put through letter boxes display all the hallmarks of the worst sorts of building scams, such as special deals for 'show homes in this area' and '40 per cent discount for the next two weeks', etc. In some cases, people have been persuaded to pay more for this unnecessary treatment than it would cost to have the house completely re-roofed. One elderly lady was defrauded of £5000 for washing the moss off and painting the tiles with red paint. The process will not even stop lichens and mosses from reappearing, as in many cases they are not growing on the tiles themselves, but on silt deposited on and between them. The growth of lichens and mosses on roofs is an inevitable part of the weathering process and many architects and conservationists welcome it as it takes the 'newness' off a roof and helps it blend in with its environment. Unless the moss growth is excessive, it is not harmful to roof tiles and there is no need to have it removed, nor to have roofs treated with water-repellent coatings. Some readers complain that moss is displaced by birds, and rolls down to block the gutters; if this is a big problem, then get the gutters cleaned out every couple of years, or fit mesh gutter guards. Pressure washing will not necessarily damage the tiles immediately, but it will remove a layer from the surface, paradoxically shortening their lives more than the lichen and moss will.

In conclusion, you should never commission building work from firms that put leaflets through your letter box; and if you are worried about moss on the roof, take a look at the property adverts for posh country houses in *Country Life* – the more moss they have on their roofs, the more expensive they seem to be!

MOSS GROWTH – CHEMICAL & COPPER WIRE TREATMENTS

Q The moss on my roof is getting more abundant and I am concerned that it may damage the tiles. I have been advised of various remedies including a chemical solution, although warned that it may cause blotchiness to the tiles. Another interesting suggestion is to affix copper wire at various points of the roof. Can you advise?

A Lichen and moss growth on roofs is a totally natural occurrence. Some people find it unsightly; others welcome it as a sign of the natural weathering and ageing of a house. The only serious damage is likely to occur on soft old red clay tiles, where the roots of button-type mosses can eat through and eventually create a leak. Even this can take many years to happen. Lichen and moss growth occur more in country locations than in cities, where air pollution prevents it. The problem with chemical treatment is not just staining, but the fact that it has to be repeated regularly. The idea of copper wire laid along the ridge is that the copper oxide is washed off by the rain and flows down the surface. Again, this can lead to staining, and water running off copper on to other metals can cause severe corrosion – aluminium gutters and window frames are especially at risk. Personally, I'd learn to love the moss, or else pay a roofer to scrape it off every few years.

MOSS ON FLAT ROOF

Q You have commented on the effect of moss on tiled roofs – i.e. that it should be left alone. Are your remarks relevant also to felt flat roofs and, if not, what treatment do you consider might solve the problem? It's difficult enough to eradicate moss from paths and patios, and I hesitate to tangle with a felt roof unless really necessary.

A Moss will always grow on unpolluted shaded surfaces that hold moisture. On flat roofs, excessive moss growth may be a sign of inadequate fall – i.e. that the slope is too flat for water to drain off – but I have never seen a case where moss has actually damaged properly laid roofing felt.

SARKING FELT

Q My valuation survey report says that the roof of my 1930s semi has no underfelt, and that it will have to be brought up to modern standards by stripping off the tiles and battens and re-roofing, including felt. The roof seems to be in good condition, both internally and externally, and there are no signs of any leaks, past or present. Is re-roofing really necessary?

A Since the 1960s it has been common building practice in Britain for roofers to drape sarking felt across the rafters before battening and tiling. The term 'sarking' originally referred to close timber boarding laid across the rafters to prevent wind-driven rain and snow from penetrating through the gaps around tiles and slates. Sarking is a good second line of defence in areas of high exposure, and the original boarding is still used in exposed areas in Scotland.

But for less exposed parts of the UK sarking felt is less of a necessity, and has generally been adopted simply to make life easier for roofers. When retiling an old roof, roofers used to have to work in sections, stripping and re-covering an area in a day, so as to leave the roof weathertight. With sarking felt they can strip the whole roof covering off in the first day and felt it, then take their time with the replacement tiling or slating.

Sarking felt has two disadvantages:

First, the idea that it is a fail-safe second line of defence encourages roofers to take less care with the final tiling or slating. This is especially notable with regard to calculating and laying the correct headlap (vertical overlap) to cope with prevailing weather conditions. Tile manufacturers (and the Building Regulations) specify a minimum lap, to prevent wind-driven rain and snow from being blown up under the lap and into the roof space. This may be as much as 60mm or 75mm, and if this measurement is adhered to, then no roof should leak. But by shrinking the headlap to 25mm, roofers can save one or two complete courses of tiles

Fitting sarking felt to an old roof can cut down on ventilation.

TRADITIONAL PITCHED ROOF

battens

wind bracing

sarking felt

roof
trusses

plasterboard

MODERN PITCHED ROOF

or slates (thus saving themselves £50 or more in materials) and if the water gets in then the sarking felt will catch it – as long as it stays intact – for maybe fifteen or twenty years. After that, the roof will start to leak in severe weather conditions, and there will be no alternative to complete re-roofing.

Second, sarking felt cuts down on the natural ventilation in the roof space, especially if it is stretched too tight (it is supposed to sag loosely between the rafters) or if it is one of the new plastic varieties. With the current high standards of ceiling insulation, roof spaces can be very cold in winter, so the water vapour, which finds its way up from the bedrooms, condenses against the cold surface of the felt, and can drip down and stain the ceilings. Some readers have reported a steady dripping of condensation from the felt, and have even thought that the roof is leaking. It is notable that other European countries, including those with cold northern climates such as Germany and Denmark, do not use sarking felt, but prefer to keep the natural ventilation that comes from air passing through the gaps between the tiles or slates.

If a roof really needs re-covering, due to a large number of rusty nails and/or a large number of slipped slates or tiles, then it is probably worth letting your roofer use sarking felt as part of the new installation, as long as it is installed properly according to Building Research Establishment standards, and adequate ventilation is provided in the form of special vents at eaves and ridge. But if an old roof is in sound condition and not leaking then there is no need to strip it off simply to install a layer of felt. This recommendation indicates a misunderstanding by the valuation surveyor.

THATCHED COTTAGE

Q Please could you advise on the implications of buying a semi-detached thatched cottage, some parts of which are believed to date back to the seventeenth century. We have always lived in up-to-date houses so have no experience of life in such a property.

A Thatch is an attractive traditional roofing material and very good for insulation – both thermal and sound. People who live in thatched houses have nothing but praise for the material. Its insulation properties are second to none, keeping a home warm in the winter and cool in the summer. And estimates of longevity are actually greater than you might think. Norfolk reed thatched roofs (the best quality material) have been known to last for over a century, with sixty years being a reasonable minimum, and even a straw roof can last a good forty years. All thatch needs re-ridging every fifteen to twenty years, and localized damage needs prompt repair, on the 'stitch in time' principle.

For details of qualified thatchers contact your local-authority Building Conservation Officer, or call the National Council of Master Thatchers Associations [ROOFING].

WHITE POWDER ON RAFTERS

Q When my ninety-year-old house was re-roofed, some three years ago, I was alarmed at seeing a white 'powder' on beams in my loft space. It looks like the sort of powdery tide mark that appears when you dry out wet shoes. The powder seems to rub off easily and the beams appear to be dry, and are sound when poked with a screwdriver. This therefore does not seem to be a fungus, but as it is extensive I would value your opinion.

A It is common to find white powdery deposits on the rafters of old houses, and on the undersides of the clay tiles that they support. This is the result of salts being leeched through the tiles by the slow penetration of rainwater over the years, and as long as the rafters are dry, is no cause for concern. The powder is usually magnesium sulfate, otherwise known as Epsom Salts.

BEDDING & POINTING RIDGE TILES

Q I think the ridge tiles on my 1930s semi need repointing. There seem to be two methods – either to remove the tiles and reset in fresh mortar, or leave the tiles in place and repoint the edges, as with brickwork. Is one method better than the other? What is the ideal ratio of sand and cement in the mortar mix, and is there an additive or adhesive that can be used to assist adhesion?

A It depends entirely on the condition of the ridge tiles and the mortar bedding. If the roof covering is original, then it is natural that the surface of the mortar will have weathered away slightly, and whilst this may look untidy, it does not necessarily require attention, other than for cosmetic reasons. If the ridge tiles have become loose, however, or if there are leaks coming through to the inside of the roof, then they will require lifting off, cleaning, and rebedding in mortar.

Be warned, though, that bedding ridge tiles and hip tiles in mortar, and applying mortar to the verges on gable ends, is one of the great unspoken contradictions in construction. Timber roofs, by their very nature, are flexible things, and a general principle of all tiled and slated roofing is that the roof should be allowed to move and to breathe. But the only material available to our predecessors for these finishing details was mortar, which is basically a rigid material, prone to cracking. Up until the 1950s, however, lime mortar was used, and this was reasonably flexible if applied with skill and care. The problems started when roofers and builders switched from lime to cement, which is a far harder and more brittle material. So any bedding mortar used in roofing should have a high lime content. It is very hard to persuade modern builders to use lime mortar, as most of them have been wrongly persuaded that, without the addition of cement, it will not set. But a 9:2:1 (sand/lime/cement) mortar will perform far better than a mortar made only with sand and cement. Plasticizer added to the water will make the mix more workable and reduce drying shrinkage, but there is no real need for any other additives. Alternatively, a bagged, pre-mixed roofing mortar is made by Feb, and sold in roofing suppliers.

FELT FLAT ROOF

Q We have a twenty-three-year-old felt flat roof on a ground-floor extension (around 5m x 5m) which is cracking and needs to be replaced. We do not want to have a 'torch-on' felt roof (neighbours had their house burnt down by contractors doing that), and the alternatives seem to be fibreglass or rubber. Is one of these inherently better than the other, in terms of safety of installation, durability and cost? The roof gets no foot traffic. Finally, is there any way we can ensure that a contractor is competent – does membership of a trade organization mean much, and, if so, which organization?

A In my opinion, the latest reinforced torch-on felts are the best material for most domestic flat roofs. They are the modern equivalent of the traditional built-up felt roof covering, where the layers of felt were bedded in hot-poured tar or bitumen. The torch-on felts are applied in the same way, in layers, with the advantage that instead of having to melt bitumen and pour it over the roof, the underside of the felt itself is softened with a blow-torch as it is rolled out. The accident to your neighbour's house is most likely to have been caused by careless or incompetent workmanship, rather than any inherent danger in the process itself.

It is true that fibreglass and synthetic rubber membranes are being marketed as the latest in flat-roofing technology, and promoted as being maintenance-free and more durable than felt. However, they are still relatively untried and the firms doing the work are sometimes franchises of bigger companies, meaning they might not be local, and might not be in business several years hence should problems arise with the installation. The twenty-five-year 'guarantees' offered for some of these products are rarely worth the paper they are written on and the prices charged by the commission-led salesmen are often much higher than for a traditional felt roof.

A properly installed felt roof should last for fifty years or more, and has the advantage that if it were accidentally damaged (by falling branches, for example), it would be repairable by local tradesmen using tried-and-tested techniques and materials.

The most important factor for any flat roof is generally not the covering, but the underlying structure. Flat roofs should have a gradient of at least 1-in-80 to ensure quick rainwater run-off, and timber roof joists need to be substantial enough to withstand sagging over time. Shallow, sagging joists can lead to 'ponding' on a roof, allowing water to find its way in through the tiniest pin-prick hole. Another common cause of failure has been the use of chipboard as a decking material – this sags under its own weight over time, especially when softened by condensation from below (insulation and ventilation are also important factors in ensuring the longevity of a flat roof).

Regular readers of my newspaper column will know that I do not generally recommend trade association membership as a mark of quality, but the roofing industry has a poor reputation, and it would be just as well to use a member of the National Federation of Roofing Contractors or the Flat Roofing Alliance [ROOFING], which also publishes a free booklet, 'The Householder's Guide to Flat Roofing'.

FLOORS

Readers' floor problems tend to fall into two main categories: solid concrete ground floors and creaking upstairs chipboard floors. Both can be equally troublesome.

Solid concrete ground floors were introduced into Victorian houses in a big way from the 1960s onwards. The rationale was that the original suspended timber floors could be affected by rot, and many surveyors, architects, housing associations and even private owners decided that it would be a good idea to do away with the timber and replace it with a slab of good old solid concrete, poured on to a polyethylene damp-proof membrane (DPM). This may have removed the possibility of wood rot, but at the same time it deprived a house of the sub-floor ventilation that had kept it dry for decades. The perceived wisdom was that the DPM would keep the floor dry, and a chemical injection damp-proof course (DPC) would stop the ground moisture from being diverted into the walls. The fatal flaw in the scenario was the blind faith in the idea that chemical injection DPCs actually worked. They don't. So tens of thousands of Victorian houses have had perfectly serviceable dry, ventilated, timber floors torn up, only to be replaced with cold, hard concrete, and with the added disadvantage of damp walls. It is still being done.

Creaking chipboard blights the lives of many people who live in 'modern' homes – by which I mean mass-produced, speculatively built houses and flats of 1970s vintage onwards. Some estate homes of this period were built with proper timber floorboards, but not many. Like concrete ground floors, chipboard upper floors were built on the misconception that being a man-made board material, tongue-and-groove chipboard was more stable than pesky old-fashioned real wood, and that it would therefore have none of the disadvantages of traditional floorboards (i.e. shrinking, swelling, twisting, splitting, creaking). What was not appreciated was that chipboard suffers from a phenomenon called 'creep', which means that over time, it sags between the joists, and in the process becomes distorted, so that it creaks when it rubs against the joists, and it squeaks when it binds against adjacent boards.

Both of these problems are examples of what can go wrong when builders fall for the idea that old-fashioned construction materials and methods must be inferior to new ones. It is a problem of the modern age.

MATCHING OLD FLOORBOARDS

Q I have been thinking about sanding and sealing the floorboards in my dining room. However, some sections of the floor have been ruined by successive plumbers and electricians, and need replacing. The problem is, the modern 6in x 1in (150mm x 25mm) floorboards from builders' merchants are narrower and thinner than the original boards. Where can I buy suitable matching replacement boards?

A The timber sold at the builders' merchants will be PAR (planed all round), sometimes called PSE (planed square edge), so the 150mm x 25mm sawn size is reduced to about 140mm x 20mm. You could try to find second-hand boards at auctions or from architectural salvage firms (or keep an eye out for boards dumped in builders' skips). These can sometimes provide a good match in colour and grain. But new sawn boards of the right size should also be available from specialist timber merchants, and any sawmill will cut boards to order. Victorian floors were often laid with rough sawn boards, which were then planed and sanded in situ. For a perfect fit buy the boards slightly over-size and allow them to acclimatize to the room conditions for as long as possible before fixing.

WIDE FLOORBOARDS

Q We have bought a redundant farm building to renovate as a house. The floor is dirt at the moment and we intend having a suspended timber floor. I would appreciate your opinion on our using scaffold boards instead of standard floorboards. They were used on a recent *Changing Rooms* programme on TV. We like the idea of wider boards.

A You can have floorboards any width you like. But if you buy scaffold boards you will just be paying extra for stress-graded timber with metal reinforcing strips fixed to each end. Any local timber merchant or sawmill will supply you with boards cut to size.

CURLING FLOORBOARDS

Q My 1930s semi has suspended wooden floorboards throughout. Over the last few months I've noticed that some of the floorboards feel through the carpet as if they are 'curling' up at the edges and coming away from the supporting joists.

This 'curling' or lifting is accompanied by the obligatory squeaky floorboard sound expected in a seventy-year-old house. Now I would like to pull back the carpets and secure the floorboards back to the joists but am unsure as to how best to do this. Should I: (a) screw the boards to the joists; (b) hammer standard nails in; or (c) use special nails?

One concern I do have is what is causing the floorboards to curl/lift on both the ground and first floors? Is it normal for this to happen or are there any other possible reasons lurking around?

A The nails to use are called floor brads, which are 60mm square-cut nails with a one-sided head. These provide a good grip into the joists, the heads are easily 'lost' in the surface of the board without splitting it, and, like all cut nails, it should be relatively easy to work them loose if the boards need to be lifted for access to the sub-floor void. (Round-head, or 'wire', nails cannot be 'lost', and leave bumps on the surface of the floor. Round-heads and ovals both grip tight into the joists and cannot be worked loose, so when the boards are lifted the nail heads rip through the boards and split them.)

Screwing floorboards is often done to cure squeaking, but it can create difficulties. Not least that if the boards have to be lifted, it is difficult to locate all the screw heads and remove the screws. And it takes only one screw to be missed and the board will split, making it unfit for reuse. It might be worth screwing the boards covering pipe or cable runs, so they can be lifted to gain access to these services, but otherwise floor brads are preferable.

The sudden recent curling of the floorboards is most likely due to drying shrinkage, perhaps due to recent increases in heating and/or ventilation.

GAPS BETWEEN SANDED FLOORBOARDS

Q What is the best way of sealing gaps between old floorboards? We have sanded and varnished the floors, but in some rooms wind blows cold through the gaps between the boards. We have tried doing an area with wood filler, wiped off with a damp cloth, but this takes ages, and does not always bridge the gap. Is there a better way?

A The main point to note is that floorboards in Victorian/Edwardian houses were not intended to be left exposed, and would usually have been covered with loose rugs or mats. Sanding softwood floorboards is very much a recent fashion, and is a poor substitute for tongue-and-groove hardwood boarding. Having said that, it is possible to make a good job of sanding old floorboards (although bear in mind the noise problems that bare timber floors can have, especially for downstairs neighbours [SOUNDPROOFING]).

The gaps between the boards are due to drying shrinkage, accelerated in most cases by central heating, which is good, because it means that the boards are well seasoned and unlikely to shrink any further. If you want to do a really good job then you should consider lifting the boards, cleaning off the edges, and refitting them, wedging them up tight to each other as you go. You will probably find that tightening up all the gaps leaves you room for almost one extra complete board across the width of the room. This sounds like a major upheaval, but if it can be combined with rewiring or central heating work, or fitting insulation below ground floors, then it is probably worth it.

If you decide to leave the boards in their original state, and the gaps are large – 2–3mm – then you could ask a local joinery work-shop to cut you tapered strips to glue into the gaps, which you then trim and sand flat. Otherwise you should save the dust from the sand-ing machine (collected in the vacuum bag), mix it with PVA adhesive or a proprietary resin adhe-sive [FLOORING] and work it into the gaps with a filler knife. Sand it flat when it has dried.

Not all floorboards are suitable for sanding and sealing.

TIMBER FLOOR IN BATHROOM

Q I want to put new flooring in my bathroom, and would like to put down a wooden floor. However, I'm worried this will be a problem due to moisture. Is it advisable to put wooden floors in bathrooms, and are there any special measures I should take?

A Timber floors can look good in bathrooms, and provided they are fitted properly and kept dry, they can provide an easily cleanable surface. The problem is always going to be moisture move-ment – timber expands when it gets wet and shrinks when it dries. The worst-case scenario would be shrinkage gaps between the boards followed by a sudden spillage as water could leak through and damage the ceiling below. The first thing to do is to ensure that your bathroom has a fairly stable internal environment. A large bathroom with good ventilation could be suitable for a timber floor; a small one where condensation runs down the walls every time you have a shower may not be. Bamboo is a hard, resilient flooring material (e.g. the charmingly named Pandafloor from Pioneer Woodfloors [FLOORING]).

DAMAGED TEAK BLOCK FLOOR

Q Our teak block floor, laid in 1949, is causing concern. A few of the blocks have become loose and can lift out. What would you suggest as the best substance to reseat and secure them?

A Hardwood block floors were originally laid in hot bitumen, so you need a special solvent-based adhesive, which will melt the bitumen and enable the blocks to be pushed back down into it. Lecol adhesive is available from Victorian Wood Works [FLOORING].

SQUEAKING CHIPBOARD FLOOR

Q Our house is only twenty years old, but we suffer from creaky floorboards in one particular area. Is there a practical solution that does not involve major work?

A Many houses built since the 1980s have chipboard flooring rather than the traditional solid timber floorboards. Over time the chipboard sags between the joists, and the edges rub against each other, which is what causes the creaking. The first step is to lift up the carpet and look to see if there are any obvious signs of movement; it may be that one or two screws have worked loose, and tightening these may effect a cure. If this doesn't work, then you may need to use some extra screws. Avoid underfloor pipes and cables by checking with a metal detector, and use screws that are twice as long as the thickness of the boards, which are probably 18mm. If this still fails to cure the squeaking, then you could try the old stagehand's trick of sprinkling French chalk or talcum powder into the gap between the boards.

New houses have chipboard floors which can sag and squeak.

TIMBER ON CONCRETE (1)

Q I have just purchased a newbuild house and have had screeding put down prior to the installation of oak flooring. How long should I leave the screeding to dry before laying the wood in order to avoid any future buckling in the floor? The screed was laid on concrete that has been in situ for nine months. I have heard from some people that I should allow twelve weeks for the screeding to dry out. My builder says that as the screed used was expensive (£40 per bag) it should dry out in a few days and the floor could then be laid.

A My first response is to ask why, if the house already has a concrete floor, you would want to screed it before fixing oak flooring on top. Sand-and-cement screed is normally used to level concrete floors before laying carpet or vinyl flooring. The best way to fix a timber floor above concrete is on timber battens, leaving a ventilated air gap between the concrete and the timber.

I must also add that although it might be trendy, oak is not an ideal material for ground floors. Oak is notoriously prone to moisture movement, and any slight differences in humidity between the top of the boards (i.e. room humidity) and the undersides (the cool area adjacent to the concrete floor, which is subject to condensation) can often result in twisting and buckling, even though the concrete sub-floor and/or screed is effectively 'dry'. The normal recommended drying time for any cement-based material is one month per 25mm (1in) thickness, so a 50mm screed should be allowed to dry for at least two months. But I think you would do well to reconsider your choice of floor finish.

TIMBER ON CONCRETE (2)

Q You have advised against using oak flooring. We would like a wooden floor over our concrete floor. Is there any wood you would advise?

A I do not advise against oak flooring as such, but oak is a particularly difficult wood to use as it has a high degree of moisture movement. Oak flooring can work well on upper floors, and on traditional suspended ground floors, where the sub-floor ventilation removes any moisture from the ground below and maintains an even humidity balance above and below the flooring. The problem with laying any species of timber flooring on top of a solid ground-floor concrete slab is that there will inevitably be dry air above the wood and moist air below it, leading to possible problems with warping and distortion.

If you are determined to have a timber floor on top of your concrete, than the best bet would probably be some type of engineered laminate, with a softwood base covered with a veneer of real timber. Buy from a reputable manufacturer and follow their installation instructions to the letter, so that if anything goes wrong you have a claim. Personally, I wouldn't recommend any kind of timber flooring on top of a concrete ground-floor slab.

CRACKED TILES

Q We bought a new flat three years ago and two of the kitchen floor tiles are cracked. I have been informed that this is due to the movement of the building. The floors are concrete and we are on the second floor. As these tiles are no longer available do we have any redress against the builder, and should this have happened after just three years? We feel that spares of these tiles should have been kept if this problem was likely to arise, considering the flats were sold as luxury apartments.

A The theory that your tiles have cracked due to building movement may or may not be true; this could only be confirmed if the alleged movement was measured. It is certainly common for new buildings to move, through settlement or drying shrinkage, and it is good practice to allow for this by bedding floor tiles on a flexible material such as asphalt rather than a rigid one like sand-and-cement. However, the ultimate reason for the cracking will almost certainly be that the tiles are too thin for the job. The term 'luxury' often refers only to the surface appearance of a new property, and not to the quality of the materials used. Since the tiles are no longer available, you could justifiably claim that the builder should re-lay the whole floor, but you may have to take him to court to achieve this.

BOUNCY SUSPENDED TIMBER

Q I own a detached 1930s house. The floorboards appear to be in good condition but when anyone moves heavily there is corresponding movement across the boards, and furniture on the other side of the room vibrates slightly. I had some building work done a few years ago, after the problem began, and was told that there was adequate ventilation under the boards and that everything was OK. What is the likely cause of this movement and what can I do to rectify it?

A Although timber ground floors are usually referred to as 'suspended', they are actually supported at intervals by honeycombed brick sleeper walls. Over time these can settle into the ground, or slight shrinkage can take place in the timber wall plates (which lie on top of the sleeper walls, and support the floor joists). Either of these causes will allow the floor to bounce, and the solution is simply to lift a few floorboards and drive new timber wedges under the offending joists. Suspended timber floors in upstairs rooms can often be stiffened by tightening up the herringbone strutting which runs across the centre of the span and is wedged to the walls at each end.

TILES ON CONCRETE

Q I have had new floor tiles laid in my kitchen. Before starting, the fitter took a meter reading from the concrete and said the floor was damp. After six months some of the tiles are lifting and the fitter is now recommending a damp-proof membrane. I am concerned as the previous floor covering, with similar tiles, was down for fifteen years with no problem. What could be the cause of the lifting tiles?

A Electrical moisture meters are calibrated for timber, not concrete, and it seems unlikely that your floor would have suddenly become damp after fifteen years. There are several things that can cause tiles to lift, usually associated with differential movement between the floor and the tiles, due to moisture, heat or structural movement. Current thinking is that rather than sticking tiles tight to the floor, it is better to separate the two with a woven uncoupling membrane, which prevents stresses in the floor from being transmitted to the tiles. For further information try Schluter Systems [FLOORING].

CHIMNEYS

In these days of central heating, it may seem strange that fireplaces, flues and chimneys should cause problems for so many readers. But most weeks my postbag contains two or three chimney queries. In many cases, the problem is due to the fact that the chimney is no longer in use. Rain landing on the chimney stack or falling into the flue via the chimney pot will always percolate down and may appear as dampness further down inside the house. When fireplaces are regularly used for their original purpose, then the heat of the fire will constantly dry things out, but when there are no fires then other steps need to be taken. It is important to maintain a drying flow of air through the flue, and if the fireplace opening is bricked up in the room, then this is best achieved by venting the flue at ceiling height. This allows a flow of warm air from the top of the room to enter the flue and flow upwards by natural convection; it also helps to ventilate the room. It is also a good idea to stop excess rain from entering a redundant flue by fitting a terracotta cowl, either into the top of the existing chimney pot, or in place of it.

Leaks at high level often manifest themselves as staining on the chimney breast within the loft space. This may look alarming but is probably not a problem as long as there is sufficient ventilation within the roof space. Regular leaks on the prevailing (windward) side of the chimney breast may be caused by inadequate flashing allowing rainwater to flow straight down the side of the brickwork, usually apparent from the staining pattern. Flashing round chimney stacks has to be applied with great care and attention. It should always be in proper lead (not stick-on 'Flashband' or similar), and tucked a good 25mm into the brick joints.

Isolated damp patches that appear further down the breast, often with a brown stain, could

Chimneys are a traditional feature of British housing.

be caused by rainwater dripping down inside the flue and hitting an obstruction or bend. If this occurs near an inside ceiling level, then the stain sometimes spreads out across the ceiling, especially if this has been repaired or replaced with plasterboard.

In neglected, unvented flues, it is not uncommon for rainwater to find its way right down to the ground floor fireplace, and over time the soot and tar can be leached out into the surrounding brickwork, where it is often misdiagnosed as 'rising damp'. The soot contains hygroscopic salts, which, apart from giving very high readings on electrical moisture meters, also absorb moisture from the atmosphere, so where a property has a condensation problem, this can concentrate moisture in the flue, and cause staining on the surface of the chimney breast, even when there are no rainwater leaks.

Another problem concerns the removal of part of a redundant chimney breast. Victorian terraced houses were built with large chimney breasts, often back-to-back on the party walls. These contain a huge number of bricks and probably weigh twice as much as the wall itself, so they provide a buttressing effect which stabilizes the building, as well as providing ventilation to the rooms. Chimney breasts are often partially removed, to create extra space within rooms, and the brickwork above is supposed to be supported by spanning across the room to the wall opposite with steel joists (RSJs). It never is. The danger is not of the bricks falling down into the room – because they are bonded into the party wall itself. Rather, it is that the centre of gravity of the wall has been shifted, and, over the long term, this may result in movement of the whole terrace.

Readers in houses where chimney breasts have been removed also report being troubled by their neighbour's noise and even their smells. So the removal of a chimney breast is not something to be undertaken lightly.

The other common problem with chimneys concerns using an old flue as a vent for a gas fire or boiler. This is a very dangerous thing to do unless the old flue has been prepared with a purpose-made flue liner.

STAINING ON CHIMNEY BREAST

Q Two of the fireplaces in my 1937 house (bedroom and dining room) are closed off and vented at grate level. The front-room fireplace is still in constant use during the winter with coal and log fires. There is now staining and dampness on the chimney breast in the bedroom upstairs. Is this because the vents are in the wrong place?

A It is more likely to be due to a build-up of tars and salts from the smoke of the downstairs fire, whose flue will pass to one side of the breast in the bedroom. These deposits are hygroscopic – i.e. they absorb moisture from the atmosphere giving rise to the phenomenon of 'chimney damp'. Staining on upstairs chimney breasts is especially common with log fires – these burn at a lower temperature than coal and produce more tar. Get the flue swept regularly, and if the problem persists, then you may have to get it relined.

CHIMNEY, FLUES AND FIREPLACES

SMOKE IN ROOM

Q I have lived in my house for about thirty years and have always had open fires. I never had much trouble until the last eighteen months, when I have had smoke returning down the chimney into the living room. It seems to come in puffs. I've had a cowl put on top of the chimney and had it swept, but the smoke still comes back down. The chimney sweep said the cowl might be too low. I do have some tall trees about 15ft (4.5m) away from that side of the house and wonder if they are causing a downdraught?

A All sorts of environmental factors can create bursts of positive pressure, which cause the smoke to be blown back down the flue. Internal draughts and kitchen extractor fans can also sometimes draw air down the flue. Are you sure you haven't carried out any draught-proofing measures in the past eighteen months, such as having replacement windows fitted? A fire will not work in an airtight room – it needs an incoming draught to feed the flames and carry the smoke up the flue. If the doors and windows are all draught-proofed, then you may need a separate air supply for the fireplace, ducted in under the floor to a vent next to the fire.

If all these factors have been accounted for, then it may be worth trying an aerodynamic cowl, which uses the wind to create an uplift. Colt make a range of these, with different models suitable for different exposure conditions. For further information call The Loft Shop [LOFT CONVERSIONS].

SMOKE IN OTHER ROOMS

Q My 1898 semi has a living room with an open coal fire, a dining room with a gas fire, and a kitchen with an extractor fan. If I light the coal fire and have the extractor fan working in the kitchen, the dining room fills with smoke! The chimneys have been swept and smoke pellets in each fireplace indicated that there is no problem.

A It sounds as though there is insufficient ventilation in the kitchen, so the extractor fan is drawing air in through the nearest inlet, i.e. down the dining-room chimney. Not only is this annoying, but it is potentially dangerous, as when the gas fire is lit, the fan will be sucking in carbon monoxide from the flue gases. You urgently need extra permanent ventilation in both the kitchen and the dining room – either airbricks or floor vents – and you should keep the kitchen door closed when the extractor fan is running.

REMOVING CHIMNEY BREAST

Q I own a two-bedroom mid-terrace Victorian house. The bathroom (upstairs and at the back of the house) has a chimney breast; the kitchen directly below it does not. The chimney breast appears to be supported with 6in x 3in (150mm x 75mm) timber, taken to the supporting walls. Should I reinstate the chimney breast in the kitchen, or at least replace the timber with an RSJ?

A For many years builders and DIYers removed fireplaces and chimney breasts in downstairs rooms without giving it a second thought, supporting the breast above by bolting a couple of steel gallows brackets to the party wall, or, as in your case, inserting some extra timbers into the floor. It is now accepted that this is not the best thing to do to an older house, and surveyors usually comment on removed chimney breasts in homebuyers' reports. This does not mean that the brickwork above is liable to come crashing down, because it will be bonded into the party wall or flank wall. But it is a warning that the equilibrium of the structure may have been altered by the removal, and that in the future some kind of movement or settlement may occur. So when chimney breasts are removed nowadays, the preferred method is to insert rolled steel joists (RSJs) to transfer the load across to the opposite wall. Unless there is obvious movement or cracking, there is no immediate need for you to do this now, but it could be done as part of any future building work in the kitchen. Alternatively, you could consider taking out the breast in the bathroom as well, thereby giving you more space, and putting the supporting RSJs in the roof space. You should seek advice from a structural engineer about this.

REMOVING PART OF CHIMNEY BREAST

Q **You have referred to the potential damage caused by removing a chimney breast from a downstairs room. Does the same problem apply to a top-floor room?**

A Yes, the problem is one of removing any section of the breast and failing to support the remaining brickwork above it. In a top-floor bedroom this would mean the part of the breast remaining in the loft space, and the chimney stack above the roof-line. This situation can be especially dangerous, as in smaller bedrooms the bed is often situated against the wall from which the breast has been removed. There have been several instances of chimney stacks being blown over in gales and crashing through roofs. Remember, there is a very large amount of weight in a chimney stack.

INSTALLING A CHIMNEY

Q **We live in a house with no chimney. What are the options for putting in a fireplace? One hears such horror stories of potentially lethal chimney/flue installations.**

A Constructing fireplace openings, flues and chimneys used to be a standard part of the bricklayer's craft, so if you can find a bricklayer of the old school he should be able to sort you out. The least disruptive option is to cut a fireplace opening in an outside wall and construct an external chimney breast. If the chimney breast has to be on the inside then it will require cutting through floor and ceiling timbers, and making sure they are adequately fire-protected.

An easier option may be to install a solid-fuel stove with a cast-iron flue pipe up to ceiling height, and a twin-walled insulated flue liner through upper floors and roof space. Ask your local-authority Building Control Department for guidance.

If you live in a smoke-controlled area you will need to buy a stove with a catalytic converter, or resort to 'coal-effect' gas fires, with a balanced flue going out through the wall. The regulations for these are the same as for any gas-fired appliance, and they must be installed by a CORGI-registered gas fitter (see CORGI block advert in the Yellow Pages under 'Gas Installers').

USING CHIMNEY AS GAS FLUE

Q **We are about to have gas fires installed in our 1934 house and our installers have said that flue lining is not necessary, but you have mentioned that flues in older houses should be lined. Is the potential danger due to age, or to the materials that were used in a particular period?**

A In 1934 the chimneys will have been built with bricks and lime mortar, and whilst probably being structurally sound, will not be airtight enough to contain the exhaust fumes from gas fires. The problem is the carbon monoxide in these fumes, which is a deadly poison; if it leaks through the brickwork into the bedrooms above, then it can be fatal. Even

Inserting a stainless steel flue liner.

houses built with purpose-made concrete flue liners in the 1960s and '70s are now thought to be inadequate for this purpose, and therefore metal flue liners must be inserted in all older flues before they are used to vent gas fires or boilers. You should use only CORGI-registered gas fitters, as they will be up to date with all the necessary safety regulations.

OPENING UP FIREPLACE

Q **We want to recommission the downstairs fireplaces to use open fires. One is currently fitted with a gas fire and the other blocked off. What is the best way to do this?**

A As long as the flues are still open – i.e. not capped at the top or lined with gas flue liners – then you will probably just be able to open them up and use them. Get a local chimney sweep round to sweep them and give his opinion. The only problem is likely to be that if the parging (the mortar lining the flue) has broken down you may, in time, get staining on the breasts above.

SMELLS FROM NEXT DOOR THROUGH FLUE

Q **How can we deal with smells from a bathroom next door coming into our bedroom? There is a chimney breast in the party wall, and we wonder if the neighbours have used it for venting. The noise is bad enough, but the smell is quite another matter.**

A If there is a bathroom vent going into a redundant flue then it should be lined with a flexible flue liner or plastic ducting. This is not just to get the smells vented to the outside of the building, but water vapour too, otherwise there could be condensation occurring within the chimney breast. It is always better for bathrooms to be ventilated directly through to an outside wall, and this can usually be achieved by ducting through the ceiling void.

SULFATE ATTACK

Q **My chimney stack has lost a brick and is leaning a little, following a few nights of high winds. I asked the insurance company whether I had a valid claim, and was told no, and that it was due to sulphate attack of the mortar. When I asked them how they identified sulphate attack, the answer was that their expert had years of experience. Are there recognized tests for this? I've scoured the Internet but can't find anything definitive.**

A Sulfate (as it is now spelt) attack occurs when sulfates from the ground, or from coal tar, react with Ordinary Portland Cement. If your house is post-war and built with cement mortar then it is possibly a cause, but if it is older and built with lime mortar then the lean is more likely to have been caused by moisture expansion on the side facing the weather, or may indeed be due to wind damage. Sulfates can be easily tested for – for publications try the Building Research Establishment [CONSTRUCTION LITERATURE], remembering to use the new spelling in your search.

DAMP BREAST

Q **About ten years ago I had my house re-roofed, and at the same time the chimney was taken down to below roof level to give a clear run for the tiler. Recently I have noticed dampness on the chimney breast in the top corner of the bedroom, which has caused the wallpaper to peel away. Is this likely to be something arising from past use of the old chimney or the capping-off of the stack? If so, why is it only in a small area right at the top, and what would you recommend?**

A Old chimney flues get a build-up of tars and salts from the coal or wood smoke passing through them and these deposits are hygroscopic (meaning they absorb moisture from the atmosphere, giving rise to the phenomenon of 'chimney damp'). Humidity within a house rises with elevation, and is often greatest at ceiling level in unheated upstairs bedrooms, so this is the point at which the chimney damp is most likely to become apparent. The simplest solution is to seal the affected area with Polycell Stain Block or Ratcliffe's Styptic before redecorating.

CRACKS

Cracks cause householders a lot of unnecessary distress, usually because of the fear that they might signify structural problems. This is largely a result of the publicity given to subsidence damage, and stories about huge insurance claims for underpinning and other structural work. Most internal cracks are actually harmless, and their only drawbacks are cosmetic. And in reality subsidence is a hugely over-diagnosed and overrated problem.

Subsidence first hit the public consciousness following the dry summer of 1976, and a little-noticed change in the wording of buildings insurance policies that enabled owners to claim for the repair of cracking damage caused by ground shrinkage. Once one owner down a street had had their house underpinned at the insurer's expense, everybody else wanted it too, and almost overnight a huge army of 'specialist' underpinning contractors sprang up ready to cash in on this lucrative insurance-financed work. Underpinning is extremely expensive and disruptive, and very often unnecessary, as when the drought ends the ground swells again, and the cracks that opened up in the summer close themselves. The insurance industry belatedly realized this, and they are now more reticent about agreeing to fund underpinning work.

What many people fear to be 'subsidence' is often just minor differential settlement. The main causes are shallow foundations below front bays (which can cause cracks to open up between the bay and the main house) and softening of the ground due to leaking drains where they run along alleys between houses. The former is often curable by tying the bay back to the house with traditional brick stitching (or resin-bonding in serious cases), and the latter by lining or replacing the damaged drain. Old houses built with lime mortar and plaster can often cope with this sort of movement quite easily, which is why you can see brickwork above windows looking decidedly lopsided, but with no evidence of serious cracks. Modern materials are much more brittle and can withstand very little movement. So cement mortars and renders, and gypsum plasters, tend to emphasize movement by opening up into cracks. It's a bit like the difference between icing and marzipan.

Most cracks in internal plaster occur in gypsum-plastered surfaces. On walls they are often nothing more than drying shrinkage, and on ceilings they usually follow the lines of the joints between sheets of plasterboard. It is also a surprisingly common practice by cowboy builders to plaster over woodchip wallpaper which looks fine for a few weeks, but then lots of cracks open up, running in all directions. I know of a house in London where a structural engineer specified £30,000 worth of structural repairs based upon such cracking, and the buyer duly got that sum knocked off the price.

One situation where cracks *can* result in serious problems is where they occur in external rendering. Most external renders are cement-based and are much too strong for the wall below, so they crack, allowing rainwater to penetrate. And once the water is behind the render, it is trapped, because strong sand-and-cement plaster is impermeable.

CRACKS IN EXTERNAL RENDER

Q **My forty-year-old bungalow is rendered and I have several vertical cracks, mostly under the window sills. In the past I have Sandtexed the whole of the rendering after filling the cracks with Tetrion. This lasts for a couple of years and then the cracks show again. How can I get a lasting solution?**

A Cracks below window sills are sometimes an indication of structural movement, rather than simply shrinkage of the surface render. You need to hack off the render in the offending areas and investigate what is happening underneath it. If there is cracking in the brickwork then this will need to be repaired by stitching-in with new bricks. The exposed area should be reinforced with expanded metal lathing and primed with a dilute PVA solution, before re-rendering with a 6:1:1 washed sharp sand/lime/cement mix. Use a mortar plasticizer to reduce the amount of water in the mix and prevent drying shrinkage.

CRACKS IN RENDER ON LIGHTWEIGHT BLOCKS

Q My Victorian house has a two-storey back addition built of lightweight blocks and rendered. The rendering has many fine cracks and one large one. Rain has penetrated through the cracks and the lightweight blocks act like a sponge, causing the internal plaster to crack and 'blow'. I bought the property eight years ago and despite having a full survey, no damp problems were found!

A External render on lightweight block walls often cracks, due to the differential movement between the hard cement-based render and the softer lightweight blockwork. Where the blockwork forms the outer leaf of a cavity wall this is not such a serious problem, but when, as in your case, the wall is solid, then it can present serious difficulties. Unfortunately, there are no easy answers. The fault lies with the original builders, who did not understand the need to provide movement joints in the blockwork, or to use a soft lime-based render. The only long-term solution would be to hack off the render and replace it with the correct material (a 6:1:1 washed sand/cement/lime mix), with the provision of a movement joint where the addition joins the main house.

CRACKS IN PLASTERBOARD CEILING

Q The plasterboard ceiling in my 1976 house suffers from cracks. I have tried many types of filler without a successful permanent cure. Apart from rejointing with scrim, or Artexing, do you have any suggestions?

A Plasterboard ceilings always crack. The cracking is worse in upstairs rooms because the plasterboard is fixed to the underside of the roof trusses, which will always move around in response to changes in temperature and moisture. In order to cope with this movement, 1 per cent of the ceiling is

Hairline cracks often occur along the joints between sheets of plasterboard.

supposed to consist of joints between the boards (so a 4m-wide ceiling should have at least 40mm of joints). Plasterboard manufacturers produce special narrow 600mm 'plank' sizes to allow for this, but most builders prefer the convenience of larger sheets, which means there are always too few joints. The best thing is to open up the existing cracks to around 10mm and cut extra joints, if needed, to reach the 1 per cent figure. Then fill the joints and replaster, with a soft plaster such as 'universal one-coat'. Even then, it may not work perfectly. The problem lies with the modern materials.

CRACKS IN ARTEXED CEILING

Q Our bungalow roof is made of pre-formed trusses and there is a large crack running across the living-room ceiling, along the joint in the boards. We had the ceiling professionally Artexed ten years ago, where the workmen sealed this crack with scrim and Artex before applying the textured coating to the whole ceiling. Needless to say the crack has returned. I have considered reinforcing the cracks from above using timber or plasterboard, but I presume I would have to get the Artex coating removed and have the ceiling recoated with either Artex or plaster. Or is there some way of repairing a crack in Artex?

A Plasterboard ceilings fixed to roof trusses often crack, as the ceiling joists move in response to temperature and moisture changes within the roof space. You could try opening up your ceiling crack to around 5mm and filling it with a soft filler such as one-coat plaster, reinforcing from above with plasterer's hessian scrim. Matching the original Artex pattern will be difficult, although the manufacturers suggest using flexible decorator's filler, blended into the existing pattern with a wet cloth or brush. But it may be better to plaster over the whole lot with a smooth finish, using Artex Ceiling Finish, as then it will be easier to repair next time the crack opens up.

CRACKS IN LATH-&-PLASTER CEILING

Q Two lath-and-plaster ceilings in my Victorian house are cracked and sagging. My builder proposes removing the plaster but leaving the laths, and then fixing plasterboard over them. Will this not make it difficult to level the plasterboards and thus make for an uneven ceiling, or is this normal practice?

A Fixing plasterboard on top of laths is not a very professional way of working. But then plasterboard is an inferior material to lath and plaster anyway. Why not simply repair the cracks and the damaged areas, using lime/sand/hair plaster to match the original? (Or universal one-coat plaster if that's all your builders can manage.) Finish with two layers of heavy-grade lining paper.

SUBSIDENCE CAUSED BY LEAKING DRAIN

Q The property we want to buy has been underpinned due to subsidence caused by a leaking drain. The repair work was carried out by the insurance company. I would be happy if I could be sure that this is a one-off problem that has been fixed and that it is not ongoing. Or should I be aware of other factors concerning this?

A As long as the offending drains have been completely renewed there is unlikely to be any further problem. My usual advice to people in cases like this is that if you like the house, buy it. There's nothing that can't be fixed later. Your main problem is likely to be getting buildings insurance on a property on which a subsidence claim has already been made. Make sure this is sorted before you incur any further expense.

These minor cracks in the brickwork would not be noticeable if the correct mortar had been used to repair them.

SUBSIDENCE

Q Our late Victorian house is built on clay and suffering badly from subsidence. We have accepted, for many years, cracks that open in summer and close in winter but now the brickwork is breaking apart and the cracks have not closed for three years – they just keep getting bigger. In 1992 we experienced subsidence on a lesser scale but although the response from the insurance company was very good we felt let down by the structural engineers and were devastated by the builders they appointed. Can we appoint our own structural engineer and if so how do we find one we can trust? Is there a book or a crash course in managing the situation?

A Subsidence occurs chiefly south-east of a line from the Severn to the Humber, where the subsoil is shrinkable clay. So cracks that appear following sustained periods of drought are often no cause for concern, as they are quite likely to close up again the following winter when the clay expands. Victorian houses are usually better able to cope with this than modern houses, because they were built with soft lime mortar, and cracks tend to follow the joints between the bricks, rather than fracturing the actual bricks themselves. However, there can sometimes be a problem with dust and debris falling into a crack, which stops it from fully closing up again. Then, next time there is any movement due to ground shrinkage, the crack will open up again from its new position, thus getting progressively wider. This is known as the ratchet effect.

When a crack opens up and fails to close again, it might also be caused by settlement rather than subsidence. Settlement is due to the one-way compaction of the subsoil, usually caused by the weight of a new building or extension, but it can sometimes affect older buildings too, if the subsoil has been disturbed by adjacent building works. And if an area of shrinkable clay subsoil gets very wet indeed – as can happen with a long-term leaking drain – then the clay might even start to behave like a liquid, allowing part of a building to settle irreversibly into it.

This is clearly a complex subject, and you need to find a structural engineer who is both expert in the field and has experience of building movement in your area. I recommend an excellent book called *Has your House got Cracks?* which explains the structural and legal implications of building movement, as well as how to find a suitable structural engineer, and how to make an insurance claim [from BRE Bookshop – CONSTRUCTION LITERATURE].

CRACKS – SKIMMED PLASTER

Q We had our 1930s house replastered ten months ago, as we wanted to paint the walls without using lining paper. Unfortunately the new plaster now has hairline cracks all over it. I have tried carving the cracks out and filling them with different kinds of filler, but this has failed to prevent the hairline cracks from returning. We hired a surveyor who said there was no building movement, and that the cracks were due to climatic temperature change. He recommended a Polycell basecoat, which we used in one room on the bare plaster, but this has not worked either. Do you have solutions to this problem?

A It sounds as though you might have had your lime plaster walls skimmed with modern gypsum plaster. When you put a hard plaster on top of a softer one, it will always crack, due to the different expansion/contraction characteristics. The only solution is to use lining paper (which you should have done in the first place), without wasting money on the replastering. Sorry, but it sounds as though you have been misadvised from the start.

CRACKS – CONCRETE FLOOR

Q My nine-year-old house has cracks in the concrete ground floor, either side of nearly every door opening. The floor away from the doorways has settled by about 5mm. Should I be worried, and do the cracks need attention before I get new carpets fitted?

A The cracks are a sign that the floor slabs have settled, due to inadequate compaction during construction. The floor at the door openings has stayed at the original level because it is supported by the brick or block footings of the walls. This is called 'differential settlement'. You need to get the floors screeded to level them up. If it's only 5mm, it might be possible to use self-levelling floor compound.

PVC-U

All materials are subject to decay, but this is not something that is much discussed by salesmen, who prefer the idea that their products will last for ever. Adverts for PVC-U replacement windows and cladding, for example, often give the impression that the material is 'maintenance free', and, for the scientifically uneducated, this must sound like a wonderful thing. Unfortunately, it is simply not true.

A recent reader's letter describes a typical scenario. The reader lives in a fairly modern purpose-built block of flats, and someone on the residents' committee has decided that, in order to 'reduce maintenance costs', all the windows, fascias and soffit boards should be replaced with PVC-U, at an estimated cost of

PVC-U roofline products.

over £100,000. The current annual amount they are spending on exterior maintenance is, of course, zero, because the windows, fascias and soffits have not actually been painted since 1976.

Imagine if we adopted the same approach to our clothes. Or teeth. Don't bother to clean them or look after them. Just let them rot away and then buy some plastic ones. Society would judge anyone who behaved like this as foolish, or deranged, or both. They would be sent for psychiatric counselling and their children would be taken away from them. But when it comes to the buildings that we live in, it seems to have become socially acceptable to allow them to rot.

The PVC-U salesmen exploit this inertia by reassuring us that it really is all right to neglect our homes. It is not our fault that the windows have rotted, they say; it is because they were made from that pesky old-fashioned stuff called wood. Time to get modern and use space-age materials that will last for ever.

Only they won't. PVC-U often becomes discoloured and brittle, and, because of its high thermal expansion coefficient, it can even crack. This last problem is especially common in PVC-U replacement fascias and soffit boards, which need very careful fixing and, dare I say it, maintenance, if they are to remain intact for more than a few years.

DISCOLOURED WINDOWS

Q My PVC-U window frames are becoming discoloured. They were installed about four years ago, and the outside surfaces have changed from white to cream. I have tried using a recommended PVC-U cleaner, and also T-cut and various other polishes, all without success. The company that installed them has since gone out of business. Do you have any suggestions?

A PVC-U windows will all eventually become discoloured and brittle, due to the action of u/v light from the sun. Those that are made cheaply, by disreputable manufacturers and installers, are liable to degrade the quickest, and it sounds as though yours fall into this category. Worse discolouration – to brown or yellow – occurs because of faulty manufacture, with an imbalance in the amount of titanium oxide in the formulation and the heat or speed of the extrusion process. The only real cure is replacement. Some installers claim they can strip off the top layer and apply lacquer, or paint them, but this will only be effective for a few years.

PAINTING PLASTIC

Q We had an extension built and now have exposed white plastic windows and waste pipes, a brown pipe going into the drain, a grey plastic soil stack, and black plastic gutters and down pipes. Would the life of all this plastic be prolonged if painted, and is there a special paint for the job?

A All plastics become brittle through exposure to u/v light, but not at the same rate. This will depend upon the type of plastic, the colour, and the amount of u/v stabilizer used in manufacture. Your white internal waste pipes are probably polypropylene, and the windows, brown and grey drainage pipes, and black guttering, are PVC-U.

The biggest maintenance requirement for PVC-U products is to keep them clean. The plastic surfaces seem to attract dust and pollutants – possibly by electrostatic attraction – and white PVC-U can quickly become dirty. So all PVC-U windows and roofline products should be washed with detergent at least once a year, and more frequently in towns or areas close to the sea. All plastics will last longer if painted. ICI/Dulux make Weathershield PVC-U paint for use on weathered PVC-U windows, which will need rubbing down and recoating every few years, like all paintwork; but ordinary spirit-based undercoat and gloss can also be used.

ROOFLINE PRODUCTS

Q I live on an estate of houses with much white boarding – soffits, fascias, etc. Firms come round offering maintenance-free white PVC. Some firms cover the surfaces of the existing wood soffits with thin plastic boards; others insist it is better to remove the original wood and replace it entirely with PVC. Few of us still have the original woodwork which, of course, has the disadvantage of needing repainting at intervals. Which is the best option?

A 'Maintenance-free' PVC-U is something of a myth. It won't last for ever. It becomes brittle through exposure to sunlight, and discoloured by airborne pollutants. PVC-U must also be fixed using slotted holes to allow for thermal movement. If this is not done then the boards can buckle and split. Fastening PVC-U boards over existing timber is a real bodge job, as it will trap moisture underneath and the timber will rot. Why do you think there are so many of these firms around touting for work? It's because they are making a fortune for doing not very much. For the money they charge you could pay to have the woodwork maintained and painted for fifty years.

NEIGHBOUR PROBLEMS (1)

Q We live in a semi-detached bungalow. We have the rainwater downpipe for the front of the two properties discharging at the front corner of our bungalow, and our neighbour has the corresponding pipe for the rear. He is going to have his original wood fascias, guttering, etc., replaced with PVC-U, and wants us to do the same. Ours is quite sound, and we do not care to replace with PVC-U in any case. What do we need to be aware of with regard to jointing, etc., and what redress would we have if there were problems in the future?

A The main thing to be aware of is that most of this kind of replacement PVC-U work is carried out by unskilled, unqualified cowboy companies, who are unlikely to still be trading in twelve months' time, when the gutters start leaking. You should make it clear to your neighbour in writing that you will hold him responsible for any problems caused to your property as a result of his actions. You should also commission a condition survey from an independent surveyor, which should include a photographic record of the guttering as it is now.

NEIGHBOUR PROBLEMS (2)

Q My guttering is the standard half-round plastic, and my neighbour has had his renewed with a square shape. His fitter joined up to our gutter with a big wedge of silicone mastic, which has now started leaking. Is there an actual fitting that will couple half-round to square gutters?

A There are various adaptors for connecting different shapes of plastic guttering together, and for connecting plastic to cast iron. The best place to ask is in a specialist plumbers' merchants, where they will have all the different manufacturers' catalogues. It will help if you find out the brand names of the two types of guttering, which should be written or stamped somewhere on the guttering, downpipes and clips. In the event that you cannot find a suitable adaptor, you will have to fit stop ends to the two lengths of guttering, and adjust the fall of the higher section so that the rainwater drains back to the nearest outlet and downpipe.

This PVC-U guttering has been melted by the heat from the boiler flue below it.

WINDOWS

Most people who have double-glazed replacement windows fitted to their homes do so under the impression that these will last till the end of their days. Unfortunately this is often not the case. Sealed double-glazed units have a limited lifespan, and the seals will eventually fail, resulting in misting-up between the two panes of glass. In the highest-quality installations this may not happen for thirty years. Some experts say twenty years is a reasonable life expectancy. But poorly installed windows can fail much sooner – sometimes within a year – which can come as quite a shock to people who swallowed the sales pitch that their new windows would be maintenance-free for ever. The catches and hinges on cheaper windows also often break, and it can be very difficult to find matching replacements.

The sales techniques used to flog double glazing are much the same as those for any other building gimmick, except that double glazing is now apparently approved by the world's leaders. The Kyoto Accord on reducing carbon emissions committed nations to cutting down fuel consumption, and the British government is amongst those concentrating on reducing home heating energy in order to reach their Kyoto targets. Since 2002, the Building Regulations have required all windows in new houses, and replacement windows in existing houses, to have an insulation value that can be achieved only by double glazing, with at least one pane being of low-Emissivity ('low-E') glass. (**Note**: the Building Regulations do not oblige you to have your windows replaced or upgraded. An existing window can still be repaired using traditional methods, even if this involves replacing or reglazing part of it. Double-glazing companies that use the Building Regs to pressurize homeowners into buying replacement windows are acting unscrupulously, and should be reported to local-authority trading standards officers.)

The problem is, double glazing requires energy to manufacture and install, and the payback period, in terms of both energy and money, is very long. Taking the average British home and replacing its existing windows with new double-glazed units, it would probably take around a hundred years of reduced heating bills to cover the cost of the installation. So the salesman who recently persuaded a ninety-five-year-old man that new windows would save him money in the long run surely deserves some kind of award.

In any case, there is no way that new, sealed double-glazed units are going to last a hundred years. They are doomed to fail eventually because of the way in which they are made. The two panes of glass are joined at the edge with a polymer compound, which by its very nature is slightly vapour-permeable (i.e. it will always allow a small amount of water vapour to enter from outside). So to keep the glass from misting up, each double-glazed unit also incorporates a desiccant – a drying agent – housed within a perforated alloy strip running around the edge. This desiccant absorbs the invading moisture and prevents misting. But eventually there will come a day when it can absorb no more. It will be saturated, and then there will be free water between the panes, which will form as mist on the glass. How long this takes depends upon the quality of the materials and workmanship.

In ideal circumstances the sealed glass unit will be mounted in drained and vented recesses in the window frames, positioned on special setting blocks, and with spacers at intervals around the edges to support it when the window is opened or subjected to wind loads. When this is not done, which is very often the case, the resulting stresses on the glass can break the seal. Units fitted into timber windows using ordinary putty or oily mastics can also fail quickly, as these dry out the sealant and cause it to crack.

When the seal is broken, any water collecting at the bottom edge of the glass will find its way through and saturate the desiccant. And once these double-glazed units mist up inside there is nothing that can be done to remedy it. Thousands of windows in hundreds of homes already have this problem, and the numbers are set to grow. As with all common building defects, there are 'quick fix' remedies being marketed, which consist mainly of drilling holes in the glass and inserting plastic stoppers or valves. These might remove or reduce internal misting, but are not really a solution, as drilling holes in the glass reduces the thermal insulation benefits of the sealed glazed unit.

Double-glazed windows can also constitute a threat to fire safety. They often have key-lockable catches, and, in many cases, homeowners keep them locked and hide the key in a 'safe place'. Some window catches are even designed so that if you try to force them open whilst locked, the spindles will actually shear off, leaving the windows unopenable. And of course the double layer of glass makes them harder to break. I am not being provocatively 'anti-double glazing' here, but experts confirm that several deaths have been attributed to the difficulty people have encountered in escaping through locked or badly designed double-glazed windows.

REPLACING WINDOWS

Q We have been advised that our two bay windows need replacing and are now considering the PVC variety. However, there are so many 'cowboys' around. Is there any trade organization we could contact for some idea of quality?

A My advice is to first try to find a good carpenter to repair your existing windows. Should this prove impossible, then consider timber replacements. The curse of the window industry is cheap plastic (PVC-U) replacement double glazing. PVC-U is a flexible material, which is why the extruded sections used to fabricate them have to be so chunky-looking (on smaller windows the PVC-U framing can take up more than 50 per cent of the total window area, seriously restricting the light coming into the room, as well as spoiling the appearance of the building). Also, because of their bendiness, PVC-U windows are supposed to be reinforced with steel or aluminium alloy inserts. Less reputable manufacturers have been known to omit this reinforcement, or to only put it down the sides where the hinges are, or where the frames are fixed to the walls of the house.

Cheap PVC-U replacement windows also suffer from problems of degradation of the rubber glazing gaskets, and early failure of the window hardware (hinges, catches, etc.), for which matching replacements are often difficult, sometimes impossible, to find.

Perhaps the greatest problem with poor-quality double glazing, however, is misting up between the two panes of glass, when the sealed glazed units (SGUs) in the windows break down and allow condensation to form inside them. This is starting to reach epidemic proportions, with hundreds of thousands of homes across the UK being affected. Sealed glazed units need to be glazed using special spacers (called 'bridges' and 'location blocks') to support them in the frame, so that the combined actions of the wind and opening/closing of the windows will not put excessive strain on the edge seals. In the case of many cheap windows that mist up prematurely, these spacers are found to be missing.

Just as important is the fact that SGUs need to be mounted in drained, vented rebates in the windows, so that any moisture finding its way into the frame – whether from outside rain or internal condensation – can drain away before it has a chance to penetrate the edge seal. This requirement has even been formulated in a British Standard, BS6262, but this is widely misunderstood, and even ignored, by many in the replacement window industry. This is a shame, because BS6262 is easy to implement. It simply requires a clear 5mm gap between the glass and the frame all round the window (the plastic bridges support the glass and maintain the gap), and the provision of 5 x 25mm slots along the bottom edge of the frame, so that any moisture can drain away to the outside.

The main trade association is the Glass & Glazing Federation, but as with all trade associations, membership does not necessarily indicate quality. There are a few good firms out there, but they are hard to find. My contacts in the trade recommend the following firms:

For timber windows – Peter Shaw Joinery, 02476 447 644, www.shaws-joinery.co.uk

For PVC-U windows – KBE Window Systems, 0845 130 6169, www.kbe-online.com

For sealed glazed units (SGUs) – Goldshield Windows, 01277 814 444, www.goldshieldwindows.com.

Details of the dry-glazed, drained and vented system are in the Building Research Establishment report 'Double-glazing units: a BRE guide to improved durability' [CONSTRUCTION LITERATURE].

REPAIRING DAMAGED FRAMES

Q Can you offer advice regarding dry rot in the bottom transom of window frames? I am thinking in particular of the use of fillers or even splices as a repair.

A Windows are unlikely to suffer from dry rot as this requires high humidity and so only occurs within enclosed spaces. Your windows are more likely to have been damaged by wet rot, caused by water running down the glass and getting in behind poorly maintained paint and putty. If the transoms, bottom rails or sills have rotted badly, there is really little point in trying to patch them up with filler, especially if the joints have been weakened, and it is better to engage a skilled carpenter to cut out and replace the damaged sections. Surface damage on otherwise sound sections of timber is best filled with a two-part epoxy filler. New timber windows, or new sections, should be given two good coats of primer before glazing, and the paintwork should be inspected annually and, if necessary, touched up to cover any damaged areas. The life of timber windows can be greatly extended by opening them at regular intervals to release water trapped between the sashes and the frames.

REPAIRS TO WINDOWS

Q Your recent comments have convinced me to try to repair the wooden bay windows in my 1930s semi, rather than go for PVC-U double glazing. But do you have any advice as to how to get in contact with reliable firms that can repair/upgrade the original windows? I am wary of the claims made in the Yellow Pages, and I'm not sure which of the various trade associations are genuine.

A Ideally, you want to find a carpenter of the old school (probably retired) who will do a slow, careful job of overhauling your windows – repairing badly damaged areas by splicing-in new sections of timber and making sure the opening lights open and close smoothly. If you cannot find any local glaziers to repair damaged leaded lights, then you can ship them to Gilbert & McCarty (020 8505 9342), who can also make replacement leaded lights based on photographs and measurements. They can also arrange for traditional window repairs in some parts of the country.

SLIDING SASH PROBLEM

Q I have a flat in a Victorian house with sliding sash windows. These all work well, apart from one in the kitchen, which will not stay open. The cords on both sides are intact, but the window falls shut unless it is propped open with something. How can there be a fault with this one window?

A The most likely cause is that the sliding sash in question has had a glass breakage, and been reglazed with 4mm glass in place of the original 3mm. On a large pane, this can represent a significant weight difference. On a top sash, it will result in the window refusing to stay shut, and on a bottom sash, in its refusal to stay open. You should be able to spot a new pane of glass by looking at the putty and paintwork. The solution is to add extra weights to the sash weights hanging inside the box frame.

REPAIRING SASH WINDOW

Q My flat in a converted Victorian house has a large twelve-pane sash window which is rotting at the bottom. It won't close properly, so I have a permanent 2in gap at the top. Does the whole window have to be replaced and what is the likely cost? I am on the first floor so I would expect it to involve scaffolding if it had to come out. Also, being in a conservation area, I would need to replace it with a wooden window, which I would prefer anyway. I have no idea who to contact for what needs doing.

A Your course of action depends on the actual state of the window, its age, and whether it has any important historical features that are worth saving (even crinkly panes of glass have a value). The total replacement scenario might not be as expensive as you fear – maybe only a few hundred pounds for the sliding sashes, depending on who you find to do it. No scaffolding is involved; sashes are easily removed and replaced from the inside. A local carpentry workshop should be able to make you a close copy, glazed and primed. Repair might also be an option, but would require an older traditional sort of carpenter.

METAL WINDOWS

Q I live in a 1930s house with many small-paned metal windows (Crittall, I believe). The majority are OK, but a couple of the upstairs opening casements have warped over time and have small areas of rust, causing cracked panes. How can I get these refurbished?

A Crittall windows are still being made by the original firm, and if you contact their technical services department they will give you a list of regional distributors who provide a repair and refurbishment service. Metal windows have performed well over the years, and it is well worth keeping them, especially in order to maintain the architectural integrity of a 1930s house. Steel windows are also supplied by other members of the Steel Window Association [WINDOWS & GLAZING].

WINDOWS – INSULATING

Q We live in an eighty-year-old house with large Crittall windows – not double-glazed, but we do have central heating. We find that in the winter, until we draw the curtains in the evening, a lot of cold comes through the glass. Is it possible to stick some kind of clear plastic insulation material on the windows, and would this help?

A It is possible to apply a heat-reflective film to the glass, which would have the same advantages and disadvantages as the low-Emissivity ('low-E') glass used in new double-glazed windows. The advantage would be a very small improvement in the thermal insulation value of the glass, which might or might not make a noticeable difference to your internal comfort. The disadvantages are that the film is best applied professionally (by a company such as the Window Film Company, [WINDOWS & GLAZING]), otherwise it might wrinkle or peel off. At around £30 per square metre, the cost is unlikely to be paid back by any savings in heating bills over its lifetime (around ten years). Also, as with all low-E coatings, the reflective film imparts a dark tint to the glass, which you might find annoying.

A more worthwhile course of action would be to make sure your Crittall windows close properly and are completely draught proof; Crittall has a network of regional distributors who provide a repair and refurbishment service. Next, consider fitting sliding alloy-framed secondary glazing on the inside of the existing windows. This will provide a further barrier to heat loss and external noise, and can also be fitted with low-E glass if you so wish. Secondary glazing (from a company such as Selectaglaze) will cost more than the window film, but will definitely improve your comfort levels, and will be a permanent improvement to the property.

DOUBLE GLAZING – LEAKING VENTS

Q I know that replacement double-glazed windows should always have ventilation slots at the top, but we had windows replaced two years ago and unfortunately when it is very windy, the wind howling through the closed vents produces a noise like elephants trumpeting! At times the noise drowns out the TV. Is there something wrong with our windows' vent system or is this inevitable with window vents?

A Other readers have complained of wind noise, and also of rain being blown in through window vents, even when they are shut. The idea of these 'trickle vents' is to provide a gentle flow of ventilation, to make up for the fact that the replacement windows have probably sealed off all the natural ventilation that was occurring before. But trickle vents should always be designed to cope with the prevailing weather conditions, and if they are noisy, or leaky, then this is because they are simply poor quality and not fit for their designed purpose. Your installers have an obligation to rectify this. A soundproof trickle vent is available from Renson, and Glazpart claim to supply a weatherproof vent [WINDOWS & GLAZING]. Both can be fitted to existing windows, although this may be more than a DIY job.

DOUBLE GLAZING – MISTING UP (1)

Q Several years ago I had my windows replaced with double glazing. After a few years, the south-facing ones became subject to occasional, unsightly internal misting. As there was a ten-year guarantee I claimed for renewal of the windows. The insurance company claimed that the condensation was normal and therefore refused the claim.

A One of the great unspoken truths of sealed double-glazed units (SGUs) is that eventually they will all mist up. The timescale should be twenty or so years in a perfectly made and installed window. But in poorly made ones it can be a lot less. Five months has been reported.

So, in a way, the condensation is 'normal', in that it will happen eventually in all windows. But I would have thought you could expect that a ten-year guarantee would reasonably cover you against misting within that time. It depends on the insurers' small print, I suppose.

Double-glazed windows will all mist up eventually.

DOUBLE GLAZING – MISTING UP (2)

Q Is it possible to have misted double glazing repaired rather than replaced? Can the two glass panes be separated, cleaned new desiccant added, and reassembled again, or is the cost of this not significantly different to that of new units?

A No, it is not possible. Nobody has yet found a way to remove the spacer bar and its sealant, and leave a clean surface able to take a new spacer bar and sealant. Any attempt to do so will cost far more in man-hours than making a new sealed unit with fresh clean glass. Some 'experts' suggest a repair trick of drilling two small holes in the outer pane, allowing the misting to clear, and then sealing the holes. This may work for a few weeks, but the glass will soon mist up again because it has not remedied the actual cause of the misting, which is water getting in through the seals and saturating the desiccant inside the spacer bar. Drilling holes and leaving them unsealed has also been suggested, but this removes the thermal insulation benefit of having double glazing. This is why it is so important that double-glazed units are installed correctly in the first place, using a drained, vented, dry glazing system, that prevents water from coming into contact with the edge seals.

DOUBLE GLAZING – MISTING UP (3)

Q **Two of my double-glazed units have started to mist. Is there a company that can supply just the sealed panes, as I am more than capable of removing and refitting them myself. But I am struggling to find a company that will supply the panes only.**

A Any local glazier or glass merchants should be able to supply new sealed double-glazed units to your measurements. However, if you fit them into the existing frames, the chances are that they will mist up again before too long. Premature misting of sealed glazed units is usually caused by incorrect fitting. The glass needs to be mounted in drained and vented rebates, supported on special setting blocks, and with spacers around the edges to support it when the window is opened or subjected to wind loads. If this is not done, then the stresses on the glass can damage the seal and allow moisture to penetrate between the two panes. Double-glazed units fitted into timber windows with ordinary putty or mastic can also fail prematurely, as these materials can dry out the seal and cause it to crack.

DRY-GLAZING SYSTEM

Q **You have advised against fitting double-glazed units in timber windows using putty or mastic, because of the problem of internal misting. Our property was built in 1987, and soon after we bought it in 1993 we had to replace ten units that had misted up. Two different glaziers said our units could be installed only with putty, the recesses not being deep enough to accept timber glazing beads. In 1994 we installed sealed Pilkington K units in a new sun lounge, which were fitted with beads but reinforced with mastic because of the local wind-driven horizontal rain. All of these have now acquired internal misting. We would dearly love to get twenty years' use out of replacements, rather than the seven to eight years we have had so far, but how can we get a glazier to use the dry-glazing method you recommend?**

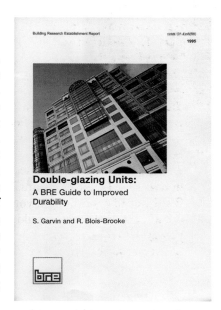

Building Research Establishment Report GRBB (31.4)ck6(R8)
1995

Double-glazing Units:
A BRE Guide to Improved Durability

S. Garvin and R. Blois-Brooke

A Sealed glazed units (SGUs) installed with putty or mastic can mist up within a short time because the oils in the putty or mastic dry out the edge seal, causing it to crack, and because these sealants also trap water, allowing it to penetrate the edge seal, saturate the desiccant, and cause condensation between the panes. A drained, vented dry-glazing system overcomes both of these problems and should help to give SGUs a mist-free life of twenty years or more.

Any competent glazier or carpenter should be able to adapt a timber window to a dry-glazing system. In the unlikely event that the existing glazing rebates are too shallow, they can easily be deepened using a router, plane or oscillating shear. The replacement SGUs should be mounted on plastic setting blocks to hold them clear of the rebate, and the bottom glazing bead should have 5mm x 35mm slots cut in the lower edge to allow water to drain away. This technique is described in British Standard BS6262 and in the Building Research Establishment book 'Double-glazing Units: A BRE Guide to Improved Durability' [CONSTRUCTION LITERATURE]. Existing timber windows can be converted using Reddiseals' patent dry glazing system [WINDOWS & GLAZING].

DRAINED & VENTILATED GLAZING SYSTEM

DOUBLE GLAZING MISTING EXTERNALLY

Q Why would my newly installed double-glazed windows mist up on the outside?

A Condensation on the outside of double-glazed windows is not uncommon, and householders often think it is due to a fault. But night-time condensation on any outside surface is nothing more than dew, which will form on any cool surface after sunset, as the warm air cools, and is no longer able to hold as much water vapour. This phenomenon occurs more often in the summer, and is therefore sometimes referred to as 'summer condensation'. It is commonly seen on car windows, but rarely on single-glazed house windows, because heat escaping through the glass from inside the house keeps the window pane above dewpoint temperature. The insulating effect of double glazing means that the outer pane of glass is relatively cooler than single glazing, allowing dew to form on it.

SECONDARY GLAZING (1)

Q My brother-in-law and I are seeking to fit secondary glazing to our houses for different reasons. My requirement is to bolster the soundproofing effect of my existing double-glazed units because of road noise. He wishes to improve the heat insulation of single-glazed windows on a north-east-facing wall. What are your views regarding secondary glazing for these purposes? Do you have recommendations regarding glass thickness or aluminium versus PVC?

A Secondary glazing is best for noise reduction, double glazing for heat insulation. But secondary glazing will also help to keep the heat in, by cutting out draughts, and your brother-in-law may achieve good results by using a single pane of 'low-E' glass from Pilkingtons. Alloy frames are better than PVC-U as they are less obtrusive and longer lasting. For optimum sound reduction, use the thickest glass you can – up to 6mm if the frames will take it. It also helps if the glass in the secondary glazing is a different thickness from that in the original windows.

SECONDARY GLAZING (2)

Q We have a 1910 house with its original windows. Most of our neighbours have had theirs replaced by horrible-looking plastic double glazing. We do not want to do this. On the other hand we would like some of the benefits of double glazing such as more warmth and less noise. What can we do?

A You should fit secondary glazing on the inside of the original windows. This is better for cutting down sound than sealed double-glazed units, and the greater the gap between the two sets of windows, the greater the sound reduction. It will also cut down the draughts. Aluminium-framed sliding secondary glazing can be made to match the fenestration pattern of the original windows, and is unobtrusive.

SECONDARY GLAZING (3)

Q Some years ago secondary glazing kits appeared to be widely available at most DIY shops, but they no longer seem to be on the market. Is it possible to purchase these for installation as a DIY project, or are they only supplied and fitted by specialist manufacturers?

A Aluminium secondary-glazing kits are still available for keen DIYers. For example Selectaglaze supply kits to builders, and also have a network of approved fabricators and installers. Many local replacement-window firms will also be able to supply made-to-measure secondary-glazing units, and you may find that these are cheap enough that you will save very little by making them yourself. Try looking up 'Window frame and accessory manufacturers' in the Yellow Pages. The Monarch secondary-glazing system is also available from a network of local fabricators and installers [WINDOWS & GLAZING].

GEORGIAN-LOOK DOUBLE GLAZING

Q I'm forever replacing putty and repainting our mock-Georgian window frames. Not only is it a constant battle against leaks, but single glazing means pools of condensation throughout the winter. You've described the pitfalls of PVC-U but my wife is adamant that she wants to enjoy the comfort of double glazing and I don't want to continue with high maintenance. Can I satisfy both of us and still maintain a 'Georgian' look?

A Yes. Modern high-performance sealed glazed units can be as thin as 14mm, so this makes it possible to double glaze your existing timber windows, or new timber replacements. It is claimed that timber windows can achieve minimal maintenance if they are painted with high-build micro-porous paint, which needs a rub down with steel wool and a single recoat every seven to ten years. And this gives you the warmth of timber, which is superior to PVC-U reinforced with aluminium. You need a vented and drained dry-glazing system (no putty or mastic bedding) to keep the SGUs from misting up prematurely.

LEAKING LEADED LIGHTS

Q My 1930s house has small leaded windows. When it rains heavily, some of the windows leak. I have tried putting putty or wood filler on the horizontal sections but it is a very protracted job and I have had little or no success. Is there a product on the market to insert between the lead and the glass or is the answer to have new sections made?

A Leaded lights can be repaired using traditional leadlight cement, which requires the windows to be taken out and laid flat on a bench. You should scrape out all areas of loose old cement, and make sure that none of the soldered joints have corroded, as these can also be points of leakage. The joints are then resealed by brushing in fresh cement. Small areas can be resealed without taking the window out, using black putty. For professional restoration look under 'Stained glass suppliers' or 'Leaded lights and windows' in the Yellow Pages. James Hetley supply books on leaded-light work [WINDOWS & GLAZING].

LEADED LIGHTS IN DOUBLE GLAZING

Q We have a 1930s semi still with the original bay windows at the front of the house, with leaded stained glass in the top sections. The wood is quite rotten in places and we need to have something done about this. Is it possible for these leaded lights to be used in replacement plastic double-glazed windows? We would prefer plastic double glazing as we aren't getting any younger and these would be easier to maintain. We currently have secondary glazing, which cuts out all draughts and stops condensation.

A Many replacement window companies offer a 'stained glass' option for 1930s houses, but they are usually only coloured paper stuck on to the inside of the sealed glazed units. More conscientious leaded light restorers will be able to reuse your original glass – set in lead strips – on the inside of the units (look in the Yellow Pages under 'Leaded lights and windows'). But before you take this drastic step, you would be well advised to see whether you can get your existing timber windows repaired. It is not always true that double-glazed PVC-U windows are easier to maintain, as they can suffer from embrittlement (caused by exposure to sunlight), misting up between the panes, and readers report that the catches and handles are prone to premature failure.

More importantly, in 1930s bay windows, the original timber frames often bear the load of the floor above, and replacing them with PVC-U can result in settlement and cracking damage. For the money that you will pay for replacement plastic windows, you could probably pay someone to repair and maintain your existing timber windows for the next fifty years.

PVC-U DOOR WON'T OPEN

Q I had replacement PVC windows and back door fitted to my small semi in June 2000. The supplier and fitter went out of business soon afterwards. In the summer of 2001 I had difficulty turning the key in the lock of the back door and called in a locksmith, who said the lock was not at fault, but that the door needed rehanging. This summer the same thing is happening again. It seems to be a heat-related problem. First thing, in the cool of the morning, the lock functions easily enough, but later in the day when the temperature goes up, I can't turn the key in the lock and have to go out the front way to get to the back garden. Short of replacing the door, can you suggest a way of solving this problem?

A PVC-U expands in heat a lot more than other materials – nearly 1mm per metre per 10°C. Dark colours absorb more heat than white, so expand more. The clearances around the door should be a minimum of 5–6mm all round if the PVC-U is white (7–8mm if any other colour). The rollers can be adjusted up and down to accommodate the expansion, and the lock clearances can also be adjusted separately, but it needs someone familiar with the mechanisms who can make the adjustments whilst leaving the door secure. Unfortunately most PVC-U replacement window firms do not have this expertise, and are only after your money. For independent advice on finding someone to solve your problem call Fenestration Associates [WINDOWS & GLAZING].

PUZZLING BREAKAGE

Q Neighbours had a stone thrown at their double-glazed PVC-U door. Strangely, the outer sheet of glass didn't break but the inner one shattered, looking like a spider's web. How is this possible?

A It sounds as though the outer pane was toughened glass, which would be able to withstand the impact of the stone, but which would deflect momentarily, to transmit a pressure wave across the air space. This pressure broke the inner pane, which was laminated glass. Both materials qualify as 'safety glass', which is required in doors.

So, you may ask, why weren't both panes made of toughened glass? Well, it's tough, but it's not that tough. It can be broken by impact from a sharp instrument such as a pickaxe, and when it does break, it disintegrates and falls out of the frame. Laminated, on the other hand, whilst it shatters more easily, still hangs together in one piece. So they each have different security advantages.

NEW WINDOW REGULATIONS

Q I am shortly to embark on an extension to my 1935 property and wish to install single-glazed wooden window frames similar to the originals. Architects have informed me that since 2002 all new windows have to be double glazed to comply with Building Regulations. This means I shall have two new double-glazed windows in the drawing room along with the three original single-glazed windows. It is most unlikely the new windows will match the old ones, and the whole issue of two types of glazing in one room seems a nonsense. Is there any way to overcome this?

A This is a typically absurd result of the new Part L of the Building Regulations that came into force on April Fool's Day 2002. All windows in new houses, and replacement windows in existing houses, are supposed to be double glazed with low-Emissivity ('low-E') glass. Exceptions apply only to listed buildings, houses in conservation areas and buildings of architectural or historical interest. However, in your case, since the new walls of your extension will presumably be built to the current Building Regulations, you could argue that you are in fact improving the thermal insulation of the room overall, and that you should therefore be allowed to trade this off against the thermal value of the new windows. Your local-authority Building Control Department does, in fact, have the discretion to consider the thermal value of the whole construction, and not simply the windows in isolation. There is much confusion over this amongst architects, surveyors and builders.

SCRATCHED GLASS

Q We recently moved house and it wasn't until we moved in that we noticed scratches on the double-glazed patio doors. They are surface scratches obviously made by the previous owner's dog. Is there any remedial treatment, in order to avoid the expense of having new doors fitted?

A The traditional way to do this is with jewellers' rouge and much elbow grease. Rouge can still be bought from glass-processing suppliers, and even some old-style builders' merchants. You wet it, apply it to the scratch and rub and rub and rub. Eventually, depending upon how deep the scratches, they will disappear.

Alternatively, find a glass merchants in the Yellow Pages – not a double-glazing supplier or leaded-lights maker, but one who really cuts and supplies pieces of glass. Most of these now have a high-speed electric buffer which can be brought along with some of the new buffing pastes, which make scratches disappear very quickly.

REMOVING OLD PUTTY

Q My architect-designed house was built forty-three years ago with wooden Georgian sliding sash windows. The original nineteen windows have been regularly painted with good-quality paint, but over the last few years cracks have appeared in the glazing putty, typically 30–50mm apart. The painter who has painted the windows several times now says that were he to try to remove the putty, not only would the pane on which he was working be broken, but also the one next to it would be at risk. Is there any solution other than replacement PVC-U windows in 'heritage' style?

A You should certainly not think of replacing your timber windows with PVC-U, as they will be unlikely to give you anything near forty-three years' service. Any competent glazier should be able to remove your cracked putty without breaking the glass, but if you (or your painter) want to do it yourself then the tool to use is the Fein MultiMaster [WINDOWS & GLAZING]. This is a power tool with a patented oscillating action and a selection of blades which will get into all sorts of tight corners. It is excellent for window refurbishment, and also good for cutting out old grout and sealants.

OVERHAULING SLIDING SASHES

Q **Our lovely Victorian house has one drawback – heavy sash windows. Is it easy to convert the lower pane – approximately 30 x 30in (750 x 750mm) – to something more manageable for seventy-year olds? We must, of course, maintain the original appearance.**

A Sash windows shouldn't be 'heavy' as they are supposed to be counterbalanced by the weights. It is possible that over the years they might have been fitted with thicker glass than the original, and this would need balancing by adding extra weights. A competent carpenter will be able to remove the sashes and weigh them (bathroom scales are suitable), and then adjust the amount of iron or lead weight hung on the sash cords. For a real expert job, the top and bottom sashes should be weighted differently. The weights for the top sash should be very slightly heavier than the window, so that it doesn't drop from its closed position, and the weights for the bottom sash slightly lighter than the window, so that they don't pull it up from its closed position.

Whilst the windows are out, the sashes and beads should be cleaned of excessive paint build-up at the sides, which can also impede smooth operation. You might also wish to take the opportunity to have brush-type draught-stripping installed in slots cut in the sides of the sashes. This will be totally unseen when the windows are reassembled. The sashes should be reinstalled using new sash cords and, if necessary, new pulleys, timber parting beads, staff beads and catches.

For sash window fittings and weatherproofing products, or to be put in touch with an experienced independent sash window restorer in your area, contact Mighton [WINDOWS & GLAZING].

DOUBLE-GLAZING HARDWARE

Q **My widowed mother has replacement PVC windows which are unlocked, and no keys can be found. We have tried all our local suppliers (B&Q, Homebase, local tradesmen) and none of them is able to help. Is there any method of making these windows lockfast as she is very worried about her house insurance and safety. The original installer appears to have vanished!**

A This is a common problem for many readers, who often believe that their missing keys are irreplaceable and unique. The reality, however, is that most replacement windows have very simple locks, and the keys for other windows in the house will probably fit them.

If this doesn't work, however, new handles are not expensive, and available from a variety of hardware suppliers [WINDOWS & GLAZING]. They will supply any number of handles, left- or right-handed, in whatever pattern and colour you require. Any local builder or odd-job man should be capable of changing a handle, by levering or pulling off the boss plate to reveal the two retaining screws, unscrewing these, throwing the old handle away, fitting the new one on to the projecting spindle and replacing the boss plate. The job should take ten minutes.

Alternatively, you could try the advertisers in the 'Double glazing repair' section of the Yellow Pages, who will probably charge around £70 for the call-out, but they will carry a limited stock, and the replacement handles might not be an exact match.

WINDOWS

DOUBLE GLAZING EDWARDIAN WINDOWS

Q Our Edwardian semi has large wooden sliding sash windows, which we would like to keep, but upgrade with sealed double-glazed units. We are receiving conflicting advice about whether this is possible, with some firms saying we will need complete replacement windows, and others suggesting 'stepped' units, with the outer panes puttied into the existing glazing rebates, and smaller panes fitted on the inside of the glazing bars.

A The problem is that normal double-glazed units (4 mm glass – 6 mm spacer – 4 mm glass) are too wide for the existing glazing rebates, and also too heavy for conventional sash weights and pulleys – hence the suggestion that you will need new box frames and sashes. This also applies to stepped-edge sealed units, and these are notorious for being fitted badly and breaking down. A better solution would be heat-strengthened 3mm glass, with 6mm spacers. This will give lightweight 12mm sealed units, which should fit into most Edwardian glazing rebates. The extra weight can be counterbalanced by adding lead circles on top of the existing sash weights.

WINDOWS – FIRE SAFETY

Q You have explained that for many years now, houses have had to be built so that every bedroom has a special escape window of sufficient size and shape that an adult can climb out through it. We live in a house which is part of a development built during the last four to six years by a national housebuilder, and which has PVC-U windows with no openings other than fanlights that not even a child could escape through. Consequently, in the event of a fire, our only means of escape from the bedroom would be down the stairs and out by way of either the front or back door. This has always been a cause for concern, but we assumed that the house must have been constructed in accordance with the relevant regulations, and that we had no legitimate grounds for complaint. Who should we approach to get this rectified?

A Until 2000, the Building Regulations on this matter were somewhat ambiguous and subject to interpretation by Building Control Officers. Rooms on a third storey (or loft rooms that form a third storey) had to have regulation-sized escape windows, but bedrooms on the upper floor of a two-storey house could have smaller windows, and a single escape route, down the staircase and out through the front or back door, as long as the Building Control Officer deemed this to be satisfactory.

However, the situation was tightened up considerably in the 2000 edition of the Building Regulations, which stated that all habitable rooms (except kitchens) in the upper storey(s) of a house served by only one staircase should be provided with an escape window with an unobstructed openable area of at least 0.33 sq m, and at least 450mm high, 450mm wide, and with the bottom of the openable area no higher than 1100mm above floor level. If you think your housebuilder has not conformed to the regulations, then your first point of complaint should be to your local-authority Building Control Department, quoting paragraphs 2.7 and 2.11 of Part B (Fire Safety) of the Building Regulations 2000 [CONSTRUCTION LITERATURE].

ELECTRICS

'**E**lectrics' is the name given by builders to anything in a house that is connected to the main power supply. So it covers the nests of hidden wires that run all around the house, and anything that has one or more of these wires permanently attached to it.

I have always tried not to get too closely involved in electrics, because (a) electricity is dangerous and (b) the regulations and the equipment are constantly changing. For example, since 1 January 2005, all electrical work (apart from simple like-for-like replacements of damaged power points and light fittings) has been subject to approval by local-authority Building Control Officers. So any DIYer who fits a new lighting circuit in the kitchen, say, or installs an electric shower, is obliged by the new 'Part P' of the Building Regulations to supply plans in advance to the council, and then pay for an inspector to come out and test the work. Professional electricians – if they wish to avoid the expense and hassle of getting a council Building Control Officer to inspect their work, have had to become members of one of the five government-approved (but privately administered) 'competent persons' schemes. This requires an annual fee of around £500 and extra fees for the registration of every completed job.

In the electrical world, the gold-standard qualifications have always been complying with the latest version of the Institute of Electrical Engineering wiring regulations (currently known as '16th edition') and City & Guilds 2391: Test & Inspection. These qualifications take years of experience and study to achieve and can cost applicants hundreds of pounds in course fees and lost work time. But time-served electricians who have these qualifications are themselves now being asked to pay £500 to prove that they are 'competent persons'. And, to add insult to injury, kitchen fitters, heating engineers and burglar alarm installers, who go on a five-day course with one of the private companies, will now be able to claim exactly the same level of status.

This new legislation is not going to raise standards. It amounts more to a collective dumbing-down of standards. And, like previous government attempts to interfere with the building industry (such as the ill-fated Quality Mark) it misses the really dangerous practitioners – the cowboys and incompetent DIYers – who will ignore the new rules and carry on as before. Instead it penalizes the good guys – the conscientious, qualified electricians who have always done things properly anyway. No wonder so many of them are saying they can't be bothered with it, and will retire early instead.

Whatever, there are some basics that everyone should know, such as the position of electrical cables under wall plaster and floors. Wall-mounted power sockets and light switches are the way in which we use and control electricity in our homes. In winter, we may use the kitchen light switch twenty times in a day, but we never stop to think about the cable route carrying the electricity from the consumer unit to the switch and then on to the light fittings. The cables are run under floors and up and down walls behind the plaster. It is useful to have an idea of where they might be, if for no other reason than to avoid drilling through them when we put shelves up.

Under timber floors, electrical cables running parallel to the joists should be clipped in place along the mid-axis of a joist. This is mostly the case with houses built since 1960. Houses older than that are likely to have been rewired since their birth, which means that new cables will have been poked or dragged into place beneath already-fixed floorboards. So the chances of the cables having been carefully clipped in place are slim. They are probably just lying on top of the ceiling plaster. Nothing wrong with that, but bear it in mind if you ever decide to drill a hole in the ceiling.

Cables which have to run perpendicular to the joists should go through holes drilled as close as possible to the vertical centre of each joist. This is the section of the joist that is in neither compression (the top half), nor tension (the bottom half), so drilling a 25mm hole through the centre of a 180mm floor joist does not, theoretically, affect its strength. Let's hope not. And make sure your electrician understands what is meant by 'centre'. (The reason these holes are usually hit and miss is that you can't fit an ordinary electric drill down in the space between the joists in order to drill square, so the holes are drilled at a downward angle. Only the most dedicated electricians carry special drills with right-angle attachments.) But as long as the cables are running through holes somewhere near the centre of the joists, at least they won't be hit by nails hammered into the floor from above. Unlike copper plumbing pipes which, because of their stiffness, have to be laid into notches cut in the tops of the joists.

Behind wall plaster, cables are supposed to be run vertically to and from power sockets and light switches. This is basic good practice, in order to give other people a rough idea of where they might be. So light switch cables will almost always drop down vertically from the ceiling. Power cables usually run below timber floors, and vertically up to the sockets, but in houses with solid concrete ground floors, they may drop down vertically from the ceiling above. Bear in mind, also, that unqualified electricians and DIYers may not always have been completely diligent about having vertical cable runs, and that cables can sometimes be found running at all angles around rooms. This is especially likely in kitchens or rooms that have previously been used as kitchens, where power circuits for above-worktop sockets may have been run horizontally behind tiled splashbacks.

If in doubt, or when drilling into walls close to sockets or switches, it is a good idea to trace cable routes using a metal detector or cable finder. These are inexpensive and can be bought from builders' merchants or DIY outlets.

Another common question concerns what electricians call 'lamps' and other people call 'bulbs'. Is it true, as some people say, that lamps blow more easily in cold weather? The only logical reason for this might be that the greater temperature difference between the 'on' and 'off' states of the light causes more stress on the filament – the thin wire inside the bulb that glows white hot and gives off the light. But, since the tungsten filament of an incandescent bulb glows at around 2500°C, the fact that it starts off at ten degrees rather than twenty, say, would appear to be neither here nor there. Neither is there any evidence that failing bulbs are a sign of faulty wiring. We must face the fact that light bulbs break more often in the winter months because there are more hours of darkness to eat up their 1000-hour average lifespans. Since this is equivalent to only three hours per day over a year, it is hardly surprising that bulbs in heavily used rooms such as kitchens should need replacing on a fairly regular basis.

As incandescent bulbs glow white-hot, tungsten molecules evaporate from the filament and get deposited as a black residue on the inside of the glass, until the filament becomes so thin that it burns through. So a blown but thoroughly blackened bulb will be one that has served its time well; a clearer one is more likely to have failed due to impact or vibration.

A more significant factor in bulb life is which way up it goes in the fitting. Bulbs are designed to hang downwards, and if they point upwards or sideways they don't last as long. This is because, as the filament becomes thin and brittle with use, if the bulb is pointing upwards or sideways the filament can eventually collapse under its own weight. The filaments in downward-hanging bulbs are subjected to less stress and will usually only break before their time if you bash them.

Another disadvantage of upward-facing bulbs is that when they do blow, they tend to short out the whole circuit, blowing the fuse or MCB (miniature circuit breaker or 'trip switch') on the consumer unit, plunging the whole place into darkness. This is because bits of the broken filament fall across the two bulb terminals and cause a surge in power. If the bulb is hanging downwards then the broken bits land harmlessly in the glass.

Lately, however, even downward-hanging bulbs have started to trip circuits, because of a lowering in manufacturing standards. Light bulbs used to have a little built-in fuse – a very thin strip of wire in the bayonet cap – which would burn out first, leaving the rest of the filament intact. But now, pressure on costs from overseas manufacturers has meant that most modern bulbs are unfused, and can blow at any point along the filament. So you can now buy light bulbs for 20p, but they won't last as long and they'll blow your fuses. You never, ever, get something for nothing.

Nowadays we are all supposed to be using energy-saving light bulbs, claimed to last for 10,000 hours. I have been a keen user of these ever since they were first introduced, but I have yet to own one that has lasted anything like that length of time. Their price has come down in recent years, but they still cost up to ten times more than incandescent bulbs. They are claimed to use only one-fifth of the electricity, but this still means they need to last at least 1000 hours before they start saving you money, and it is not unusual for them to break before reaching this age. When you put one in, write the date in felt-tipped pen on the side of the plastic base, so you can keep a check.

Energy-saving bulbs are more accurately called 'compact fluorescents' and the latest versions consist of two or three fluorescent glass loops attached to a chunky mounting block containing the electronics needed to keep it working. This means they cannot always be used directly in place of incandescent bulbs. The light quality is cold, as with most fluorescent tube lighting; they cannot be used with normal dimmer switches; and they are too bulky for some light fittings and shades. The packet advertising which states 'interchangeable with an ordinary bulb' does not seem to mention any of this. Like all fluorescent lamps, they have a high initial rate of electricity consumption until they have warmed up, so they only save energy in situations where a light would normally be left on for long periods. They lose light intensity with age and their life is shortened by regular switching on and off. Readers have also pointed out that they may be dangerous if used on dark stairways, because of the time taken to warm up and give full illumination.

With the advent of Home Information Packs, and their associated Energy Performance Certificates, readers might be under the impression that replacing a few incandescent light bulbs with compact fluorescents might be a good way to improve their homes' energy ratings. Not so, unfortunately. The only low-energy lamps that will be registered by the energy assessor are permanent light fittings that can take only fluorescent tubes.

And, like all fluorescent lighting tubes, the compact fluorescents contain mercury and need to be disposed of as hazardous waste since, if crushed as landfill, the mercury may find its way into the water supply. Local-authority waste sites are supposed to be equipped to deal safely with fluorescent tubes, and householders should be allowed to deposit a maximum of six tubes at a time (this being the number used in a sunbed, I am told). Electricians are obliged to dispose of redundant fluorescent tubes via specialist contractors – a service for which they have to pay a fee. This is why so many tubes are dumped illegally in builders' skips, and why anyone driving through a city centre early in the morning will have noticed forests of fluorescent tubes apparently sprouting out of litter bins. Any government worth its green credentials would obviously provide free recycling for such a hazardous material. Ours appears keen to persuade us to use the bulbs, but doesn't want to think about the consequences.

REWIRING (1)

Q We have lived in our 1961 semi since it was built. Over recent years a number of neighbours have had their houses rewired. As far as I am aware this has been done because the owners felt it was time to do so, rather than as the result of any specific problems. Should ours be rewired?

Rewiring.

A It depends upon the type of cable. The 1960s saw the changeover from rubber-sheathed cable to PVC. The rubber (usually black) had a life expectancy of around twenty-five years, so it would almost certainly be in need of replacement now. PVC-sheathed cable (either white or grey) has no known life expectancy, and should still be perfectly serviceable. However, up until about 1970, lighting circuits were usually wired in twin PVC cable with no earth wire, and whilst this is still acceptable for plastic light fittings, anything metal (such as some types of wall light) would need an earth cable running to it. Also, in the same period, it was usual for one 30-amp ring main to supply power for the whole house, whereas now, with the increased number of electrical appliances, it is normal to have one ring main for downstairs and one for upstairs. Upgrading does not necessitate a complete rewire, as the circuit can be cut in half and reconnected to provide two separate rings.

It would also be advisable to replace an old fused consumer unit with a modern one with miniature circuit breakers (trip switches), and incorporating a residual current device (RCD), sometimes also referred to as a residual current circuit breaker (RCCB). You might also consider having your old light fittings replaced, as these become brittle with age and heat, and having your power points inspected and replaced if necessary. The NICEIC recommend that household electrical systems should be inspected at least every ten years.

REWIRING (2)

Q My house, built in the 1960s, has a 13-amp ring main with PVC cable connected through a cartridge-type fuse box. On attempting to have installed a modern consumer unit with earth bonding, I was informed by the electrician that for the unit to be fitted, the whole house would have to be rewired. Is this the case under current electrical wiring regulations?

A No, there is nothing in the IEE wiring regulations that requires your house to be rewired. If you want your wiring system to be upgraded to the latest standards, or if the electrician has spotted that parts of the current system are unsafe, then that is a separate matter. In order to have a modern consumer unit installed possible additional work would be to upgrade the main earthing and equipotential bonding conductors (i.e. thicker earth bonding cable to the water and gas pipes). Note that replacing the consumer unit is notifiable under Part P of the Building Regulations, and either your electrician should be a member of a recognized competent persons scheme, or the work should be pre-notified to your local-authority Building Control Department.

OLD CABLE DANGERS

Q I moved into a first-floor flat conversion, in a 1920s semi-detached house, about two years ago. The wiring was fairly old, so I decided to have it completely renewed at considerable expense. But, with proper earthing and new trip switches, I feel a lot safer. However, when the electrician was doing the wires under the floorboards he disturbed the wiring to the lights of the ground-floor flat below, which he showed me. He said it was lead-covered cabling, not used since the 1940s, and that it was a potential hazard. The people in the flat downstairs are neither particularly house-proud, nor well-off, but is there any way I can legally (or otherwise) persuade them to rewire?

A There are thousands of homes that still use the old lead-sheathed cables, and the good news is that – as long as the cables are not disturbed or overloaded – they are not an immediate safety hazard. The bad news is that where a fault does occur, the circuits are usually protected only by the old wire-type fuses, which do not cut the power off as quickly as modern miniature circuit-breakers (MCBs), so that there is more chance of an electrical fault leading to a fire.

You should certainly try to persuade your downstairs neighbours that it is in both your interests that they have their electrical system upgraded. If they object, and if you are leaseholders, then you should ask your freeholder to intervene. If you are joint freeholders, then you may have to take legal advice about how to enforce the upgrade. It may also be worth asking advice from your building insurers.

CORRODING CABLES

Q I have lived in my house since it was built in 1967. The wiring is of the twin-and-earth type (for lighting and power), covered in grey PVC. There are two separate lighting circuits. Recently I have noticed a green tenacious substance seeping out from a number of light switches (particularly on the two-way circuit to the hallway). On closer inspection this seems to be coming from out of the cable itself. Is this a chemical reaction between the copper and PVC, or is it caused by something else?

A This happens to some cable installed in the 1965–70 era. Although the outer sheathing is PVC, the inner red and black sheathing on the conductors was a different plastic, known as 'capathene', and it does seem that it reacts with the copper wire to produce a green runny liquid. It is likely to be happening on all the cabling, but will be most noticeable on the light switch cables, as these drop down from the ceiling, and the liquid runs out under gravity. You should get the cabling checked by an NICEIC-registered electrician [ELECTRICS].

SENSITIVE CIRCUIT BREAKERS

Q My friend, who is eighty-eight years old, lives alone and is registered blind. He has had numerous instances of a 'trip switch' operating when a light bulb blows. This means he has to grope his way to the consumer unit, open it, and feel along the switch knobs for the one that needs to be reset. Is this not evidence that these switches are excessively sensitive, and is there any way of overcoming the problem?

A Miniature circuit breakers (MCBs) in the consumer unit are designed to trip whenever a particular circuit is overloaded. In addition, the whole electrical system will be protected by a Residual current device (RCD) – also known as an 'earth-leakage circuit-breaker' – which detects the amount of current flowing in through the live conductors and the amount flowing out through the neutral conductors. If there is an electrical fault allowing current to leak to earth, then the RCD will shut the whole system down in a fraction of a second. Both the MCBs and the RCD are there for one important reason, which is safety.

When a light bulb blows, pieces of the broken filament can fall across the conductors, causing a surge of power, which is most likely to trip the individual MCB protecting the lighting circuit. It is worth noting that light bulbs are designed to hang down, from ceiling fittings, in which case the pieces of filament usually fall harmlessly into the bottom of the bulb without tripping the circuit breakers. The problem is far more likely to occur with wall lights and table lamps in which the bulbs face upwards. Also, good-quality British Standard bulbs have built-in fuses, which should burn out at a lower current than that which trips the circuit breaker; cheap imported bulbs do not have these fuses, so the only protection is the circuit breaker.

If these suggestions do not solve the problem then your friend may consider having an emergency lighting circuit installed, which would come on when the main circuit fails. Seek advice from an NICEIC-registered electrician [ELECTRICS].

CIRCUIT BREAKER TRIPPING

Q I recently had my place rewired to current standards, including a new-type fuse box (probably not called a fuse box these days!) Whenever there is an interruption of supply, the main circuit breaker trips, turning off the power sockets, meaning that my freezer and central heating boiler will not operate until the trip is reset. As I am working away from home for weeks on end this is a huge problem. I have twice returned to find the freezer defrosted and the contents ruined. And if the boiler were to be off during a prolonged cold spell, damage could occur to the house. I have spoken to the installing electrical company and they say the trip is designed to kick in when there is a power interruption. Have you come across this problem before and do you have any suggestions as to what I can do?

A There are some stand-alone RCDs that plug into socket outlets – for example to protect lawn-mowers and power tools – and these are designed to remain 'off' after a power failure until reset. But there is no RCD designed to fit into a consumer unit that is intended to trip when the mains supply fails. So the likelihood is that either the installed RCD is itself faulty, or else you have a faulty appliance somewhere in the house that is tripping the RCD when it comes back on following a power failure. The key suspects would be appliances with motors, as these use a large amount of current when they start up; it may even be the freezer itself that is the problem.

It is also possible that when the electricity supply resumes, the surge of power to all the switched-on appliances is causing the RCD to trip. RCDs are available in a range of different models – class AC types are the most widely used, but there is also a class A type, used to protect electronic equipment such as computers, a class B type for direct current (DC) installations, and a class S type, which has a built-in time delay to allow other 'downstream' devices – such as MCBs – to operate first.

Note that not all the circuits in the consumer unit are protected by the RCD. The general principle is that downstairs power sockets should be protected because they might be used for portable outdoor equipment. But upstairs power sockets do not have to be protected, and nor do circuits that power the lights, water heater, cooker or central heating. So you might also elect to have your freezer connected to the non-protected side of the consumer unit, provided it is wired to a switched fused spur rather than plugged in to a socket.

EXPENSIVE LAMPS

Q About a year ago I installed three sets of lights in my house, each with nine bulbs. These are the 240-volt version of the halogen-type lights that are so fashionable. The advantage of the 240v version was quick installation and no need to put a transformer in the ceiling. The disadvantage has become apparent in that the bulbs blow frequently and cost £8.99 a go. In fact it is cheaper to buy a complete new light fitting with three bulbs included than to buy one replacement bulb! Could you advise me where I might buy 50 watt, 240 volt GU10 bulbs wholesale?

A My local electrical wholesalers sell GU10 bulbs for £3.50 each plus VAT (£3.25 each if you buy a pack of fifteen). Look in the Yellow Pages under 'Electrical Supplies Wholesalers'. Any out-of-the-ordinary type of lamp will sell at an inflated price in a supermarket or high-street retailers. I have seen screw-in 40w reading-lamp spots on sale for £2.85 (packed in individual blister packs) when I know they can be bought for around 60p at an electrical suppliers. Similarly, 15w screw-in 'pygmy' lamps for cooker hoods and under-worktop fittings cost 99p in the shops, but 25p from electrical suppliers. The trick is to buy in bulk, and not to be afraid to ask advice from the guys at the trade counter. It also helps if you know the trade parlance. For example, you want 'lamps', not 'bulbs' (lamps are for lighting; bulbs are for growing). Screw-in continental lamps are called ES (Edison screw – either large or small), and conventional British-style lamps are called BC (bayonet cap).

And anyone contemplating fitting halogen lighting from scratch should consider the cost of the replacement lamps – the low-voltage variety are usually cheaper, which makes up for the extra initial cost of the transformers. (Plus, low-voltage lights can be used safely in showers and bathrooms.)

DOWNLIGHTERS & CONDENSATION

Q I have recently had a new shower room built (en suite to the top-floor master bedroom) and was dismayed to find, after only a week, water stains appearing on the plasterboard ceiling. Upon going up into the loft, I found the whole space dripping with condensation. There is white mould growing on the rafters, and water is literally dripping off the felt between the rafters. A surveyor friend says that the shower room ceiling should have incorporated a vapour barrier to stop water vapour getting into the loft, but it seems likely to me that the moisture is rising up around the bulbs of the downlighters, and it says in the instructions for these that they should never be covered. Is there any solution to this problem, or does it mean that downlighters are not suitable for bathrooms?

A It would have been a good idea to incorporate a vapour barrier but, as you point out, this would be pretty ineffective if the water vapour was able to escape around the downlighter bulbs. There are special sealed downlighters made specifically for wet rooms, but ordinary downlighters also come in a wide range of styles – some of them are open around the bulb, like yours, notably the 'eye ball' type with a moveable directional spot bulb. In this case, the heat of the bulb is likely to create a convection current and actually draw moist air up into the loft, like a flue. In other types of downlighter the bulb fitting is integral with the surround and these will present less of a gap for the water vapour to escape. With luck, you may be able to find some of the latter, which are similar in size to the ones you have to replace, and so avoid the need to make new holes. In any event, it sounds as though you need much more efficient air extraction in the shower room (see CONDENSATION), and you will also need to look at the ventilation in the roof space (see ROOFS).

Downlighters are very popular but they can compromise fire safety and sound insulation.

DOWNLIGHTERS & CEILING FIRE RESISTANCE

Q I have discovered another problem with downlighters – that cutting the holes in the plasterboard apparently compromises the fire resistance of the ceiling. I am in the process of converting a house into three flats, which means the separating ceilings must have a one-hour fire rating. The Building Control Officer says that cutting holes in the plasterboard for downlighters weakens the integrity of the ceiling, and he will not permit them.

A Low-voltage downlighters cut into ceilings are all the rage with interior designers and architects, but few of them consider the implications for fire safety (or noise or moisture transmission) of cutting 65mm holes all over the ceiling to fit them in. Fortunately, some manufacturers are grappling with the problem and there are now several brands of downlighters that are claimed to have 60-minute fire resistance, and to stop sound and moisture transmission through ceilings [ELECTRICS].

DOWNLIGHTER DANGERS

Q We have recently moved into a newly built bungalow which has downlighters throughout for lighting. We are told by the developer that the downlighters are of a variety that have their own containment capsule, but our concern is that the loft-insulating blanket has been placed over these units, and therefore they have no air circulation around them and this may cause overheating. Should we be concerned?

A Halogen downlighters and their associated transformers are commonly pushed up into the ceiling void. Where this is the top-floor ceiling, they are clearly likely to be covered over with loft insulation. It is obvious that downlighters generate a lot of heat, and the electrical wiring regulations state that they should, therefore, be contained within fireproof enclosures. Until a few years ago, this regulation was dealt with on a rather ad-hoc basis, and conscientious electricians used to make their own enclosures using pieces of plasterboard or other fireproof materials (one contact of mine prefers inverted terracotta flowerpots!) More recently, manufacturers have produced intumescent cowls and perforated aluminium boxes to reduce the risks of fire, and these are claimed to meet with all relevant Building Regulations and NHBC requirements and still allow the insulation to be laid on top of them. Personally, however, I wouldn't risk it, and would remove the loft insulation for a 50mm radius around all halogen downlighters [ELECTRICS].

DOWNLIGHTER FIRE HAZARD

Q Low-voltage downlighters can actually start fires. In old houses, the space between ceiling and floorboards is often liable to periodic inhabitation by rodents. The materials that they use for their nests – scraps of paper, hair, dried vegetation, etc. – is highly flammable. When shown a low-voltage downlighter by the designer revamping my kitchen I was alarmed enough to carry out a test. It did not take long before smoke was rising from the scraps of rodent bedding with which I had covered the (normally concealed) top of a downlighter. Needless to say, I refused to countenance their fitting.

A You are right to be concerned. Low-voltage downlighters are currently in vogue and they are being fitted in their thousands in every conceivable situation. But few people realize just how hot they get in the part of the fitting that is hidden above the ceiling, and that this may create a fire risk. Where downlighters are fitted in top-floor ceilings the loft insulation should be removed from at least a 150mm (6in) radius around them, and care should be taken that stored goods do not come into contact with them. Where loose granular (vermiculite) insulation has been poured between the joists, the top of the downlighter should be covered with a fireproof enclosure. In downstairs ceilings similar precautions should be taken; if it is not possible to access the ceiling void by lifting floorboards from above, then there are flexible downlighter fire protection covers that can be pushed up through the hole from below (e.g. Tenmat [ELECTRICS]).

But obviously many downlighters are just pushed up into ceiling voids without any precautions and, as you have pointed out, they can get very hot, and present a fire risk. I am afraid it will take a few disasters before anything is done to regulate the use of these trendy light fittings.

MODERN LIGHT FITTINGS

Q We live in a modern house with loop-in lighting circuits, i.e. all wiring connections take place in ceiling roses or batten holders. We want to replace the batten holders in our kitchen with spotlights, but every spotlight assembly I have looked at has only live, neutral and earth connections, but no terminal to connect the loop-in, loop-out and switch cables. What is the best way of wiring these spotlights? I have been told by some to use a terminal block, but this doesn't sound very safe to me, as it would just be hanging in space, i.e. connections would not be in a fireproof enclosure. I cannot alter the cabling easily as it is not readily accessible.

A Most modern homes are wired in this way – known as three-plate wiring – where all the connections are made at the lighting point. Yet very few manufacturers consider this in the design of their light fittings. So the new fitting comes with connectors for the earth, neutral and switched live conductor to operate the light, but no provision for terminating the permanent live conductors which, although they do not connect to the light fitting, must all be connected together to carry the supply on to the next lighting point.

Regulations and good practice require that all connections are made in an 'appropriate enclosed accessory', which is often not easy, given that there is very little space in the mounting. Some fittings come with strip connectors and instructions that clearly encourage the installer to push them up into the ceiling void above the fitting, which is not advisable. Strip connectors (or 'choc block', as they are known) may be used provided they can be enclosed in the housing or mounting of the light and that they are of good quality – i.e. either Bakelite or self-extinguishing PVC (you can always check this with a match). But if there is insufficient room you will have to fit a small four-terminal joint box in the ceiling void. These can be as small as 50mm in diameter, which means they can be pushed through the hole made for a downlighter, for example.

HALOGEN LAMPS

Q What are the advantages and disadvantages of mains halogen and low-voltage halogen lamps?

A Halogen lamps give a very white light and come in mains voltage or low voltage, usually 12V. The main differences are cost. The low-voltage lamps are cheaper, but you have the initial additional cost of a low-voltage transformer. There is a wider variety of fittings to choose from in the low-voltage range, and, if the transformer is fitted remotely, they can be used in more situations where mains voltage would not be acceptable (such as bath/shower rooms or saunas). As far as lamp life and running costs are concerned, I suspect there is little difference.

FUSE ALWAYS BLOWING

Q We have a peculiar problem with our downstairs lights. Every twelve to fourteen weeks the 5-amp fuse blows on the lighting circuit. We replace it, but it blows again, several times on the same day. On two occasions when this has happened we have engaged a qualified electrician to locate the fault. He has put his meter on the fuse box and told us that there is no fault indicated. He says it may be due to condensation or dampness entering one of the lights or switches, and this is the reason why the fault is only occurring every twelve to fourteen weeks.

A The first thing is to do a rough calculation to check that the lighting circuit is not overloaded. The formula Watts = Volts x Amps indicates that a 5-amp circuit on a 240-volt supply should be able to carry 1200 watts – equivalent to 12 x 100W lamps or 20 x 60W lamps. If you are at or near this limit, then the fuse wire will be getting hot, and gradually burning out. If the fuse wire is tarnished and dull looking, and if, when it blows, the ends remain intact, but a little blob burns out in the middle, then overloading is very likely the cause. If, however, the fuse explodes with a bang, and burns out along its whole length, then a localized electrical fault is probably to blame.

Dampness or condensation could well be the cause, and you will have to do a bit of detective work by inspecting the fittings in the bathroom and kitchen, and the outside lights. Any fitting that is faulty will usually show evidence of scorching, or a black carbon trace where dampness has allowed the electricity to short-circuit between the terminals. Obviously you should isolate the circuit at the fuse board before you open up any electrical fittings.

EMERGENCY POWER SUPPLIES

Q We are told that flooding, gales and blackouts may become more common. What are the practicalities of installing some form of generator-based emergency light and power supply that would enable family life to go on – albeit in a reduced way – until proper power is restored?

A Petrol-powered generators have become remarkably small and quiet in recent years, and if you live in an area prone to power cuts then it may make sense to keep one in the garage for emergency lighting using extension cables. Prices start at around £400 for a 1kW model. The other main 'essential' is to power the fridge and freezer, which may need more power (the compressor on a chest freezer may use only 500W, but it needs a higher surge of power every time it kicks in). It would also be useful to be able to power the central heating pump and boiler (without which the gas or fuel oil are of little use) but this would require wiring in to the existing house electrical system. You should consult a qualified electrician for advice about installing the necessary switching gear. At the upper end, a 10kW diesel generator with automatic start which will power the whole house could cost between £6000 and £10,000. The market leaders are Honda [ELECTRICS].

WORKING AROUND OVERHEAD CABLES

Q I would like your advice on how to work safely around the electricity supply cables to our cottage. I want to replace the guttering and paint the walls but there are two electrical cables attached to insulators screwed to the wall. One appears to be sheathed but the other is bare. The chances are I will touch the cables with a scaffold pole or something whilst carrying out the work. Am I correct in thinking the results could be electrifying?

A Recently connected overhead electricity supplies usually have a single insulated twin-core cable coming into the house, and this should be safe to work around. The older two-cable system has separate live and neutral cables. The top cable is the live one, and will be insulated over the span between the house and the nearest pole. The lower, uninsulated cable is the neutral. Theoretically there should be no danger of electrocution from accidentally touching the cables, but to be on the safe side, you should call your electricity supplier and tell them you want to carry out some maintenance work in the vicinity of the cables and they will send an engineer round to cover them with temporary protective plastic sleeving.

HEATER IN BATHROOM

Q For some thirty years my cottage bathroom has been heated cheaply, safely and effectively by a single-bar radiant heater above the end of the bath. This failed recently, and I have been told by three electricians and a council Building Control Officer that, under the new electrical regulations, I may no longer have an electric heater in the same place. The bathroom is very small – only just large enough to accommodate the bath, washbasin and WC. There is about one square yard of standing space, into which the door opens. The ceiling is 2m (6ft 8in) high, so there is no wall space above the door. All other wall space is taken up by the window, the WC cistern and the mirror over the washbasin. I do not have gas or central heating. In many older properties like mine, bathrooms have been fitted into odd spaces under sloping roofs, etc. and surely, as houses and bathrooms get smaller, my problem cannot be not unique. Do you have any suggestions?

A Electric heating in bathrooms has to be treated with caution, as water is a good conductor of electricity. The regulations are certainly tighter now than when your radiant wall heater was installed, but it is not true that electric heaters in bathrooms are not permitted. They must be fixed and permanently wired – i.e. not plugged into a socket – and must comply with a zonal positioning system. Areas further than 600mm from baths, showers and washbasins are classified as Zone 3, and any type of heater can be used. Closer than 600mm to water is Zone 2, and any heater must have an IPX4 rating, meaning that it is splash-proof, and has pre-set controls or a pull-cord switch. Zone 1 refers to the most hazardous area – directly above a bath or shower, up to a height of 2.25m, and the IEE wiring regulations state that when a heater or other appliance can reasonably only be sited in Zone 1, it must be IPX4 rated and protected by a 30mA RCD (residual current device). There are several IPX4-rated heaters on the market, including wall-mounted downflow fan heaters and radiant infrared heaters. You might also consider a ceiling-mounted infrared heat-and-light bathroom unit, which fits in place of the existing ceiling light, and contains a light bulb surrounded by a circular radiant heating element. You just need to find a qualified electrician who understands the IEE regulations.

BATHROOMS & KITCHENS

Q It is well known that you cannot have a power point in a bathroom lest you get murdered by someone dropping an electric fire into your bath. However there is almost as much water in a kitchen where there are power points galore, and it's quite easy to have one hand in the sink whilst putting the other into the toaster. Is there a rule that power points should be out of reach from the basin, and if not, why not?

A The wiring regulations for bathrooms are stricter than for kitchens for several reasons. In a bathroom people are likely to be not only wet but also unclothed, and hence electrically uninsulated, and there are more potential metal contacts in the form of baths, taps and pipes. So there is a higher risk of electric shock by a current flowing from a metal tap, say, through wet hands and wet bare feet, to earth. So the rule is no power points at all, apart from shaver sockets, which have an automatic cut-out.

In kitchens, the dangers are far fewer, and so the regulations are less prescriptive, and less precise. The main requirement is that power points should not be in places where they can be accidentally splashed, and this is usually interpreted by electricians' organizations to mean that they should be at least 300mm, and preferably a metre, away from the sink or draining board. Naturally this means that a toaster or kettle, with their trailing cables, can be unwisely positioned a lot closer than this, but the wiring regulations only cover the siting of the power points, not the use of electrical appliances.

LOW-ENERGY LAMPS

Q I have been using energy-saving light bulbs since they were first introduced. But the packaging states that an 18W bulb gives the equivalent light output of a 100W tungsten filament lamp, and I don't agree – they seem quite dim. Further, the light output falls appreciably over time to the extent that most need replacement after about a year. Now there is a threat to tax tungsten bulbs, perhaps to price them off the market. Can you comment on the performance of these energy-saving bulbs to enable the best choice to be made? It might be of great interest, especially to the elderly who, due to failing eyesight, require much brighter illumination.

A Compact fluorescent lamps are a sacred cow for the green lobby, but their energy-saving properties are as much a matter of faith as of science. Like all fluorescent tubes, they do take a while to warm up from cold, so do not give a good light in situations where they are turned on and off frequently. And, whilst much is made of their supposed longevity, it is rarely mentioned that they lose light intensity after a few months. The alleged energy savings are also questionable, since electric lighting is mostly used in the winter, when the waste heat from incandescent lamps goes to warm the room. So in a house with central heating, the room thermostat should take account of this and burn less fuel to compensate. Compact fluorescents also contain mercury, and need to be disposed of as hazardous waste, not crushed in landfill sites, where they might contaminate the groundwater. Local authorities are obliged to provide suitable waste-disposal facilities, presumably paid for from council tax revenues – in effect, a hidden tax subsidy that the green lobby does not acknowledge. I have so far been unable to obtain the figures showing how much energy is used in manufacturing compact fluorescents, and in disposing of them in an environmentally friendly way (assuming that this is done).

Some readers have argued that compact fluorescents are useful in homes using off-peak electricity for heating, where the daytime electricity tariff is currently around 12p per unit, as opposed to 10p for the normal tariff. In that case an 18W compact fluorescent, saving 82W over its 100W incandescent equivalent, and switched on for 20 hours per week, would be saving about £10 per year. But if you deduct the heating effect mentioned above, the benefit would be closer to £4 per year. With the lamp itself costing some £3, the energy saving is at best, marginal.

LIGHT BULBS BLOWING

Q **My daughter's house has the conventional lighting set-up, with separate circuits upstairs and down. Upstairs is no problem but on the downstairs circuit light bulbs blow with monotonous frequency. She buys quality bulbs, some of which face upwards and some downwards. There are also some mains halogen bulbs which do not last long either. Sometimes (but not always) they blow when the lights are switched on and sometimes (but not always) they trip the circuit breaker in the consumer unit. There appears to be no consistency in the failures. Have you any suggestions as to how this problem can be solved?**

A The first step is to keep a record, to ascertain whether the light bulbs really are blowing before their expected lifespan. Traditional incandescent lamps have a life expectancy of around a thousand hours, which is equivalent to only three hours per day over a year. It would not be unusual for upstairs lamps to last longer, as bedroom and landing lights might be used for only one hour a day, meaning they should last three years or more. Lamps in a lounge, kitchen or downstairs hallway, however, might be on for six hours a day or more, meaning that they should not be expected to last longer than about six months.

If the record shows that lamps in one particular fitting really are regularly blowing early, then check the fitting. A faulty fitting might show evidence of scorching, or a black carbon trace where electricity has short-circuited between the terminals (isolate the circuit at the consumer unit before investigating any fitting). Note that as a lamp ages, the filament evaporates, and gets deposited as a black residue on the inside of the glass, so a blown but blackened lamp is likely to have served its time, whilst a clearer one might have failed through impact or vibration. I suspect, however, that if you faithfully record the number of hours that each lamp is turned on, you will find that most of them do last for 1000 hours or more.

TRACE HEATING

Q **The utility room of our Victorian farmhouse is in an adjoining single-storey outbuilding, and the water pipes feeding it from the main house enter at ceiling level. The utility room is heated, but the pipes cross an exposed passageway only about 1m (3 feet) wide. During the recent cold snap, both hot and cold pipes froze solid, despite being lagged with thick foam sleeving. I was surprised that the pipes froze so easily, as I had thought the foam lagging would prevent this. Does lagging serve any purpose in this kind of situation, and if not, what can I do to prevent frost damage in the future?**

A Lagging will stop pipes freezing as long as warmer water is being drawn through them occasionally. But insulation in itself does not make the pipes warmer – it only slows down the rate at which heat escapes from them. If water is standing still in the pipes and the temperature drops below freezing for more than a couple of hours, then even the best-lagged pipes will freeze. One short-term solution, the next time sub-zero temperatures are forecast, would be to leave the taps slightly running in the utility room, but clearly this wastes water (which is especially significant if you are on a meter).

In the longer term, you might consider rerouting the pipes by burying them underground – 760mm (2 feet 6in) below ground level is reckoned to be deep enough to avoid the worst frosts. It would probably be easier and cheaper, however, to install electrical trace heating. This entails taping a thin heating cable along the length of the exposed pipework, under the insulation, and connecting it to the mains electricity supply. Trace heating uses a very small amount of power (around 10 watts per metre of pipe) and is self-regulating – i.e. it only draws current when the temperature is low enough to require it. Contact a local qualified electrician, or, for more details and to buy the materials direct, try Trace Heating UK [ELECTRICS]. Prices start from around £30 for the heating cable and connectors to protect a short run of exposed pipework, and thereafter work out at around £7 per linear metre.

SMOKE ALARMS

Q **As a small landlord, some ten years ago I converted a building into three flats. Smoke alarms were not required by law at that time, but I wonder whether they are now a legal requirement, and whether I should install them.**

A The Building Regulations covering fire protection are being constantly updated, and the mandatory provision of smoke alarms depends on the layout of the property. As a general rule, they are required in common areas such as shared lobbies and staircases, but not in self-contained accommodation up to two storeys high. However, as a responsible landlord, I am sure you will want to provide the best possible fire protection measures for your tenants and the property. Smoke alarms can be battery operated, or mains powered with emergency battery back-up. They can operate singly, or be linked together, and there are also versions that incorporate emergency lighting. I think you should ask your local-authority Building Control Department for advice, and fit the best system you can. Smoke alarms save lives.

PLUMBING, HEATING & DRAINAGE

In a temperate climate like Britain's, homes need heating for three-quarters of the year. And since over 70 per cent of us own our homes, or are responsible for the heating in the homes we rent, it is no wonder that when the heating goes wrong, we are prone to being held to ransom by the trade. The fact that almost every house or flat has its own central-heating system – with boiler, radiators and controls – is one reason why Britain is so inefficient in its use of energy. Some other European countries make much better use of energy, with blocks of flats and even whole streets sharing heating systems.

The majority of us use natural gas as a fuel, which heats water in a boiler, to be pumped round a wet radiator circuit. Oil, solid fuel, and LPG (liquified petroleum gas or propane) are also used to fuel the same type of heating system. The principles are very simple, but the equipment gets more complicated by the year. It's very similar to cars. The first few cars I owned were noisy, dirty and not particularly efficient. But when they went wrong (which was often) I could usually open the bonnet, spot the problem and fix it with a screwdriver and a pair of pliers. My current car is quiet, clean and hardly ever goes wrong. But when it does, I open the bonnet and I haven't a clue how to fix it. It has to be towed into a garage where they plug it into a computer which diagnoses the fault, the remedy often being the wholesale replacement of a chunk of electronics, costing hundreds of pounds.

Where old central heating boilers differ from old cars, though, is in the fact that they shouldn't wear out as quickly. A boiler is basically a cast-iron vessel with a burner underneath it. The water is circulated through it and around the radiator system by a separate electric-powered pump. So there are no moving parts in the boiler itself, and nothing much to go wrong. The old pilot lights were pretty infallible and cost maybe £25 per year to run, but this was deemed to be wasteful, so electronic ignition systems were introduced. When these go wrong the parts have to be replaced, at a cost of maybe £150, or six years' worth of pilot light fuel.

Nevertheless, the industry is geared up to 'upgrade' the nation's boilers, which means selling new, complicated boilers with lots more electronic circuitry, rather than keeping the old ones going. At the forefront of this sales push are British Gas Services, formerly known as the Gas Board, but now privately owned by the Centrica Corporation. British Gas Services operate the Three Star Service contracts, whereby customers pay an annual fee as a kind of insurance against breakdowns. Except that many readers report that when they call the engineers in, they are told either that their problem is not covered under the terms of the Three Star Service contract, or that the boiler is beyond repair because parts are no longer available. An increasing number of readers report being told this in the course of their annual Three Star boiler safety check.

This idea that boilers can become 'obsolete', or that 'parts are no longer available', is disputed by some independent gas engineers, who point out that just because a particular manufacturer no longer supplies original catalogue-numbered parts, this does not mean that equally effective replacement spares are not available from other sources. Pressure switches, gas valves, pumps, fans and timers, for example, are all pretty much standard components which will fit a variety of appliances. Potterton may no longer supply a cut-to-length section of asbestos rope for the door seal of a 1969 floor-standing boiler, but the equivalent modern material is available by the reel from plumbers' merchants.

Going back to the car analogy, it's like saying that a 1990 Ford Sierra is beyond repair because Ford no longer manufacture replacement windscreen wiper blades. There are always replacement parts that will fit the bill – witness the large number of Ford Sierras still being driven around.

The prices that British Gas Services quote for supplying and fitting a new boiler are also consistently high at £3000 or more for a boiler whose trade price is nearer £650. So if you have trouble with your boiler, or are thinking of upgrading, then it is always best to get two or three estimates from independent CORGI-registered gas engineers before coming to a decision.

Apart from central heating problems, most readers' queries concern poor water pressure, noisy plumbing systems, toilets that won't flush, and leaking shower enclosures. These are all things that should be within the remit of any half-decent plumber, but unfortunately there are lots of guys calling themselves plumbers who don't seem to have a clue.

What to do if you are a Three Star Service customer, and you have had a letter from British Gas/Scottish Gas, telling you that the 'manufacturer has stopped making some of the spare parts'. Most boilers are put together using standard parts from a variety of third-party manufacturers and these parts are usually easily available from specialist spares suppliers, if not from the boiler manufacturers themselves. In some instances, the only part that is 'unique' to a particular model is the boiler casing with the manufacturer's name stamped on it. (Note, however, that the casing can sometimes be important. 'Positive pressure' boilers, such as the Potterton Netaheat, can leak fumes into the room if the casing corrodes.)

If British Gas has told you that a particular part is unobtainable, the first step is to check this with the boiler manufacturer. Some of them are still carrying large stocks of spares, especially for models less than ten years old. Next, get a second opinion from an independent CORGI-registered gas engineer (look in the CORGI block advert under 'Gas installers' in the Yellow Pages). An experienced gas engineer should know where to obtain parts anyway, but, more importantly, should advise you on whether your boiler is worth repairing. For example, if £250 worth of repairs will keep a boiler running for another ten years, this works out at £25 per year and is worth doing, but if a £100 repair is needed on a boiler that will only last another year or two, then it may be wise to think about a replacement, since a decent new boiler can now be bought for as little as £650.

If your gas engineer cannot find a particular spare part, then try the local spares firms that advertise under 'Central heating services' in the Yellow Pages, or the following companies, which operate mail-order services:

Curzon Components, 0870 510 3030
FMT Ltd, 01245 357993
HRPC, 01282 834400 (parts availability can also be checked on their website)
Thermagas, 01257 275080

In addition, Peter Porter Electronics Ltd (01920 871711) sell refurbished components, which they will exchange for your old components, at a considerable cost saving. They will also repair damaged components, including electronics and printed circuit boards.

If you order parts yourself, then you will need to give the supplier as much detail as possible, i.e. the exact boiler model and Gas Council number ('GC:—:—:—' on a data plate somewhere on the casing). You should not attempt to fit parts yourself, but should always engage a CORGI-registered engineer to do the work.

What to do if your boiler really needs replacing. If you have decided that you really want a new boiler, or if a trusted independent gas engineer has convinced you that your existing boiler is not worth repairing, then you should think carefully about which replacement model to choose. Since 2005 the Building Regulations have required all new boilers to be condensing models (with a few exceptions – see the reader's query headed 'Back boiler replacement'). These are said to be much more economical than conventional boilers – '15 per cent more efficient' is a common claim. These figures are almost certainly over-optimistic, and based upon the manufacturers' own

TRADITIONAL CENTRAL HEATING CIRCUIT

COMBI CENTRAL HEATING CIRCUIT

best-case laboratory test results, rather than actual use in people's homes. Also, the alleged improvements in efficiency are often reached by comparing the new boilers with the most inefficient type of older boiler, complete with its gas-guzzling pilot light.

The official test results can be found on the website www.sedbuk.com (Seasonal Efficiency of Domestic Boilers UK), and the difference between the lower end of the condensing boilers list (84 per cent) and the most efficient of the conventional boilers (82.1 per cent) is insignificant. And what the list omits to measure is the poor performance record of condensing boilers and the frequency of repairs needed to keep them running. Some independent gas engineers who have installed condensing boilers say they have had to return three or four times in the first few months to attend to breakdowns and replace parts. As one of them said, 'Every time I go back to fix it, driving my diesel van and stopping for a bacon sandwich on the way, it does more damage to the environment than their old boiler did in five years.'

Condensing boilers gain their extra efficiency by extracting the latent heat from the flue gases, which condense out on a secondary heat exchanger. This condensate liquid, which is slightly acidic, has to be piped away to the drainage system. The flue gases are much cooler than those from a conventional boiler, and therefore often emerge as steam, causing the phenomenon of 'pluming'. However, to run in this most efficient condensing mode, the water returning to the boiler has to be at 54°C, which is considerably cooler than the 80°C of a conventional boiler. So to distribute the same amount of heat around the house, they need bigger pipes and larger radiators. Once the reliability problems have been sorted out, condensing boilers may be something for the future if they are built into new houses, with new radiators (or under-floor heating pipes), as part of a designed heating system. But they are unlikely to produce significant efficiency gains when bolted on to an existing central-heating system as a replacement for a conventional boiler. However, since 2005 there is no longer any option, which makes it all the more important to keep your existing boiler going if at all possible.

Combination or 'Combi' boilers are also heavily promoted. These are basically glorified versions of the old 'geysers' or instant gas water heaters. Most Combi systems do not have separate hot-water storage tanks, but rely on heating the mains cold water as it flows through the boiler. In winter, when the incoming mains water is very cold, it can take a long time to run a bath. Combis can be useful in one-bedroom flats, or where there is no loft space for water tanks, but they are not generally suitable for larger flats or houses, where more than one person wants to use water at the same time. There *are* new Combi systems with higher outputs, and various forms of pressurized hot-water storage tanks, but they are expensive. If you have an existing conventional system with a cold-water tank in the loft, there is usually nothing to be gained from replacing your boiler with a Combi. If your heating engineer advises you to fit a Combi, it is most likely because it involves considerably less work for him.

My independent gas engineers recommend Vaillant and Worcester Bosch, and stress that if you buy a new boiler, you should take up the manufacturer's extended warranty or breakdown insurance for as long as it is available.

PLUMBING

MAGNETIC/ELECTRONIC LIMESCALE INHIBITORS

Q We live in a hard-water area, and a plumber has recommended that we install a device that he called a limescale inhibitor. We understand it is fitted to the mains water pipe and by magnetism it causes the lime particles to separate out, thus giving us softer water. It sounds like a good idea. Or are we being conned?

A Instead of installing a proper ion-exchange water softener, which requires plumbing in and the monthly application of a dose of salt, manufacturers of these devices advocate cutting into the mains pipe and inserting a chrome tube containing a magnet. There are also electrical versions involving wrapping coils of cable around the pipe.

The companies marketing this equipment produce lots of glossy brochures with artists' impressions of pipes, water, wires and coloured blue and red arrows showing how their patented electro-magnetic waves will save your immersion heater. They are not so keen on producing independent research supporting their inventions, though, because there isn't any. Well, perhaps – in anticipation of the abusive letters that the manufacturers of these devices will be writing to me – I had better qualify that.

Work at Cranfield University has shown that, under certain conditions, some magnetic water conditioners do reduce limescale formation. The bad news is that nobody knows exactly what these conditions are, or why the devices work when they do work. There are theories, but none of them tells the whole story, and no experiments have stood up to the test of scientific repeatability.

What is known is that the devices can be made to work in closed industrial processes – i.e. where the same water is recirculated at a known flow rate and constantly remagnetized. These conditions do not exist in the average home's plumbing system, where the device is fitted to the incoming pipe and the water passes through it once only, and at a varying rate of flow.

The manufacturers' literature does not make this clear. And it often makes selective use of the research by reproducing data from the experiments that worked, but omitting the data from those that did not. On the other hand, those who market the devices claim that British Water, the trade association, is dominated by companies selling ion-exchange water softeners, and there are even dark mutterings that favourable research is being deliberately suppressed by the salt manufacturers. Skulduggery indeed in the murky world of water treatment.

Many readers ask whether these magnetic or electrical water conditioners actually work, and the answer has to be … maybe. But since they cost between £50 and £150, and since proper ion-exchange softeners now cost as little as £200, it would seem sensible to pay the extra and buy something that is proven to work. And, as a footnote, some readers have suggested that in cases where electromagnetic water conditioners do stop limescale formation, they may do so by causing the inside of the copper pipe to gradually dissolve. This would have the twin effects of gradually weakening the pipes, causing possible leaks, and raising the level of dissolved copper in the drinking water. Since raised copper in tap water has recently been linked with Alzheimer's disease, this is possibly not a risk worth taking.

If your only concern is to stop limescale forming on your immersion heater element and bath taps, then the simplest option is to dose your water with phosphate by suspending a bag of Fernox Limescale Preventer in the cold water tank. These cost around £8 and last for six months.

WATER SUPPLY PIPE INSURANCE

Q We have received several letters from our water supply company inviting us to pay £17.99 per year to insure against leaks in our water supply pipe. Is this a good idea?

A The water supply pipe (also known as the service pipe) runs under the front path or garden and connects a property to the water main. Strictly speaking, the supply pipe is the responsibility of the building owner. But following the Deputy Prime Minister's 1997 'water summit', the water companies agreed that, in order to help with their leak-reduction targets, they would undertake to repair customers' leaky supply pipes for free. Water regulator Ofwat maintains that this agreement is still in operation, and that there should be no need for owners to take out additional insurance cover. Details are in the Ofwat report, 'Security of supply, leakage and water efficiency', which can be obtained from Ofwat by calling 0121 625 1373, or downloaded free from www.ofwat.gov.uk (click on 'Publications' and choose 'S' from the A–Z list).

However, homeowners the length and breadth of the country have since been receiving letters, sometimes bearing the letterheads and logos of their water supply companies, inviting them to pay £17.99 per year for Supply Pipe Cover. The insurance is actually provided by a private company called Homeserve GB Ltd, which was formerly part of South Staffordshire Water Plc, and is now a separate company. Homeserve GB Ltd has financial relationships with the water supply companies, which result in some of them actually receiving commission on each policy sold. So not only is Supply Pipe Cover not needed, but if you take it out, then you may even be giving extra money to your water supplier whilst, at the same time, absolving them of their obligation to fix your leaks.

Readers who feel pressurized into taking out supply pipe insurance cover from Homeserve GB Ltd should read the small print very carefully, as it mentions limits on length of pipework and other exclusions, which might make it no more beneficial than the free repair service offered by your water company. The only people who might usefully benefit from paying for this insurance cover are those whose supply pipes are very old, who have a water meter under the pavement (rather than inside the house), or who have already availed themselves of one free repair from their water company. In all other cases, my view is that water supply pipe insurance is a waste of money.

GAS PIPE INSURANCE

Q I have received an offer of insurance for my internal gas pipes against leakage. It is not that costly, at £14.99 per year, but the offer is similar to all those from Homeserve GB Ltd, containing the usual 'frighteners', so I binned it. I expect you have heard about this from other readers too. Is it possible I have missed out on the one worthwhile insurance offer, doubtful though it seems?

A Transco are responsible for the gas supply pipe to your home, right up to the gas meter. This insurance is therefore for the pipes feeding gas from the meter to your gas cooker, boiler and gas fires (should you have them). These pipes are in a very stable environment. They are dry, so are not subject to corrosion. They are inside your house, so will not be affected by ground movement. The only thing that might cause a leak would be accidental impact damage, and this should be covered by your existing home insurance. I cannot see the need for anyone to insure their gas pipes.

WATER SOFTENERS – BLUE STAINING

Q Since we installed a water softener water drops left in baths and sinks have been tinged with blue, which, we understand, is due to copper sulfate being leached from the pipes. We have slightly reduced the hardness setting on the softener, but this has not solved the problem. Is there a solution apart from bleeding untreated water into the system (as recommended by the manufacturer), which rather defeats the object one would have thought?

A Soft water dissolves salts, which is why rainwater (soft) extracts calcium and magnesium salts from the ground it passes through to become hard. Green or blue salts are a common corrosion product in plumbing systems that contain a mixture of copper pipes and other metals (usually steel or zinc), and the softened water will be dissolving these and washing them out. Readers with water softeners also report green staining on clothes and hair. It sounds as though your water may be too soft, and the manufacturer's suggestion is the correct one, i.e. to increase the hardness by mixing a proportion of unsoftened water into the supply. This does not defeat the object, but adjusts the hardness/softness to a suitable level, where you get the advantages of softened water, but not the blue staining problem. As a first step try reducing the hardness setting on the softener by turning the dial right down. If this doesn't work, then you will need to have a bypass pipe fitted, with a valve, to mix a proportion of unsoftened water into the supply. The water that arrives at the taps should ideally contain 50mg per litre hardness (measured as calcium carbonate equivalent). The softener manufacturer should be able to provide you with a kit to test for this. Water hardness test kits can also be bought from plumbers' merchants and aquarium suppliers.

Trade association British Water publish ten free fact sheets on all aspects of domestic water treatment [PLUMBING, HEATING & DRAINAGE].

NOISY PIPES

Q **We recently moved to a refurbished 1930s house with polished floorboards. When the heating is on, we hear a high-pitched ringing noise, presumably from the pipes. Can we remedy this by carpeting the room?**

A Central-heating systems make noises for a lot of reasons, but bare floorboards should not be one of them, and whilst carpeting the floor might muffle the sound, it would be better to fix the problem at source. Noise can be caused by thermostatic radiator valves, or may be due to the circulating pump being on too high a setting. Ringing noises can also be caused by a small blob of loose solder running up and down inside the pipes when the pump is circulating the heating water.

Pipes can also be noisy if they are not clipped securely enough to the joists, or if they are clipped too securely. (Pipes need to be supported but also allowed to expand and contract.) A common problem occurs where pipes have been run across shallow notches in floor joists, and the floorboards have been screwed down tightly on to them. So it would pay to do a bit of under-floor investigation before you pay for that new carpet.

NOISY CISTERN

Q **Is there such a thing as a silent-filling domestic lavatory cistern? My twenty-year-old model needed a new valve and ballcock. The old one filled through a silencer tube, but the plumber fitting the new valve told me that it was designed not to take a silencer tube, and that this was illegal anyway (something to do with back-siphonage). The new system is much noisier. Is there any legal remedy?**

A Silencer tubes direct the incoming water below the surface, rather than allowing it to splash down from a height. The problem with back-siphonage is that should there be an interruption to the mains supply, then it is theoretically possible for the water in the cistern to be siphoned back through the tube, down the rising main, and thence to emerge through next door's kitchen tap. However, there are ways of getting around this problem, either by using a collapsible polythene tube, or by having a small hole drilled in the tube above water level. Examples are the Torbeck and the Fluidmaster, both of which comply with the Water Regulations, and are available from plumbers' merchants.

COWBOY PLUMBERS

Q **After a week away during freezing weather, I came home to find water cascading down from the loft. I called an emergency plumbing company from the Yellow Pages. The plumber charged me £180 plus VAT and said he had replaced two sections of split pipework and two tank connectors. But when I went up to check, I couldn't see anything that looked as if it had been replaced. It looks as though I have been 'had'. But the leak was real enough – so how has this con man repaired the split pipe, and should I be expecting fresh leaks any time when his bodged repair fails?**

A It is unusual for pipes to 'split' or 'burst' when the water freezes, although these are common expressions. Water expands as it freezes, and what usually happens is that the expansion pushes the copper pipes out of the compression fittings connecting them to the water tanks. It is often possible to push them back into place and re-tighten them, and it sounds as though this is what your plumber has done. You should contact your local-authority Trading Standards Officer to complain about the fraud, and in future remember not to pay for any new parts or materials unless you have actually seen the old ones removed, and been given an itemized receipt.

WATER HAMMER (1)

Q I live in a semi-detached house, and have started to suffer from water hammer at various times of the day, seemingly affecting all the pipes in the house. We are not using the water when this occurs, but find that if we turn on the cold-water tap for a few minutes it stops. The main water supply comes from across the street to a stopcock under the pavement and a spur then goes to our house and the neighbour's house by separate pipes. My neighbour says she does not have any problems but I am doubtful of this.

A Water hammer can travel along any interconnected pipework. It is quite possible that you are hearing the effects of a faulty ball valve in your neighbour's property, which should really have its own stop valve and service pipe. If the source of the noise cannot be traced, a skilled plumber can insert a 'dead' vertical length of pipe, containing air, in order to absorb the pressure fluctuations causing the water hammer.

WATER HAMMER (2)

Q I get a heavy vibration from the water tank in the loft which occurs just as the tank is close to filling up (i.e. just before the ballcock reaches its stable floating level). The problem has been isolated to the inlet valve which generates a strong suction noise that reverberates throughout the house, particularly late at night. This can last for one to two minutes. I have tried the following without any real improvement: changing the inlet valve; removing, cleaning and greasing the piston in the inlet valve; firmly fixing the connecting pipes into the tank to minimize any vibration there; cleaning the water tank and refilling it; and adjusting the stopcock to reduce the water pressure entering the tank.

I think a longer stopcock arm will close the piston quicker and may reduce the period of time that the suction noise is heard throughout the house, but I have only been able to find standard length stopcocks in plumbers' merchants. Any idea what may be the cause of this problem and how it could be cured once and for all?

A This is a common problem which really needs to be diagnosed by a skilled plumber. The noise is not suction and is always pressure induced. A ball valve slide should never be greased, as it risks contaminating the water supply, producing ideal conditions for triggering bacterial growth. The valve is brass or plastic on brass, and is water-lubricated. Adjusting the stopcock only reduces the flow rate – the pressure remains constant and can only be reduced by a spring diaphragm reduction valve.

You could try fitting a new 'equilibrium' ball valve with a long arm and 200mm plastic float. Any decent plumbers' merchants should be able to supply this. You might also try fitting an extra loop of pipe to form a water cushion above the level of the tank cold feed at the ball valve. This should cure the problem. If not, check that the house main stopcock does not have a loose jumper, and also check for any unclipped vertical boxed-in pipes, which can amplify the noise. This problem can be complex, often being affected by the other take-off points on the same cold line, such as WC cisterns. Sometimes, however, a single check valve fitted before the tank entry will cure the problem, saving time and money.

NOISY WASTE PIPE

Q My kitchen sink, when the water is let out, makes a loud 'glug glug glug' sound, which goes on and on. Could anything be done to stop that?

A This usually happens when the waste pipe to the soil and vent stack is too long, or at too steep an angle. (The maximum length is 1.7m, and the slope no more than one-in-ten.) Or maybe the soil and vent stack has been blocked at the top by a bird's nest. What is happening is that the water flowing out through the waste pipe is acting like a piston, lowering the pressure and drawing air in through the trap (the 'U' bend) under the sink.

POOR WATER FLOW

Q I have had the water company and plumbers out to try and find out why the flow of water from cold taps reduces when more than one tap or appliance is being used. The standing pressure from the mains supply measures 11 bar. It has been suggested that the problem is that we are supplied from the mains by a half-inch (15mm) copper pipe.

A Eleven bar is a comparatively high pressure for a mains supply, so it certainly sounds as if the problem is with flow rather than pressure, i.e. the bore of the pipe is too narrow. Whilst this will not affect the standing pressure reading, it means that there is simply not enough room inside the pipes for the water to get through quickly enough to feed more than one outlet at a time. The service pipe connecting the house to the mains would normally be in at least 22mm pipe; 50m is a long length for a supply pipe, so whilst you are at it, you might as well replace it with an even larger bore pipe – maybe 32mm.

LOW FLOW FROM NEW TAPS

Q I recently changed my kitchen taps from the conventional 15mm pipe single hot and cold to a mixer tap with smaller bore supply pipes, and the hot water pressure is now much lower. Cold water supply is from the mains, and the hot water is from a header tank in the loft. The hot water pressure has remained good to the bathroom basin tap which has a 15mm supply pipe. I do not understand why having a different size pipe should lower the pressure. Is there any way of overcoming this problem?

A Many kitchen mixer taps are of European origin and have 10mm or even 8mm feeds, soldered on to 15mm tails for the British market. Reducing the pipe diameter does not lower the pressure, but it does lessen the flow, which is especially noticeable with the small vertical head of pressure that you will have from a roof tank in a bungalow. There is no solution, short of an electric booster pump.

SHOWER PUMPS

Q We are unable to use our shower attachment over the bath at a sufficient height to use as a shower. The hot water is by electric immersion heater, and is situated at floor level. The cold tank is above the hot water cylinder, but obviously at insufficient height to give adequate pressure to the shower attachment. Is there any way we can incorporate a pump to achieve better pressure without spending an enormous sum?

A This is a common problem in flats where there is insufficient head of water to provide a good shower. There are several types of shower pump that can solve your problem, depending upon the exact layout of the plumbing. If the base of the cold-water tank is even slightly above the level of the shower head, and provides a gravity flow of half a litre per minute (a mere trickle), then you can install a positive-head pump (cost from around £120) into the existing pipework. This has a reed switch which detects water flow and switches on automatically when the taps are opened. If you do not have this minimal pressure then you will need a more expensive negative-head pump, containing a pressure vessel, which will cost from around £350.

NOISY SHOWER PUMP

Q Some time ago we had our bathroom modernized and, because of poor water pressure, had a power shower installed. We now seem to be getting continual noise from the shower pump; there is a whirring and knocking noise as though it is trying to function although not in use. The refurbishment is now out of guarantee and the company that did it do not want to look into the problem. Can you offer any solution?

A Shower booster pumps are activated by sensitive reed switches which detect water flowing through the pipes and complete an electrical circuit to start the pump. Sometimes, if the pump is situated some distance below the bath or shower, the convection currents in the hot water on the shower side of the pump can be sufficient to trigger the switch, and since there is no outlet turned on, the pump 'hunts' for water by cycling on and off. This can be stopped by reconfiguring the pipework, or by installing a less sensitive reed switch. Alternatively, one or both of these switches may be causing the problem, and they are not difficult to replace. Contact the pump manufacturer for advice.

SHOWER

Q I have a shower spray on a flexible hose above the bath. When I slide the spray to a lower position on its wall bracket, the water suddenly gets hotter, sometimes dangerously so. Would a thermostatic shower tap be the answer?

A It sounds as though your shower is receiving hot water under tank pressure and cold water from the mains. When you move the shower spray up and down, you are altering the head of pressure, whilst the cold water pressure remains constant. The best solution would be to replumb the bath and shower so that both hot and cold supplies are coming from the tank.

SHOWER LEAKS

Q Despite constant inspection and repair, I am plagued with recurrent leaks through the grouting of our tiled shower cubicle, which have damaged the ceiling of the kitchen below. I have been told there is a special waterproof grout to cope with power showers but I cannot find a stockist. Would this be a cure anyway?

A Tiled shower enclosures are never going to be fully watertight. The term 'waterproof', applied to tiles, adhesives and grouts, means that the materials will not break down in wet conditions; it does not mean they will stop water seeping through them. Even a completely waterproof grout (if such a thing existed) would develop movement cracks, and would allow water to seep between itself and the tiles. The way to stop leaks is to build your shower enclosure out of water-resistant tile backer board (not plasterboard), which laps over the edges of the shower tray so that any water leaking through the tiles drains down into the tray, and does not find a way past it.

SHOWERS – PLASTERBOARD

Q I am having a shower cubicle built in a corner of my bathroom, the internal walls of which are constructed of plasterboard on timber studding. Thus, two of the cubicle sides would be of plasterboard (suitably tiled) and two of glass (side and door). But from your comments it seems this is not a good idea, so could you please let me know why plasterboard is unsuitable and suggest how this problem might be overcome?

A Ordinary plasterboard consists of a slab of plaster-of-Paris sandwiched between two sheets of paper. Both of these materials absorb water readily and so are unsuitable for shower cubicles. The water will always be absorbed through the grouting between the tiles and will wet and soften the plasterboard underneath. After a couple of years the tiles will fall off, exposing spectacular outbreaks of mould growth. Shower cubicles are better lined with one of the proprietary brands of lining boards (Knauf Aquapanel or similar). The only plasterboard suitable is British Gypsum's moisture-resistant (MR) board.

SHOWERS – SILICONE SEALANT

Q You have said that the weakest point in a shower is always the joint between the tiles and the shower tray, and that the usual thin smear of silicone mastic is unable to cope. Is there nothing that one can use that will do the job satisfactorily or is there a particular mastic or method of applying it that would give optimum results?

A Silicone mastics will absorb around 20 per cent movement, and the weight of an adult on a plastic or resin shower tray on a timber floor may move it by 3–4mm, so the mastic joint has to be at least 20mm deep. The mastic joint should be as thick as it is deep, so you need a 20mm square bead of mastic all round. The joint should be clean and dry before application and, if necessary, treated with the manufacturer's recommended primer. Shower trays and enclosures should be thoroughly cleaned with methylated spirits before application. Very few builders follow these basic principles.

RE-ENAMELLING BATHS

Q Our bathroom suite with cast-iron bath is champagne colour. We would like to modernize it, keeping the bath and having it re-enamelled in white. There are numerous companies advertising this, some do the job in the house and others take the bath away. Ideally, we do not want to have to move the bath, so would prefer the first option; however, we are worried about how successful the outcome is and how strong the new enamel would be. Also, what would be a reasonable cost?

A Having a cast-iron bath properly re-enamelled would be an expensive and disruptive undertaking, as enamel is powdered glass, melted on to a surface in a kiln. What is more commonly offered is bath resurfacing, i.e. the application of an epoxy paint. If done properly, resurfacing can be very effective, and it avoids the disruption of removing the bath and disturbing the tiling and pipework. Resurfacing is available in a choice of colours and should last from five to ten years before it needs doing again. For a professional job try Renubath; prices start from around £180, depending on the condition of the bath. Or for keen DIYers, the Jaeger Bath Resurfacing kit costs £55 [PLUMBING, HEATING & DRAINAGE]. I have never resurfaced a whole bath myself, but I have carried out minor repairs and a good finish is surprisingly easy to achieve.

MOULD ON SHOWER SEALANT

Q Sealants used around baths and showers all seem to become infested with black mould within a few months of application. I have tried various brands of both acrylic and silicone sealants, which are claimed to have 'superior mould resistance', or 'continuous built-in protection against bacteria and mould growth', but after a time black spots appear, which quickly spread into a band of black/grey mould. Is there a truly mould-resistant sealant, or any other solution to this problem, apart from regular removal and resealing?

A Sealants that are claimed to be mould-resistant incorporate one or more fungicidal chemicals, but in such low concentrations that the sealants are not subject to the Control of Pesticides

Regulations (which would impose restrictions on their sale and use). So their fungicidal properties are limited to start with, and it is also accepted that fungicides have a high vapour pressure, meaning that they evaporate quickly. Therefore it is unlikely that any type of bath sealant will have an effective fungicidal component after a month or two of being applied. If you read the instructions on the packaging you will notice that the manufacturers do not claim any kind of time-scale for their alleged mould resistance.

Moulds grow from airborne spores, which are present in their millions in every cubic metre of air, whether indoors or out, and they will germinate and grow on any surface if the temperature and humidity conditions are suitable. Bathrooms provide the ideal conditions, and the only way to ensure a mould-free bathroom or shower room is to provide much higher levels of heating and ventilation than most people are prepared to countenance. And although silicone sealant is a wonderful material, it does seem to provide an ideal platform for black mould growth. Some experts suggest that the problem is exacerbated by the common practice of using a wet finger, or a tool dipped in soapy water, to smooth off the sealant when it is applied, since this moisture is absorbed into the surface of the sealant as it cures, allowing for rapid mould growth. So the current thinking is to avoid wet smoothing methods, and to use a dry smoothing tool such as the Fugi [PLUMBING, HEATING & DRAINAGE]. Readers have also suggested using a finger dipped in white spirit rather than water. If you already have mould-stained silicone sealant, try a sodium hypochlorite-based cleaner such as HG mould spray (from tile shops and plumbers' merchants), but once white silicone has been stained, it is very difficult to get clean.

LEAK DETECTION

Q A friend tells me the water companies use an instrument which they place on a pipe to detect leaks in the water supply into houses. Is such an instrument available for householders?

A The water companies check for leaks by listening for the sound of water flowing through pipes. At its most basic, this involves placing one end of a metal rod on to a pipe or valve, and putting the other end to the ear. More sophisticated instruments for detecting very small leaks use the same principle, by amplifying the sounds picked up from a microphone. The Ecosave water waste alarm is a small battery-powered sound sensor that clamps to the incoming water main and detects unusual water flow patterns. If it hears water running for more than an hour or two (the user can pre-set the period) either inside or outside the house, then an alarm sounds. It's a kind of smoke alarm for the plumbing system. The Ecosave costs around £20, but the manufacturers tell me they will shortly be introducing a more sophisticated model, which will include a valve that shuts off the water, and which will cost around £50 [PLUMBING, HEATING & DRAINAGE].

O-RINGS

Q Our house has solid brass plugs in the baths and basins, all fitted with rubber sealing 'O'-rings. These perish with time and use, but obtaining replacements gets more and more difficult, as none of the DIY stores stocks them, or has any advice about where to look. Can you help?

A Synthetic rubber 'O'-rings are used for many plumbing applications and, like all rubber products, they have a limited life. So it is strange that replacements are so hard to find. However, you can buy a box of eighty 'O'-rings in assorted sizes from RS Components for around £8. You will find many uses for them, from quarter-turn kitchen taps to push-fit garden hose connectors.

DUAL FLUSH CISTERNS

Q **In the interests of water economy, is it possible to have lavatory cisterns adapted to half and full flush? I have been told by a bathroom fitter that this is only possible if I buy new cisterns.**

A Dual-flush cisterns were widely fitted in the 1970s and '80s, but later ran into trouble with the Water Regulations. The market leader was the Dudley Duoflush, whose cistern carried a label saying, 'Short flush – pull and let go; Full flush – pull and hold.' Unfortunately, some people didn't read the instructions, so that they were often used only for the short flush, and developed an unjustified reputation for poor performance.

An American-style flush valve can be fitted in place of the existing siphon, but these are prone to slow leakage, which might counteract any water savings. Dudley has now redesigned its Duoflush siphon, with a different action, so that 'letting go' gives a full flush, and 'holding down' gives a short flush. It is available from all good plumbers' merchants for around £20, and can be exchanged for the existing siphon in most types of cistern.

Alternatively, for low-level cisterns with front-mounted flush handles, there is a device called the Interflush (also costing around £20), which can be fitted to the existing plastic siphon, and flushes for as long as the handle is held down [PLUMBING, HEATING & DRAINAGE].

PLUMBING MAINTENANCE

Q **We have lived in our house since 1966 and the plumbing has not been touched except that we have had a water softener put in and a new hot water cylinder. We have oil-fired central heating so there are copper pipes under the floorboards. I would just like to know if you think it is all right to leave it as it is, or should we have someone impartial to have a look at the plumbing. The reason for this is that I am worried about leaks.**

A There is no requirement to have plumbing systems routinely inspected (unlike electrical wiring, which should be inspected every ten years). The most likely cause of plumbing problems in the south-east of England is a build-up of limescale in the hot and cold water supply, and since you have a water softener fitted, this should not be a problem. The softener should be serviced and have its resin beads replaced according to the manufacturer's recommendations (every three to five years is usual).

Any leaks that do occur would most likely be at the compression fittings (i.e. screw joints) where pipes are connected to the taps or hot-water cylinder, and these are generally minor, and easily fixed by tightening the joints. There would be little to be gained from routinely tightening them, as this might even cause unnecessary strain on the fittings.

The central heating pipes under the floorboards should have very few joints, and those that there are will probably be soldered, and so very unlikely to leak. Again, the most likely points of leakage will be the compression fitting where the pipes join the radiators, and these are above floor level. Any slight leak will result in the tell-tale green staining that comes from copper oxidation, and will be easily fixed by tightening the joint. The water that circulates around the boiler, pipes and radiators is in a sealed system, and should have been dosed with a corrosion inhibitor. You can have this tested by a heating engineer, or you can do it yourself by running off a small amount of water into a glass jar from the bleed nipple on one of the radiators. Add a copper coin and a steel nail (to replicate the mix of metals found in the heating system) and see how it looks after a few weeks. If the nail has corroded, then the system needs draining down and refilling, with the addition of a suitable corrosion inhibitor.

COLOURED SEALANTS

Q Is it possible to get bath/shower sealant in any colour other than white, grey or transparent? I would like to use red grout between the tiles, but have been advised I need a 'flexible joint' in the corners. It seems a shame to spoil the effect by using a white sealant in the corners and around the edge of the bath.

A It is a good idea to use a mastic joint where dissimilar materials meet, notably where a timber stud partition butts up to a brick or block wall. Silicone mastics in a wide range of colours can be bought direct from AB Sealants [PLUMBING, HEATING & DRAINAGE].

IMMERSION HEATERS

Q My immersion heater has failed with age. I have read somewhere that there are three types of heater element produced, but I can no longer find the information. Can you help?

A The cheapest (around £10) immersion heater elements are copper-sheathed, and these can fail quickly where the water is acidic or has a high nitrate content. Rather more resilient are various grades of nickel alloy element (sold as 'Incoloy' or 'Aqualoy' – which cost from around £15. However, these can also fail prematurely, especially in hard-water areas, or where the water has high concentrations of chloride. The most corrosion-resistant immersion heater elements are titanium-sheathed, and cost from around £25. Titanium is also more resistant to scale build-up than the other two materials, enabling the water to heat up both quicker and more efficiently.

HOT WATER TEMPERATURE

Q What is the recommended minimum temperature for hot water in the home, and what is the reason for keeping water at this temperature?

A The British Standard recommended minimum temperature for hot water storage is 60°C (140°F). This is to ensure that bacteria are not able to breed, but it can represent a scalding risk. For this reason, legislation is currently being proposed that hot water from a storage cylinder is automatically blended with cold water, using thermostatic mixing valves, so that the temperature at the outlets is no higher than 41°C (106°F) for a shower and 44°C (112°F) for a bath.

SURESTOP WATER SWITCH

Q What is your opinion about the 'SureStop' water switches that my local water authority is plugging in its magazine? The mains stopcock in my house does not completely stop the flow of water through the cold tap, even when fully turned off, and I am tempted to have one of these water switches installed. They sound too good to be true!

A This device consists of a pressure-operated valve connected by two thin plastic pipes to a rocker switch, which can be sited up to 8m away, and so positioned at a convenient height on a wall, or kitchen splashback. When the switch is turned off, the change in water pressure operates a diaphragm, which closes the valve. I have had one on trial for several months, and it seems to work OK, except when sediment in the water supply got into the diaphragm and stopped it working. The manufacturers tell me they are now adapting the design to include a filter, but until this is done, it would be a good idea to fit a separate sediment filter on the mains pipe upstream of it. This can be a useful device for turning the water off in an emergency, but it should be considered as an addition to a manual stopcock, not as a substitute for it. You will still have to get your original stopcock overhauled or replaced so that it can be turned on and off easily. Note that the device also reduces the water flow through the rest of the system, so if fitted to the incoming rising main, it might interfere with the operation of direct pressure hot water, instant electric showers, or combi boilers.

LEAK REPAIRS

Q I have a small weep on a straight joint in my half-inch (15mm) mains-pressure cold-water pipe to a basin. The pipe and fitting are plastic. I have tried to fix it with a silicone jointing compound, without success. Do you know of any other product that I could try?

A In my experience it's a waste of time trying to seal a leak from the outside. Bite the bullet and remake the joint properly. You can take the opportunity to fit an isolating valve on the pipe at the same time, which will probably mean you can just cut out the straight coupling and fit the valve in its place. Don't forget to buy the metal sleeve inserts for the plastic pipe; absence of these is often why the joints leak in the first place.

MACERATOR TOILET

Q A builder has told me that you are allowed to install a macerator toilet only if you have another, conventional toilet in the house as well. Is this strictly true? I would like to do away with the huge bathroom/WC in the downstairs room of my Victorian conversion flat, in order to use the space. I would instead create a smaller shower/WC in a corner upstairs. But the distance from the drains is apparently too far to have a normal WC. Is there any way round this?

A Building Control Officers do not like macerator WCs because they are unreliable, and they are right to insist that you have a proper toilet as well. Macerator WCs use an electric-powered mincer to chop up the contents of the bowl and pump it through a 40mm waste pipe. They were originally marketed for basement conversions below the level of the main drain, in which case they represent the only possibility for installing a bathroom. But they are notorious for breaking down, particularly as the macerator teeth are easily snagged by cotton fibres – some plumbers say that women should not be allowed anywhere near them! Macerator toilets are also very noisy, which can lead to disputes between neighbours.

But there are very few situations where a normal 100mm WC waste pipe cannot be installed in an older house. The pipe needs a fall of 1 in 40, which can usually be achieved within the ceiling space of a Victorian house. And if not, then the pipe can usually be raised at the bathroom end or lowered at the outlet end to achieve the required fall. Ask an experienced architect or surveyor to design your new bathroom for you.

HEATING

BOILER VENTILATION REQUIREMENTS

Q Following this year's annual service of my gas boiler (under a Homecare agreement), British Gas have written to me to say that the ventilation arrangements for my boiler do not meet current safety standards. They say that as the boiler has passed a safety test, it can remain in use until 1 June 2008, after which date, if the ventilation has not been upgraded, it will be categorized as 'at risk' and should be turned off. I think I read in your column that existing safety arrangements do not have to be upgraded when the standards change; they only have to be revised when a new appliance is installed. My recollections on this are reinforced by the fact that British Gas only say it 'should be' turned off, which does not indicate that turning off is obligatory, even though they are probably trying to give that impression. However, I am not sure of the significance, if any, of the date 1 June 2008.

My boiler has been operating satisfactorily for nearly ten years with the existing ventilation arrangements (a grille in the floorboards allowing air to enter from under the kitchen floor) and I see no reason why I should upgrade now. I should be grateful for your advice.

A   I have been getting a large number of readers' letters about this subject, which concerns open-flued or 'chimney' boilers, where the combustion air enters the room through a ventilation grille, and the exhaust gases exit via a conventional pipe or flue. (Most modern wall-mounted boilers are 'room-sealed' and have fan-assisted balanced flues, with the combustion air entering through the flue and the exhaust gases exiting the same way. These do not require extra room ventilation.)

The fact is that there is no 'new regulation' or 'new safety standard' regarding this issue, and ventilation requirements have not changed. If a boiler was installed from new according to the manufacturer's instructions, then there is no reason why it should suddenly have become unsafe. The only reason British Gas or any other CORGI-registered gas engineer should have for advising an increase in the ventilation would be if the boiler was wrongly installed in the first place, or if the ventilation had since been reduced (such as by air bricks or ventilation grilles being blocked up), or if a free-standing boiler had since been 'compartmentalized' or enclosed in a cupboard.

The current confusion stems from the publication in August 2005 of the fourth edition of the Gas Industry Unsafe Situations Procedure, which specifies the steps to be taken in the event that a gas appliance is genuinely poorly ventilated. This states that an appliance with 39 per cent or less of the manufacturer's ventilation requirement should be classified 'at risk' with immediate effect and turned off (or less than 90 per cent of the required ventilation for a compartmentalized appliance); if the ventilation is between 40 and 89 per cent of the requirement, then the user must be informed that they have until 1 June 2008 to rectify the situation, and that if they don't, it will be deemed to be 'at risk' from that date. If in doubt, consult the manufacturer's instructions for your boiler, or contact CORGI [GAS].

CONDENSING BOILER PLUME (1)

Q   **Our neighbour has a condensing boiler plume which jets out at about 8 feet (2.5m) high and 3 feet (900mm) from our dividing fence. In the immediate vicinity of the plume as it blows over the fence, we have a patio where we sit and our grandchildren play, garden plants, and a small pond used by the local wild life, including frogs. You have mentioned the acidic discharge. Is this likely to affect any of the above?**

A   No, the acidic discharge is the condensate liquid, which goes down a pipe into the drains. The flue gases are only the usual mix of water vapour and carbon dioxide, which appears as a plume of steam because it is cooler than that from a conventional boiler. Other readers have asked about what effect the acidic discharge might have on local water tables and whether there is a potential risk of it entering into the water-supply system. Boiler manufacturers claim it is about as acidic as vinegar, so it is unlikely to have any significant effect when diluted in the drainage system. However, it could cause localized corrosion where it discharges regularly into a cast-iron soil pipe, which is why in some cases a separate soakaway has to be used. Some heating engineers, however, have questioned the possible effect of an acid build-up in the ground in these cases.

CONDENSING BOILER PLUME (2)

Q   **Our neighbour has a boiler plume which also projects about 8 feet (2.5m) high but is only just over 1 foot (300mm) from our boundary. The plume of steam blows over our patio and obscures our windows. Your reply to the question was that this may not be dangerous, but it is none the less annoying and detracts from our quiet enjoyment of our property. Is there** anything in the planning or Building Regulations which would require our neighbour to mitigate the nuisance, e.g. by extending the outlet to roof height? Or do we have any other remedies?

A This is an increasingly common readers' question, as more and more condensing boilers are installed. The flue gases from a condensing boiler have the same composition as those from a conventional boiler, being mostly carbon dioxide and water vapour. The difference is that, being cooler, the water vapour turns more easily to steam, even in warm weather. And also, being cooler, the gases do not rise up to disperse in the air, but tend to hang around at low level.

Regarding the regulations governing this issue, the answer is far from clear cut. The only definitive 'rule' for flue siting is in Approved Document J of the Building Regulations, which specifies that a fan-assisted balanced flue – for any type of boiler – should be a minimum of 600mm 'from a surface or a boundary facing the terminal', i.e. if the flue is pointing towards your boundary. I suspect from your e-mail that the flue in question is not actually pointing towards your boundary but out towards the back garden, in which case the minimum distance is only 300mm. However, 'guidance' (not compulsory) in the government document 'Guide to the Condensing Boiler Installation Assessment Procedure for Dwellings' extends the 600mm to 'a minimum 2.5m from a facing wall, fence, building, or the property boundary' for condensing boiler models. Again, this applies only to a flue pointing in that direction. This document also states, 'It is necessary to site a condensing boiler flue terminal such that the plume of wet flue products does not impinge on or significantly affect the use of the householders' dwelling and also the neighbouring buildings.' British Standard BS5440–1 'recommends' (again, not compulsory) that condensing boiler flues should not be sited where the plume is 'likely to cause a nuisance'.

Manufacturers have recognized that pluming is a problem, and supply 'plume management kits' – basically a plastic pipe that can be fixed to the flue terminal to direct the plume upwards or sideways. You might suggest to your neighbours that they have one fitted. If they refuse, then you might approach your local-authority Environmental Health Officer, to whom you would have to demonstrate that the pluming is causing a nuisance to you. All the documents mentioned above can be downloaded free from www.planningportal.gov.uk

BOILER SETTINGS

Q Could you please advise me which setting I should use on my central heating boiler and why. The boiler has settings from Low through numbers 1 to 4, and the last position for the setting is High. (I use number 3 all year round.)

A The dial on the boiler controls the temperature of the water circulating through the pipes and radiators. It is a separate control from the room thermostat, which turns the boiler on and off in response to the air temperature. Most people have the boiler setting on Medium, or 3, or whatever is in the centre of the range. In very cold weather, or to warm the house up quicker, you could turn it up to High, and this will make the radiators hotter. In warmer weather, if you still want a bit of background heat, you could turn the dial down to Low. When leaving the house unoccupied in very cold weather, you could also turn the dial down to Low, set the programme timer to 'Constant', and the room thermostat to 15°C, and this will ensure a low level of background heat to prevent condensation occurring.

OFF-PEAK ELECTRICITY

Q We have storage heaters in our living rooms connected to Economy 7 but have electric convector heaters in the bedrooms which can be timed. Would it be possible to change the convection heaters for storage heaters? Is it just a matter of swapping them over or would they have to be rewired and reconnected at the fuse box?

A Night-storage heaters on the Economy 7 tariff are becoming steadily more attractive as a heating option. Following the recent spate of energy price rises, off-peak electricity is now effectively as cheap as piped natural gas, and has the benefit of low installation costs and almost zero maintenance costs. Ideally, each storage heater should be run off its own spur – a dedicated single cable running from the off-peak consumer unit. But to save the costs of rewiring, it is also possible for a storage heater to be plugged into an existing 30-amp ring main, using a time switch to ensure that it draws current only during the off-peak period. If you are planning to connect more than one storage heater to the same ring main, you should ensure that the total extra load does not exceed 4kW, or 3kW if the ring circuit includes a kitchen. If in doubt, consult a qualified electrician.

Also note that having storage heaters in bedrooms does not suit everyone. Modern storage heaters are very well insulated, but they still leak heat into the room, even when the output controls are turned down to the minimum, and the maximum heat leakage occurs when the core reaches its hottest period (from around 3 o'clock in the morning). This may be welcome in very cold weather, but in milder conditions, some people find it uncomfortable.

BACK BOILER

Q **During a recent British Gas annual inspection of my central-heating system I was informed by the engineer that my twenty-year-old Baxi back boiler was working well, which was fortunate as should it require replacement I would be unable to replace it with another back boiler as they are now banned. This is rather worrying as I would be hard pressed to find the space elsewhere for a replacement boiler. Is this statement by the engineer correct regarding the banning of back boilers?**

A No, this is not correct at all. Your British Gas engineer must have been misinformed. The current situation is that new boilers are supposed to conform to a certain standard of energy efficiency, effectively limiting the choice to a condensing boiler. It happens that, at present, all the condensing gas (but not oil) boilers being manufactured have balanced flues, and thus need to be mounted against an outside wall (unlike conventional boilers, which take their combustion air from within the room and vent the waste gases up a stove pipe or lined chimney).

But the Building Regulations do allow for conventional back boilers (i.e. gas fires with boilers, fitted in fireplaces) to be replaced like-for-like in situations where it would be difficult to fit a new condensing boiler against an outside wall. The exemption formula is worked out on a points basis, with 1000 points being required to allow replacement with a similar back boiler. A mid-terrace house starts with a points score of 640 and a flat with 710. Moving the boiler to a different room with an outside wall (usually the kitchen) incurs another 350 points. If the property has cast-iron drainage pipes – which would be damaged by the acidic discharge from a condensing boiler – then it would be necessary to install a soakaway at ground level to accept the condensate, and this adds 100 points. Should the new boiler position require a flue longer than 2 metres, this adds another 200 points. So in many cases the 1000 points total is easily achieved, and a replacement conventional back boiler would be perfectly acceptable. [Condensing boiler installation assessment procedure is available on www.communities.gov.uk/index.asp?id=1131465]

OIL TANK REGULATIONS

Q **I have oil-fired heating and have been told that my steel tank has to be replaced with a plastic one before any more oil can be delivered. Also that the new tank will have to be a certain minimum distance from my bungalow and encased in a wall of either brick or steel. As I have only a small garden this is a big worry. Do you have any firm information on the laws concerning oil tanks?**

A This is a common rumour but not true. There are regulations covering the installation of new oil tanks, but these do not apply retrospectively to existing installations. As long as your tank is not leaking, there should be no need to replace it (and even leaking steel tanks can be repaired). Should you decide that you want a new tank (and you could choose either steel or plastic) then it would have to be sited a minimum 1.8 metres (6 feet) away from the house. Only if a tank has to be closer than this to the house would a fireproof wall need to be constructed. Another false rumour circulating is that all oil tanks have to be sited in secondary containment enclosures, or 'bunds', but again this applies only to new installations, and generally only to tanks larger than 2500 litres (550 gallons). Full regulations and advice are available from Oftec (Oil Firing Technical Association) on 0845 658 5080. Technical publications can be downloaded free from www.oftec.org

POWER FLUSHING

Q **My heating engineer has told me that where a new boiler is being fitted, it is now a requirement under the Building Regulations that the existing radiators and pipework must be 'power flushed' by a qualified person, and that this is subject to enforcement by the local authority. Is this correct? If not, could you tell us what the requirements are, and under exactly which regulations?**

A Power flushing is a process where an electric pump is used to force water through a central-heating system in order to clear out sludge and blockages. As I have written before, power flushing is rarely needed and often mis-sold. It is only likely to be effective when the system has been pre-treated with chemicals to dissolve sludge, and heating engineers tell me that once this chemical treatment has been carried out, simple draining down of the system is usually all that is needed. In cases of severe system corrosion (where radiators or pipes have been totally blocked with sludge) then even power flushing is unlikely to be effective, and it is usually cheaper and easier to remove and replace the offending radiator or section of pipework.

There is nothing in the Building Regulations that requires a central-heating system to be power flushed when fitting a new boiler. There is an 'associated document' to Part L of the Building Regulations, called the Domestic Heating Compliance Guide, which states that 'Central-heating systems should be thoroughly cleaned and flushed out before installing a new boiler', but using a chemical system cleaner, draining down, and flushing through with clean water under normal water pressure would satisfy this requirement. In my opinion, power flushing has been over-promoted by companies who manufacture the flushing equipment, and by central heating servicing companies who make a profit by persuading customers to pay from £500 to £800 for power flushing, whilst sometimes paying the subcontract heating engineers who carry out the operation only £150 to £200.

CONFUSION RE CONDENSING OR COMBINATION

Q **I have read with interest your advice to avoid combination boilers. However, my boiler is twenty years old and will need replacing soon and I have been told that new regulations mean I must replace it with a 'combi' boiler. This will involve major changes to the pipework and cost several thousand pounds. If I could replace the existing boiler with one of the same type it would be much easier and cheaper. Are there any circumstances which will allow replacement with a traditional boiler?**

A You are not the only reader to be confused by the similarity of the words 'combination' and 'condensing'. All new boilers have to be condensing models, but there is no regulation that requires you to alter a traditional indirect heating and hot water system to a combi system. A new condensing boiler can be fitted to an existing traditional system without extensive alterations to the pipework. You should also get a second opinion on the state of your existing boiler. Just because it is twenty years old does not mean it has to be replaced.

RELATIVE COSTS OF FUELS

Q We heat our house by a modern, conventional oil-fired boiler and, up to now, our domestic hot water too. However, the price of oil has increased from 10.5p to 35.5p per litre in the past eight years. Standard rate electricity has gone up only slightly, to 9.4p per unit. Would we be better off heating our water by electric immersion heater or is it still better to use oil, given that the boiler is already working to heat the house?

A Relative costs of heating by different fuels are difficult to work out, as the suppliers' invoices record their calorific values in different ways. Prices also vary in different parts of the country, and between different suppliers. The standard 'unit' of electric power is the kilowatt-hour (kWh), which will heat a one-bar radiant electric fire for one hour, and costs around 9p. Off-peak electricity (e.g. 'Economy 7') costs around 3p per kWh, but usually with a higher standing charge, and/or a higher day-time rate, and is used with night storage heaters, which many people find inconvenient. Natural gas piped into the house ('town gas') costs around 2.5p per kWh, but gas boilers may be only 75 per cent efficient, giving a truer cost of nearer 3.5p. Heating oil and LPG (propane), which are delivered by tanker and stored in tanks outside the house, provide roughly 10 kWh per litre, so at current prices this is around 3.5p per kWh (say 4.5p allowing for boiler efficiency) more expensive than off-peak electricity but half the price of standard rate electricity.

Anyone thinking of switching from one fuel to another, or considering upgrading to a new boiler, needs to calculate the payback period for the costs of the new installation. In most cases installation will cost thousands of pounds and this will take many years, or even decades, to show a profit. So it is usually better to stick with the system you've got, unless you have a very large house and/or very high heating bills, and can accurately calculate that a new installation will start saving you money within five years.

For anyone starting from scratch, with no existing heating system, off-peak electricity is probably the cheapest fuel source and has the lowest installation and maintenance costs.

WHICH FUEL?

Q We are negotiating to buy a 1960s-built bungalow for our retirement. The heating is currently electric storage radiators, and an immersion heater, which together with the wiring are of unknown age and condition. Gas has apparently been connected to the other bungalows in the cul-de-sac, so is 'in the road outside'. We have always had heating via gas boiler and pumped water radiators. In the light of current energy price trends what form of replacement heating would you advise in terms of both comfort and value for money? We are anticipating a fair amount of restoration and improvement work, including an extension to increase the kitchen and living area. One of us thinks under-floor heating would be a good idea!

A With current trends in fuel prices, off-peak electricity is roughly the same unit price as gas, and modern gas boilers have limited life, high installation and maintenance costs, and are liable to frequent breakdowns. Electric under-floor heating is a good idea under concrete, stone or brick floors (provided there is good insulation underneath) as the floors act as big storage heaters. If you have timber floors, then modern off-peak storage heaters are much more efficient than their predecessors, and if you are having the place rewired anyway, it is easy to have twin circuits put in whereby each heater has two supplies – one off-peak storage and one for a convector or fan heater boost if needed during the day. Modern hot-water cylinders have two immersion heaters – the bottom one heats the whole thing on off-peak electricity, the top one is for emergency toping-up if you run out of hot water during the day. Taking into account the installation and maintenance costs (and depreciation of gas boilers that might last only five to eight years) electricity almost certainly works out cheaper in the long run. The recent government decision to go for nuclear power will ensure that cheap off-peak electricity will be available for the foreseeable future (because nuclear power stations can't be shut down at night).

RADIATOR SIZES

Q Our bedroom never really gets warm in the winter. It's a north-facing room, with two largish sash windows, in a Victorian terraced house. The central heating radiator is on the opposite wall to the windows, and is a single panel, without 'fins', measuring about 1950mm x 530mm. It must be at least twenty years old. Would replacing it with a taller, double panel, radiator give us a cosier room?

A The science of central heating involves calculating the heat losses in each room, the temperature desired, and then choosing a radiator of the correct output. Heating engineers use tables that include the aspect, the areas of outside walls, and the number and size of windows. Obviously these figures can vary enormously from house to house, and you do not say how big the bedroom is, but as an example, an average large bedroom, say 5m x 4m, would need a heat input of around 3kW to keep it at a comfortable temperature of 21°C.

A single panel radiator of the dimensions you describe probably has an output of only about 1kW (assuming you have your boiler temperature on 'Max'), so you would need to treble it. If you want to replace the radiator with one with the same height and width (which will minimize alterations to the pipework), a modern single panel rad with convector fins will have an output of about 1.8kW, a double rad with single convector fins will be about 2.5kW, and a double-panel rad with double convector fins will be about 3.1kW, which should just about do the trick.

THERMOSTATIC RADIATOR VALVES (TRVS) (1)

Q When we refurbished our bungalow we had central heating fitted with thermostatic valves on every radiator. I imagined that this would enable us to set the room temperatures to within a few degrees, but it has not worked out that way; a fair bit of fiddling seems to be needed to adjust to hot or cold temperatures. You mentioned recently the use of a thermostat in the hall, rather than controlling individual radiators; is this a possible solution?

A Thermostatic radiator valves are fairly crude devices that are slow to respond to changes in room temperatures, and might allow differentials of five or six degrees before they turn themselves on or off. They are prone to sticking (usually in the closed position), and because they do not control the boiler, you might end up with a situation where the radiators are all cold, but the boiler continues to fire up.

Every central-heating system should have a wall-mounted room thermostat, wired with four-core ('triple and earth') cable, so that the accelerator heater is working. This controls the boiler directly and should keep the room temperature to within one or two degrees of your preferred setting.

TRVS (2)

Q I note that new central heating installations require zone controls. Do thermostatic radiator valves (TRVs) fulfil this requirement?

A The latest version of the Building Regulations requires zone controls to save heating energy by allowing for different temperatures in different parts of the house. The idea is that it is wasteful to heat the bedrooms, say, when there is nobody in them. The downside to this, however, is that water vapour from the warmer living areas will find its way into the cooler bedrooms and cause condensation on the windows and walls. TRVs can be used, but they do not have a good track record. Separate room thermostats, connected to motorized valves on the pipework, are a more reliable option.

HEATING CONTROLS

Q My central heating radiators all have thermostatic valves, apart from the one in the bathroom, which is supposed to provide a safety outlet in case the boiler overheats. The thermostatic valves have a 'Frost' setting, which I intended to use when away from home in the winter, but as the bathroom radiator is uncontrolled, it stays hot all the time, even if I turn the temperature control on the boiler to its lowest setting. The bathroom is too hot, and I am wasting gas. What can I do?

A Your central-heating system is missing one vital component – a room thermostat to turn the boiler off when the house has reached the desired temperature. Thermostatic radiator valves on their own will not control the boiler; they simply shut down the radiators, but the boiler will continue to pump hot water around the rest of the system. When you are away from home you should leave the thermostatic valves on full, the boiler heat setting turned down to '1', or 'Min', and the room thermostat on the frost setting. Contact a CORGI-registered gas installer to have a look at your system.

INSENSITIVE THERMOSTAT

Q What would you advise for a central-heating system that blows either hot or cold, but nothing in between? The wall thermostat has to be turned to 24°C to activate the boiler but then lowered to 20°C to turn it off. Any setting between these two levels has no effect. Three different thermostats have all produced the same result.

A A four-degree differential (or 'hysteresis') is about what you'd expect on a normal cheap room thermostat wired as an On/Off to the boiler. However, you may find that the thermostat can be persuaded to perform better by changing the wiring so that the small 'accelerator heater' in it is brought into the circuit. Plumbers often use only three-core cable ('twin and earth') to wire up room stats, whereas they really need four-core ('triple and earth'), with the live and switched-live conductors routed through the thermostat, and a spare neutral connected to the accelerator heater. The current through this, when the thermostat is 'On', keeps the thermostat closer to room temperature and can reduce the hysteresis to plus-or-minus 1°C. If rewiring presents a problem, and if your room thermostat has no exposed metal parts (and the air grilles are proof against small fingers), then you may be able to sacrifice the earth wire and use it as the neutral connection to the accelerator heater. This is probably not a DIY job. For totally accurate control you will need a more expensive digital thermostat, such as the Honeywell CM67.

THERMOSTAT POSITIONING

Q In most houses the central heating room thermostat is mounted in the hall next to the kitchen door. Why? I have been doing some work in a bungalow with a narrow hall and the family kept arguing about the setting on the thermostat. I went through the sequence of their life – cooking with or without the kitchen door open, lounge door open or not, etc. They have now asked me to move the thermostat into the lounge.

A The usual reason for siting the room thermostat near to the kitchen is that the boiler is in the kitchen, and the installing engineer wants to use the minimum amount of cable. More rationally, the hall is often chosen because when the front door is opened, cold air enters, and the thermostat will turn the heating on to counter the cooling effect that this cold air will have as it circulates around the house. Of course, this can lead to the lounge and kitchen becoming hotter than required. But the problem with having the thermostat in the lounge is that when the lounge reaches the required temperature, the heating is shut down in the whole of the rest of the house, leading to condensation problems. The only real answer is a zoned heating system, with separate thermostats controlling different areas.

RENEWABLE ENERGY

Q I would like to use renewable energy to heat my conservatory. But I have looked into solar, wind and ground heating types of systems, and I seem to have drawn blanks. I contacted the local-authority building engineer and was informed that I needed to contact a renewable energy helpline, which still seemed limited regarding information.

Can you recommend the best type of heating to suit a conservatory, renewable if possible? I am quite surprised at the lack of information and potential uses for renewable energy.

A If you want to be 'green' in your approach (which I guess you do, from your references to renewable energy) then the best thing would be to not heat your conservatory at all. To keep a standard double-glazed 30 sq m conservatory at a 'habitable' temperature in winter would mean pumping heat into it at a rate of around 3–5 kW, and all that energy will quickly find its way out through the glass roof and windows. There has been a lot of publicity recently about solar and wind power, but an affordable domestic solar or wind installation will produce only a small amount of energy – enough for a few electric lights, and to preheat the hot-water system, but nowhere near enough for space heating.

Ground-source heat pump systems cost upwards of £5000 to install, and have a minimum payback period of twenty to thirty years. They are also likely to use more energy in their manufacture and installation than they will produce over that period, so they are not necessarily 'renewable' themselves. There is a high level of misunderstanding about the renewable energy issue, which is not helped by propaganda from various government departments.

HEAT PUMPS

Q I am investigating the different types of under-floor heating systems available, and have been told that the way forward in the twenty-first century is to draw heat direct from the subsoil, in a manner somewhat similar to solar heating panels on the roof. Do you know anything about this seemingly inexhaustible source of cheap heat?

A The system you are describing is a heat pump, which operates in the same way as a fridge, by using a compressor to pump a refrigerant gas around a circuit, extracting heat from a low-temperature source (the ground) and delivering it at a higher temperature – like the heat from the coil at the back of the fridge. Theoretically, for every unit of electricity to power the pump, three units of heat can be delivered into the house. However, with installation costs starting at around £5000, a heat pump would take twenty to thirty years to pay for itself, and is unlikely to be worthwhile in a domestic setting.

COMBINED HEAT & POWER UNITS

Q I have read about central-heating boilers that also produce electric power for the house, which are supposed to be the latest thing in 'green' technology. Do you have any experience of these, and would you recommend installing one instead of a conventional boiler?

A These are called 'Micro CHP' units and are being promoted by some gas companies who are eager to be seen to be 'doing their bit' for the environment. They are basically gas boilers fitted with generators that produce a small amount of electric power. The house is still dependent on mains electricity for most purposes, but the idea is that when there is no electrical demand in the house, the excess electricity will be sold back to the power company. Critics say that Micro CHP is unproven technology, and that the small amount of power produced is unlikely to compensate for the high installation and maintenance costs of the units.

PIPE NOISE

Q **Our central heating comes on at seven every morning and operates quietly until about 7.50am, when it develops a rapid clicking noise for about twenty seconds and then is quiet again. The same noise crops up at irregular intervals during the day and seems confined to the pipework upstairs, towards the front of the house. The house is about thirty years old. What causes this problem and is there a solution?**

A The clicking noise is almost certainly the result of thermal expansion and contraction in the pipework. It is rare for any heating system to be completely silent in operation, and most people would consider a bit of clicking in the pipes to be insignificant. However, if you want to silence it, then you will have to locate precisely the problem area and investigate it further. A common cause of noisy pipework is the pipes being run through notches cut in the tops of the timber floor joists, and the floorboards being nailed or screwed down tight on top of them, restricting their ability to expand and contract. The notches should be a few millimetres bigger than the pipes, and conscientious plumbers even line them with felt. If the pipes are running parallel to the joists, they may have been clipped too tightly to them. Modern polypropylene pipe clips are quieter than the old copper ones.

BOILER SERVICING STANDARDS

Q **The annual service carried out by British Gas under the Three Star contract seems to have been replaced by a 'Healthcheck', which is not necessarily annual. Do you know if this is an official change to the contract, or just a way for the engineer to save time? The last British Gas engineer to inspect my boiler said it was best not to look for trouble!**

A For a few years now the terms of the British Gas Three Star Service contract have provided only for a 'yearly safety and performance check', in which an electronic instrument is used to analyse the content of the boiler flue gases. This is at odds with the recommendations of the boiler manufacturers, which specify an annual strip-down service. This entails removing the boiler's casing, removing and cleaning the gas burners, cleaning the fan and heat exchanger, and checking the ignition spark (or pilot light) and the gas pressure. You will find full details of what is required in your boiler's customer manual. A proper annual service should also include inspection and testing of header tank, radiators and pump.

When I last mentioned this, the Managing Director of British Gas Services wrote in to *The Sunday Telegraph* defending his company's practice, and claiming that it allowed their engineers to service and repair boilers 'forensically'. I have also had more than 300 letters from readers who claim that these visits do not occur annually, but at ever-increasing intervals. I can only remind readers that British Gas is no longer 'the Gas Board', but a private, profit-making company.

LEAKING PIPES BELOW CONCRETE FLOORS

Q **A reputable firm of plumbers has told us that our central heating and hot-water problems are caused by a leak from a pipe somewhere in our concrete floors. If they found the leak and dug up the floor to repair it, then another leak could occur at any time. They say the solution is to fit new pipes for the ten downstairs radiators, running down the walls from the ceiling above. Won't the pipes exposed look awful, or is there some way to disguise them?**

A Copper pipes buried below concrete floor screeds are corroded by the cement. This was not fully appreciated until the 1980s, and many systems installed before this are prone to sub-floor leaks. Copper pipes should only be used below solid floors if they are sheathed in plastic, or laid in open ducts. Dropping new pipe runs down from the ceiling above is a good solution, and the new pipes are usually situated in the corners of rooms, and disguised by boxing in.

REFLECTIVE FOIL BEHIND RADIATORS

Q **I have recently received a booklet containing 'handy tips and neat tricks' to improve my home comfort. One of them, about fitting radiator covers, added 'but remember to fit reflective foil to the wall to boost heat output'. Surely this is nonsense. We all learned at school that the only form of heat reflected by a silvered surface is radiant heat – the kind given out by glowing red coals or an electric fire. Radiators, despite their name, do not give out radiant heat, but work by convection, warming currents of air which circulate around the room. Would you agree with me that fitting reflective foil behind radiators is a waste of money?**

A Shiny metallic foil will reflect some heat back into the room, whatever the temperature of the radiator. The reflective effect is most obvious in the visible range of the electro-magnetic spectrum – the red-hot and white-hot temperatures – but also occurs at lower, non-visible temperatures. This is why chocolate is wrapped in aluminium foil. Foil behind a radiator might stop a very small amount of radiant heat entering the wall, although it is questionable whether this would justify the cost of the more expensive type of insulated foil reflector panels.

A more important question, however, is whether the foil is actually a good idea. Radiators on outside walls are often fitted below windows, and the wall below a window is always prone to being wetted by rainwater running down the glass, especially if the sill overhang is insufficient or the drip groove on the underside has been blocked with paint. Keeping the wall warm will help to keep it dry, and avoid the maintenance and repair costs of dealing with blown plaster, stained decorations and possibly rotted skirting boards. So, on balance, I would say the soundest financial option is to not fit the foil.

RADIATOR COVERS

Q **Do radiator covers reduce the efficiency of the radiator in heating up a room? I am thinking of buying one for a bedroom, to stop the heat going up behind the closed curtains, but wonder if it might stop the heat going out into the room, and warm up the wall instead.**

A The term 'radiator' is rather misleading, as the main way in which heat is transferred from those ribbed steel objects to the air of the room is by convection, not radiation. The heating industry now tends to call them 'emitters' rather than radiators. The 'efficiency' of an emitter in heating up a room is also not quite the right word, as what is really important is speed. So a large emitter, or one with lots of fins (i.e. a large surface area), will heat up the air in the room quicker than a small, compact one.

If you want your bedroom to feel warmer quicker, then it would be a good idea to direct the convection currents out into the room first, and allow the air behind the curtains to warm up later. The easiest way to achieve this is with a simple shelf. A radiator cover is really just a shelf, with some perforated decorative panels enclosing the space below it. If properly designed, with large air gaps at the top and bottom, a radiator cover can actually increase the heat transfer rate, by acting as a kind of flue, drawing air across the surface of the emitter. But a shelf will be cheaper.

ELECTRIC CENTRAL HEATING

Q Is there such a thing as electric-fired central heating? Not Economy 7 or storage heaters but something that does exactly the same as a gas-fired system?

A Electric flow boilers do exactly the same job as gas or oil-fired boilers, heating primary water which is pumped round a conventional wet radiator circuit. It is claimed that this is more efficient and more controllable than other forms of electric heating, and allows conventional central heating to be easily installed in homes with no access to mains gas. One supplier is Electroheat, whose boiler prices start at around £500 [PLUMBING, HEATING & DRAINAGE].

COMBI BOILERS

Q After twenty trouble-free years with a 'bog standard' indirect gas-fired central-heating system we are about to have a change, in order to recapture the efficiency of our system when it was younger. All we hear is combi, combi, combi, extolling the virtues as being: 'You only pay for the gas you use; the radiators heat up quicker; and no need for a hot water tank'! But we cannot get any real advice regarding the advantages of the traditional indirect system, apart from the fact that you can use a power shower off an indirect system but not a combi system. What are the pros and cons of the indirect and combi systems?

A Combination, or 'combi', boilers allow hot water to be drawn from only one outlet at a time. So if you are taking a shower and someone else turns on the kitchen tap, then you are in trouble. Also, in winter, when the incoming mains water is colder, you will get less of a flow of hot water, and it can take ages to run a bath. There should be no difference in the speed with which the two different types of boiler heat up the radiators. Some heating engineers try to sell combis because they are easy for them to install, but in your case you already have a cold-water storage tank and hot-water cylinder, so I can see no advantages of a combi boiler at all. And before you rush out to buy a new boiler, it may be worth asking a CORGI-registered gas installer for an opinion on the existing one.

Combi boilers are only suitable for small flats, not bigger properties.

COMBI BOILER – SLOW BATH FILLING

Q I have recently had a new central-heating system installed, using a combination boiler instead of the ordinary type used previously. I have now found that the water pressure is extremely low (it takes ages to fill a bath). The heating engineer says this is because a combination boiler takes its water directly from the mains and the mains pressure is low (although, apparently, within the guidelines). Is there anything that can be done to increase the pressure?

A Check that your heating engineer has used 22mm pipe for the gas supply, rather than 15mm. Combi boilers need a greater flow of gas for heating the hot water than they do for the central heating. But apart from that, there's not much you can do, unless you buy a bigger boiler. Combi boilers rarely provide a good flow of hot water, and they are only really suitable for small flats with showers, not bigger properties with baths.

COMBI BOILER WON'T FIRE

Q The central heating radiators in my one-bed basement flat were hot at the bottom but cold at the top. Following a friend's advice I bought a 'bleeding key' from a plumbers' merchants and bled the air out of them. They are now completely cold and the boiler refuses to fire up under any circumstances. What have I done wrong?

A Combi boiler systems do not have a header tank but rely on mains water pressure. What has probably happened is that there is a slight leak in one of the radiator valves which has allowed the pressure to drop. This is not unusual and is not a disaster. You have done the right thing in bleeding the air out of the radiators. Now all you have to do is recharge the boiler up to working pressure. There should be a flexible filler loop (a rubber hose covered with metal braid) somewhere around the pipework feeding the boiler. This is supposed to be disconnected after the system is pressurized, but because combi systems need repressurizing on a regular basis, many heating engineers leave them connected. Opening up the valves at either end of this will allow mains water to flow into the system. Make sure you locate the water pressure gauge before you start and turn the valves off when you reach one atmosphere pressure.

CENTRAL HEATING WON'T WORK

Q We have just turned our central heating on for the first time since May, and the radiators stay cold. There does not seem to be any fault with the gas boiler, which is firing up and heating the hot water as usual. Is there likely to be a simple problem we could fix ourselves, without the expense of calling in a heating engineer?

A The fact that you have hot water indicates that both the boiler and circulating pump are probably OK. The most likely culprit is the motorized valve on the radiator circuit. These often get blocked with sludge during the inactivity of the summer months. Turn the boiler on, and find the motorized valve, which is a rectangular metal box about 75 x 50 x 50mm, usually somewhere near the pump. (If the pipes are hot either side of the valve, then it will be the one that controls the hot water; you need to locate the other one, which controls the radiators.) There should be a manual over-ride lever sticking out of the end, and if you slide this to one side or the other then the valve should open and there will be a gurgling noise as the water flows through. This is usually all that is needed to clear the blockage, but at some stage you should have the system drained down and refilled, using a corrosion-inhibiting additive.

CENTRAL HEATING WON'T TURN OFF

Q I have a baffling problem with my central-heating system, which my regular plumber is unable to diagnose. Whilst the heating usually switches on and off as ordered by the programmer, and usually responds to adjustments on the room thermostat, there are times when the boiler fires up for no apparent reason (i.e. in the middle of the night or when the temperature is too warm for the thermostat to switch on). When this happens, the only way to stop the boiler running is to turn off the electrical switch which supplies it with mains power.

A The most likely cause is a defect in one of the motorized valves. These are fed with electric current via the programmer, and open up or close off parts of the system to allow hot water to flow through them (to heat either the hot water cylinder, or zoned parts of the heating circuit), turning the boiler on in the process. Sometimes motorized valves can get jammed in the 'open' position, and feed current back to the boiler, which makes it fire up, even though the programmer is set to 'Off' and the room thermostat is below ambient temperature. If your motorized valves are more than ten years old, then it is probably worth getting them replaced (about £30 each), rather than trying to fix them.

OVERFLOWING HEADER TANK

Q My boiler is regularly serviced by a qualified gas engineer, but the header tank has been gently overflowing for some months. The ballcock and valve assembly has been renewed, to no effect, and the engineer says he is mystified as to the cause.

A If there have been no other changes in the system, then the most likely cause is a corrosion hole in the secondary heating coil inside the hot-water cylinder. The head of pressure from the cold water cistern will be pushing water through this hole into the central heating circuit and causing an overflow from the 'f & e' (feed and expansion) tank. Check by turning off the mains feed to the cold-water cistern, leaving all the taps off, and seeing if the water level falls by the same amount as the water coming out of the overflow. The answer is to fit a new hot-water cylinder.

CORROSION INHIBITOR

Q How can I tell whether enough (or any) corrosion inhibitor has been added to my central-heating system? A British Gas saleswoman ran some water from a radiator into a glass and told me that because the water was black, the system was sludged up, and that I would need to pay extra for a power flush. But I am sure that the system was drained down and a corrosion inhibitor added when we had a new radiator installed in our bathroom two years ago.

A You cannot tell the condition of the system, or diagnose the presence of excessive sludge, from looking at the colour of the water. Even in a clean central-heating system, with corrosion inhibitor added, the water can still appear dark from dissolved oxides and residues. The presence of an inhibitor in the system water can be tested for by any heating engineer (e.g. by using a Fernox Protector test kit, which costs around £20 for fifty tests, or a Sentinel X100 test kit, around £1 for two tests). Both can be used to test the concentration of the inhibiting chemical (sodium molybdenum), by collecting a little water from a radiator bleed valve, adding tablets, and noting the colour. Betz Dearbon also offer a complete analysis for system water and mains water for around £10, which involves sending samples away for a laboratory report. Test kits can be bought from PlumbCenter or Plumbase, or call Betz Dearborn [PLUMBING, HEATING & DRAINAGE] for stockists. Alternatively, a simple DIY test is to bleed some system water into a glass jar and drop in a couple of steel nails and a 1p coin (to simulate the metals in the heating system). If, after a month, the nails have gone rusty, than that will be what is happening to the inside of your radiators, too. If the nails remain clean, then the system has enough corrosion inhibitor in it.

PUTTING ADDITIVES IN COMBI SYSTEMS

Q I understand that in central-heating systems where steel radiators are connected by copper pipes it is advisable to add inhibitors to the water to slow down corrosion. How is the inhibitor fluid added to the combi boiler system?

A The corrosion is a result of electro-chemical reaction between the two different metals. This corrosion is also responsible for the formation of sludge in the system, which can block radiators and clog circulating pumps. In a conventional wet central heating circuit, inhibitor is poured into the feed-and-expansion tank ('header' tank) in the loft. A combination boiler operates on a sealed system with no header tank. The easiest way to introduce an inhibitor, or any other additive, into a combi system, is to inject a concentrate into one of the radiator vents. These are available from plumbers' suppliers, or for further information call Fernox [PLUMBING, HEATING & DRAINAGE].

RADIATORS COLD AT THE BOTTOM

Q My twenty-year-old central-heating system has nine radiators, all with thermostatic valves. The circulating water contains Fernox inhibitor, which I have tested for using the copper coin and steel nails and which seems to be working well. The problem I have is that in the fifteen years I have lived here, some of the radiators, one by one, have gradually run cooler from the bottom, so it is not an air problem.

A If you can feel a distinctive cooler 'triangle' at the bottom of the radiator, between the two valves, then the most likely cause would be a severe deposition of sludge. In this event, it is often easier to replace the radiator rather than attempt to clear the blockage.

However, your inhibitor test seems to have ruled out the possibility of sludge, so the most likely cause is that the thermostatic radiator valves (TRVs) are jamming in a near-closed position, allowing only a trickle of water to flow through the radiators. This is a common fault and one which the government's 'energy-saving' advice never mentions when it encourages us all to fit these troublesome gadgets. When cold, the pin on a TRV is held in the open position by a strong spring. When it gets warm, the expansion mechanism pushes the pin closed. Over the years, the spring will get weaker, and the pin will corrode, and it will gradually fail to return to a fully open position. You may be able to strip your TRVs down and free them up (after draining down the central-heating system).

To avoid recurrence of the problem, TRVs should be opened and closed once a month, to keep them working freely, and left in the open ('hot') position over the summer months, or whenever the central heating is left unused for a period. Readers have also suggested freeing jammed TRVs by taking off the valve head, squirting WD40 around the pin, and tapping it with a hammer or rotating it with a pair of pliers. It is certainly worth trying this if it avoids having to drain down the whole system. Heating engineers tell me that the latest TRVs are less prone to sticking than some of their older counterparts.

RADIATORS ALWAYS HOT

Q When my hot water is on, but the central heating is switched off, some of the upstairs radiators get hot anyway. The engineer who serviced the boiler said that this is the problem with gravity-feed systems and there was nothing I could do about it. Is this so? Is there not a valve or something that could be fitted to prevent it?

A The problem is one of pipe geometry and it affects lots of systems, including those where both the central-heating and hot-water circuits are fully pumped. It is a simple matter of hot water, being less dense, rising to the highest part of the system. In some cases the water flowing to the hot water cylinder passes a 'T' joint connected to the radiator circuit, and is able to divert up it.

In other cases the 'flow' side of the pipework is laid out properly, but hot water still gravitates upwards along the 'return' side. The answer can be to insert a loop at the problem point, so that the water has to flow downwards before it goes up – then it will only take this route when it is pumped. If this doesn't work, then a check valve or non-return valve can be fitted, but the first solution is more elegant. Any experienced plumber should be able to rectify the situation for you.

CONDENSING BOILERS (1)

Q I am considering buying a condensing oil boiler for our house, which we are in the process of renovating. I would be interested to hear your comments on condensing versus conventional boilers.

A Condensing boilers – both gas-fired and oil-fired – are promoted as being hugely efficient converters of fuel into heat. Efficiency gains of 15 per cent are commonly claimed by manufacturers and retailers, but this is actually a myth. They would only achieve this sort of advantage if they were constantly running in fully condensing mode, which would mean an operating temperature of 54°C (as opposed to the usual 60–80°C for a conventional boiler). In practice, in a domestic central-heating system, a condensing boiler will be firing up from cold, running for two or three minutes, and then turning itself off again, just like a conventional boiler. It will thus only be running in condensing mode for a few seconds in each on/off cycle, and this is the period when a plume of steam can be seen shooting out of the flue (a phenomenon known as 'pluming'), which some owners and neighbours find alarming. Energy-efficiency savings will be slight, and the industry has yet to produce any reliable independent figures to support its claims.

In return for this theoretical efficiency, condensing boilers are more complicated, need more regular servicing, and have many more parts to go wrong and be replaced. So condensing boilers are really only worth installing if you have a very big house, or hotel, and very high fuel bills. And it is worth noting that if the boiler does actually run in fully condensing mode (54°C), then that is as hot as the water flowing from it will ever get, which means radiators will be cooler, and may need to be replaced with larger-sized models in order to emit the same amount of heat to the rooms. The domestic hot-water supply will also only reach 54°C, which is, incidentally, below the British Standard recommended minimum of 60°C.

CONDENSING BOILERS (2)

Q All the hype I read about condensing boilers led me to believe that I should tear out my twenty-year-old conventional boiler and install one of these gismos. Being a sceptic, I asked if there was any downside. After some waffling, I was told that my system would need to be chemically cleaned every three or so years at a cost of up to £200 a time. Surely this will eliminate most of my savings?

A Maintenance and servicing on condensing boilers is certainly more extensive, and expensive. Neither the manufacturers nor the Government's energy-saving promotional literature make this clear. If your conventional boiler is giving no trouble after twenty years, it is highly unlikely that replacing it would save you any money, or save the planet any energy.

CONDENSING BOILERS (3)

Q I bought a condensing boiler and after two years I returned home one day to find it leaking very badly. Investigation revealed that the aluminium heat exchanger was completely corroded, which the manufacturers said was due to 'over-condensing'. They said this happens when the flow/return temperatures are not controlled to within 11°C. I argued that this was impossible to achieve when a boiler is installed in an existing radiator system, and that I had not been told that the boiler would only work properly with new radiators, etc. Unable to obtain any recompense, I replaced it with a conventional boiler, which has given me no trouble and is, interestingly, just as efficient as the condensing boiler in terms of gas consumption.

A The condensate produced within a condensing boiler is acidic, and the boiler therefore requires regular (six-monthly) servicing to clean out the drainage tubes and prevent corrosion. It is also true that condensing boilers work best as part of a new, specially designed heating system with aluminium radiators, and that they often fail when fitted to existing systems. Word in the trade is that there are many more technical problems to be solved before condensing boilers will be worth buying.

QUICKER HOT WATER

Q When we want hot water in our kitchen, we waste a sink full of cold water before it runs hot. Is there a relatively unobtrusive instant water heater we could have fitted?

A This is a common problem, especially annoying for people who pay for their water via a meter. If you have a conventional system with a hot-water cylinder, then the problem is that the pipe run from the cylinder to the kitchen is too long. If you have a combi boiler, then it doesn't matter how long the pipe run is – a whole boiler-full of water always has to be run off before the water runs hot. The simple answer is to get a small, unvented under-sink electric water heater. These are simple to plumb in, and can be powered from the nearest 13-amp socket. They are usually 10- or 15-litre capacity, which means they heat up quickly and supply enough hot water for washing up. Have it fed by cold water from the mains and use your existing hot-water system only for the bathroom. Manufacturers include Ariston and Heatrae Sadia [PLUMBING, HEATING & DRAINAGE].

UNDER-FLOOR HEATING

Q What are the advantages of under-floor heating as against radiators? If you had to choose from either one (to go with a condensing boiler) to go into a new bungalow which we hope to get built within the next few months, which would you choose and why?

A The advantages are that you don't have radiators taking up wall space and getting in the way of furniture placement, the floor is nice and warm to walk on and the heat is spread evenly throughout the room.

Disadvantages are that under-floor heating works best on solid floors – concrete, brick or tiled finish – which can have their own disadvantages. It also needs fitting in conjunction with under-floor insulation, and so means a lot of excavation and building work. Of course, if you are building from scratch then this is not a problem. UFH *can* be used under timber floors, and there are various systems involving metal plates to spread the heat around. But obviously you would have to make sure that the floorboards were totally dry before fixing to stop shrinkage gaps opening up. And then, if the heating was left off for any great time, the boards could absorb moisture and swell and buckle.

Because the floor itself becomes the emitter, rather than radiators, it may take some time for the house to warm up and cool down – i.e. response times are slow. Obviously the under-floor piping has to be installed to a very high standard, as it would be very disruptive to take up the floor to repair leaks. But the biggest difference between UFH and radiators is that the water temperature from the boiler has to be lowered, otherwise the floor would be too hot to walk on. The water temperature is adjusted by using valves to mix cooler water from the return pipes with hot water in the flow pipes – another complication. Many installations have UFH below a solid ground floor and radiators upstairs.

Electric under-floor heating is cheaper and easier to install than a wet system and can be timed to use cheaper off-peak electricity.

KETTLING NOISE IN BOILER

Q My five-year-old boiler is making increasingly loud 'kettling' noises. I have been told that this is due to limescale, and that the whole system needs to be power flushed, at a cost of £550. My local plumbers' merchants tells me that for £600 I could buy a new boiler. Is it worth paying so much to descale the present one, especially since the problem will presumably recur?

A 'Kettling' may well be caused by limescale on the heat exchanger. This traps steam bubbles which expand and explode, causing the noise. Power flushing will only clear out the limescale if descaling chemicals are introduced into the system first, and if the scale is removed by chemicals then it may be possible to drain the system down manually without the expense of the power flush. Sentinel or Fernox descaler costs around £20 from plumbers' merchants and can be added to the system and left to act slowly. I would give that a try before embarking on the expense of either a power flush or a new boiler.

POWER FLUSH OR BALANCING?

Q Some of my central heating radiators get very hot, whilst others are barely warm, even after bleeding. I have heard that the radiator system should be balanced, but the British Gas Service engineer does not seem keen on this and recommends that the system is power flushed instead, at a cost of over £600. Can you tell me how to try balancing the system myself, before I incur unnecessary expense?

A Power flushing is rarely needed. Balancing the system will often direct more heat to sluggish radiators, but it is a time-consuming process, and engineers and plumbers often cannot be bothered to do it. But it is a relatively simple DIY operation. At its most basic, balancing involves restricting the flow through the radiators nearest to the boiler, so that more heat reaches those further away. Each radiator has two valves – the On/Off valve (usually, but not always, on the right-hand side) and the balancing or 'lockshield' valve at the other end. The balancing valve is shielded by a loose cap that can be removed by undoing a screw, and the valve can then be adjusted using a small adjustable spanner.

Open all the On/Off radiator valves fully and then, starting with the radiator nearest the boiler, turn the balancing valve right off and then open it a one-quarter turn. Do the same with the next radiator, opening it three-eighths of a turn, and so on down the line, until the last radiator has the balancing valve fully open. Further 'fine tuning' may be needed to ensure that the heat is evenly distributed around the whole system.

A more sophisticated approach is to use a pair of clip-on thermometers on the flow and return ('in' and 'out') pipes either side of the radiator (e.g. Brannan pipe thermometers from B&Q at about £12 per pair). Again, starting nearest the boiler, adjust the balancing valve until you get a temperature drop of 11°C across the radiator, then move on to the next one.

FLUSHING RADIATORS

Q There are four radiators in my one-bedroom flat. The two situated closest to the boiler are working but the two at either end of the flat are not. It is not an airlock problem. I think the system needs flushing through. Is there any way I can do this myself?

A First try turning the two hot radiators off and see if that forces some hot water through to the others. You may need to turn the pump speed up a notch. If that does the trick, then it's just a case of balancing the radiators. If not, then the next step is to try draining the system down to see if that removes the blockage. If that fails, then use Fernox or Sentinel Central Heating Restorer to clean the system out before draining down and refilling again [PLUMBING, HEATING & DRAINAGE].

AIR IN RADIATORS

Q I have a conventional central-heating system with boiler, pump, etc., and thirteen radiators. Of these, two have to be bled regularly to release air and no matter how often I bleed them, within a week or two they need bleeding again. There is no sign of any water leak. How can the air be getting into the system?

A The two problem radiators are probably on the return, or suction, side of the pumped circuit, and it is quite likely that there is a leak in one of the radiator valve joints. On the flow side of the pump, a leak would result in water dripping out, but on the return side it can draw air in, with no sign of water leakage. The only cure is to remake the joints in turn, making sure they are thoroughly sealed with jointing compound. Start with the first joint on the flow side, i.e. 'upstream' of the two problem radiators. Then it's a trial-and-error process of elimination until you find the guilty joint. (If the bled gas smells like rotten eggs, then this is a sign of hydrogen sulphide – a gas produced by metal corrosion within the system. It may also burn with a yellow flame, although this is not a recommended way of testing.)

DRAINAGE

SEPTIC TANKS

Q My new house has a septic tank. As we are not allowed to use bleach, what is the best alternative?

A People whose houses have septic tanks and micro-sewage plants are often told that bleach will kill the anaerobic bacteria in the sludge chamber, but this is not actually true. The main active ingredient of household bleach is sodium hypochlorite – basically a solution of chlorine – the same as that added to the drinking water supply. So the water that runs out of baths, basins and WCs already contains chlorine, and adding an extra splash of bleach down the lavatory bowl, or a cupful to the washing machine, will not make a significant difference to the concentration of chlorine in the septic tank. Especially when you consider that it will be dissolved in the 5000 litres or so of water that it already holds.

Another common myth is that septic tanks need a biological 'starter' to get them going. Some firms make a living selling these 'enzyme enhancers', but there is no independent scientific evidence to show that they make any difference. The bacteria needed to decompose sewage are already present in the raw sewage, in the same way that the yeast required to ferment wine is already present in the grapes. In any event, research has shown that even if a septic tank were dosed with a huge concentration of bleach or other chemicals, which did actually kill all the bacteria, it would take only between twenty-four and forty-eight hours to recover, with or without additives.

SMELLY SEPTIC TANK

Q All sewage from our house runs into a set of underground brick chambers, with concrete tops and inspection/access covers. There is often quite a strong sulphurous/sewage-works smell. Concerned that the system wasn't working properly, I sought advice. A salesman explained that the levels and quality of final effluent could not be improved with the existing system, and that the only solution would be a 'packaged sewage treatment system', which could be installed for £7863 plus VAT. Am I being sold something that I don't really need?

A A considerably cheaper option for your problem would be to install a pumped aeration device in the last chamber downstream. But be warned, all these systems pong a bit when the wind is in the wrong direction.

If you do decide to go for a new system, then it is still quite permissible to install a plain septic tank, costing around £500, and have the run-off filtered through the ground using 'Y'-shaped rubble-filled drainage channels. Reed beds are also quite the rage, being environmentally friendly and all that. See Building Research Establishment Good Building Guide 42, 'Reed beds' [CONSTRUCTION LITERATURE].

EMPTYING SEPTIC TANK

Q Since moving in sixteen years ago, we have never had our septic tank emptied, and neither had the previous owners. It has two covers, and is situated on a slope below the house. We have never used bleach or biological detergents. My question is, now I have recently extended the property, can I safely divert rainwater from the new roof (approx 8 square metres area) into the septic tank, and should I have it emptied?

A Septic tanks have two chambers. The first one collects the solids, or 'sludge', which is broken down by anaerobic bacteria. The second one holds the liquid run-off, or 'liquor', which is purified by aerobic bacteria – either by bubbling air through it, or allowing it to percolate into a soakaway in the ground. Eventually the first chamber will fill up, and should be 'desludged'. It is generally recommended that this is done every three to five years, but, depending upon the size of the chamber and the amount of waste, and how effective the biological activity is, it is sometimes possible to go for many years without emptying.

When a septic tank is established, and in equilibrium with the waste flowing into it, then the bacteria should break everything down with the minimum of smell. Septic tanks should not be used for rainwater drainage, however, as this will dilute the contents, and interfere with the bacterial activity. You should pipe the rainwater from your new extension into the nearest ditch or gulley.

CELLAR FLOODING

Q I have a leaking cellar wall in a house that was built in 1910. This particular part of the wall does not have a cavity, only a single layer of bricks and was possibly where some kind of fire or range had been. Every time it rains the water pours in through the wall, gathers at the bottom and is drained away by the sloping floor to a drain. This is a real shame as the cellar is otherwise in great shape and very useable. I would dearly like to stop this water penetration as I live in Manchester and we have more than our fair share of rain! What if anything do you think might be the right approach?

A I have surveyed many Victorian houses in your area (Manchester) that are similarly afflicted. The problem is usually that the rainwater downpipes lead into silted-up soakaways, so that when it rains all the water from the roof is directed straight into the ground, halfway up the height of the cellar or semi-basement walls. Since the soakaways are blocked, and the ground is saturated, the only route for the water to take is in through the cellar walls. The solution is to excavate the ground around the foot of the rainwater downpipe and either reinstate the soakaway or, preferably, pipe the water away into the main drainage system.

SOAKAWAYS

Q I have a bungalow built in the mid-1960s, and all the surface water is directed into soakaways around the property. Over the years I have cleared the pipes of roots, etc., to ensure a free flow of water, but recently I have seen a build-up of water around some of the drain covers, and in one spot in the garden, over a soakaway, a large puddle appears during heavy rain. Do soakaways have a finite life, and need to be remade, or is this just an effect of a higher water table, due to recent wet weather?

A Soakaways do have a finite life, as they fill up with silt, leaves and other debris, which gradually prevents the water from draining away into the surrounding ground. The traditional soakaway is a hole in the ground filled with rubble or stone and covered with a sheet of corrugated steel to stop the earth washing into it. They can be dug out and renewed, or a more modern solution is to use a purpose-made perforated plastic box, wrapped in a geotextile to stop soil from getting in through the holes. These can be used individually or in groups to provide the required drainage capacity. Details from Hoofmark [PLUMBING, HEATING & DRAINAGE].

SOAKAWAY REBATE

Q I understand that there is the possibility of a rebate from my water company if my rainwater goes into soakaways and not into the main drain. Is there any easy way to tell if surface water runs off to a soakaway, without digging big holes in the garden?

A Find the inspection chamber where your waste water joins the main drain. Lift the lid and check that you have the right inspection chamber by getting an accomplice to flush the toilet or run the kitchen tap. Then get the accomplice to pour a bucket of water down a yard gulley. If the water ends up in the inspection chamber then you are connected to the main drain; if not, then it may be going to a soakaway.

(Rebates vary between different water companies at roughly between £15 and £35 per annum. This rebate is available to consumers who pay a fixed annual charge for water and drainage; those who pay by water meter will have their bills reduced by a percentage figure. In order to qualify for a rebate in any particular year, the application must be made before 31 March.)

CAST-IRON GUTTERS

Q My parents' home has cast-iron gutters and in recent years they have been plagued with dripping from the joints and corrosion. Several roofers have performed repairs but with little success. I have been told that replacement sections are no longer available because of the change from imperial to metric. Is that true, and can you recommend a source of cast-iron guttering formed to imperial sizes?

A No, it is not true. Cast-iron guttering is far superior to plastic, and is well worth keeping if possible. It should be overhauled by separating at the joints, painting and reconnecting with a fresh putty seal and a new nut-and-bolt. Replacement sections, in a range of imperial sizes, are available from several suppliers. Try J and JW Longbottom Ltd and Saint-Gobain [PLUMBING, HEATING & DRAINAGE].

REPAIRING CAST-IRON GUTTERS

Q My generally solid house was built around 1930 and has cast-iron gutters and pipes. My builder has advised replacing the gutters – which he has just painted inside and out, and resealed the joints – with plastic ones in due course. He says that if the cast-iron ones are to be renewed they will have to be taken down, cleaned and reinstalled, and he thinks this would cost more than new plastic ones. Is he right? My neighbour is already on his second set of plastic guttering, the first evidently not having stood up to the weather. Replacement would, of course, detract from the originality of the house.

A I think you should learn from your neighbour's mistake and stick with the original cast-iron guttering. If it is carefully overhauled and replaced it should last another seventy years, whereas the plastic replacement is unlikely to last more than fifteen. You are lucky to have a builder who at least understands the nature of the material, so you should try to persuade him to do a proper overhaul job by rubbing each section down with a wire brush, priming and painting, then re-assembling with new bolted joints sealed with linseed-oil putty. It will be cheaper and more reliable in the long run. Cracks can be repaired by conventional electric arc welding, using cast-iron welding rods. Replacement sections are available from J & JW Longbottom Ltd and Saint-Gobain [PLUMBING, HEATING & DRAINAGE].

SEWER PIPE LINING

Q My house is connected to a private foul drain common to seven properties before it discharges to a public sewer. Following clearance of a blockage caused by root growth, the firm involved have recommended relining the 6-inch (150mm) diameter clay pipe with a plastic membrane. I understand that the lining is inserted as a flat tube and then inflated to adhere to the pipe wall; this seems to me to be liable to cause an even worse blockage should it collapse in the future. Do you have any views on this type of lining system?

A Drain lining has been used for around twenty years, and it can be a cheaper alternative to digging up and replacing, especially for deep pipes, or ones that pass beneath buildings. Several different kinds of materials and techniques are used, but the basic principle is that a fibreglass or polyester textile liner is impregnated with resin and inflated inside the pipe, where it becomes rigid. If done correctly, there should be no danger of the liner collapsing into the pipe at a later stage.

If your blockage was caused only by roots, then drain lining may well be a good solution, as the liner will be jointless and seamless, and therefore impermeable to future root growth. Not all damaged pipes are suitable for lining, however. If a pipe has collapsed or become badly displaced (by more than 5 per cent of its diameter) then lining alone will not correct this.

Finding a conscientious contractor is not easy. There are hundreds of firms offering drain lining as a service, but no independent trade body. Some of the 'household name' firms advertising in the Yellow Pages are only local franchises whose prices will be higher to cover the cost of the franchise, but their use of the trade name does not infer any extra legal protection should things go wrong. Some of these firms have been known to mis-sell drain lining when it is not needed. A typical sales tactic is to offer a CCTV survey, and then to use this to persuade customers that the drain needs relining. For example, a slight misalignment of sections of old vitreous clay drains is not uncommon and should not usually interfere with the flow, but this may be represented as a 'displaced' section in order to sell relining.

You should get several quotes from different firms or get a local structural engineer to recommend one. Reasonable prices should be in the region of £55 per metre run for a 100mm diameter drain and £65 per metre for a 150mm drain (plus VAT and extra for root clearance and physical repairs). Most firms charge for a minimum of 9 metres.

RAINWATER COLLECTION

Q I have tried to obtain details from local builders' merchants of tanks suitable for installing underground for collecting rainwater. At present the roof water and surface water run to a rubble soakaway. The only suggestion so far has been for a septic tank. I have also contacted the manufacturers of plastic oil tanks, but they inform me that they are only suitable for installation above ground.

A Most people who install DIY rainwater collection systems use recycled orange juice tanks. These hold 1500 litres and can be purchased from Tank Exchange. Two or more can be linked together to provide extra storage.

Recycling rainwater does not just save on water company drainage charges, but if you pay for your water via a meter, then by using rainwater or filtered 'grey' water (bath and shower waste) for garden irrigation, flushing WCs, etc., you can save even more. Advice on partial or complete systems can be obtained from Aquarius Water Engineering [RAINWATER HARVESTING].

DRAIN SMELLS IN CONSERVATORY

Q I have had a conservatory built at the back of my terraced house, and find that at times it is unusable because of the drain smells emerging from the vicinity of the manhole cover. Does this mean there is something wrong with the drains, and is there any solution short of relocating the manhole?

A Even the best-constructed and ventilated sewer will be smelly on occasions. It sounds as though your conservatory has been built over an existing manhole with a loose-fitting cover. Now that the manhole is inside, it needs to be fitted with a special double-sealed cover, which is screwed down on to a rubber gasket. These are also available with tray-type lids that can be tiled to match the surrounding floor finish.

UNBLOCKING DRAINS

Q Having previously paid an £80 call-out fee to a plumber to unblock a drain (when it turned out to be caused by food in the sink outlet) I feel I should learn how to do this myself. But I really haven't a clue what to do, and I am afraid of flooding the floor, which is the ceiling of the flat downstairs. Any tips for a complete idiot?

A Clearing blocked kitchen waste pipes is easy. There is a U-bend below the sink where the offending detritus collects. This is known as a trap. Not because it traps solids, but because it forms a water-seal to stop foul air from the sewer rising up into the house. To clear a blockage, you put a bucket or bowl underneath, unscrew the two plastic collars holding the 'U' to the inlet and outlet pipes, and wriggle it free. It will be full of grease, hair, rice and unidentifiable black sludge, which you scrub off into the bucket and flush down the toilet.

This is not a pleasant job, but it's better than paying a small fortune to someone else to do it for you. If, instead of a U-bend, you encounter a bulbous plastic object, this will be a bottle trap, which you remove by unscrewing the whole thing. In both cases, once you have scrubbed everything clean, reassemble in reverse order and run some clean water through whilst you check for leaks.

BLOCKED DRAINS – WHOSE RESPONSIBILITY?

Q Who is responsible for clearing blocked drains? The council tells me that I have a 'private' drain, even though it is shared by three other properties, and runs beneath the pavement.

A The definition of a drain is a pipe which carries waste water and sewage from a house, up to the point at which this joins with a drain from another house, whereupon the two combine to become a sewer. Now, whether a sewer is private or public (i.e. owned by the water company) depends upon the age of the house – the critical date being 1st October 1937 (or 1st April 1965 for the inner London boroughs). For properties built before these dates, the sewers are public, even if the pipes themselves run beneath private property. So if you live in a Victorian terrace, for example, with a sewer running beneath the back gardens of the houses, then this will be a public sewer, owned by the water company.

For a 1970s house, however, the sewer will be private, and jointly owned by all the properties connected to it, right up to the point at which it connects to the public sewer – possibly under the road at the front.

POOR FLUSHING WC

Q I have an oldish low-level cistern lavatory. When it is flushed, the solid waste swirls around the bowl but does not disappear up and over the U-bend. The lavatory has to be flushed several times before it clears. I am assured by my plumber that there is no blockage anywhere, and he admits defeat. Because of a leak under the bathroom floor some years ago, the lavatory was taken out and then reset in the floor; could this be significant?

A Badly flushing lavatories can be infuriating, and the worst culprits are usually low-level cisterns, which naturally do not deliver the same force of water as high-level cisterns. The first thing to do is to check that there is sufficient water in the cistern – i.e. to adjust the ball valve so that it fills up to the line marked. If you live in a hard-water area, it is possible that the syphon and/or flush pipe may have become partially blocked by scale, so get your plumber to take the whole thing apart and clean it. The other possibility is that when the lavatory was moved, the flush pipe may have been pushed too far into the housing in the pan – it should be seated firmly within the rubber connecting sleeve, but not pushed tight into the porcelain socket, as this can restrict the water flow.

REMOVING VENT PIPES

Q In our bathroom we have a boxed-in section running from floor to ceiling and out through the roof that encloses the stench pipe from the bathroom toilet and the downstairs toilet. We are considering having a new bathroom fitted and have been told by one of the salesmen that the stench pipe can be cut off and capped with a valve that redirects the gases back down the pipe. Is this feasible, safe and wise?

A Vent pipes serve two purposes. One is to allow air to enter the system from the top whenever toilets are flushed or basins are emptied; this stops the outflowing waste water from drawing the water out of the drainage traps (or U-bends), and this function may also be served by an air-admittance valve. The other purpose of the pipes is to ventilate the entire sewage system, preventing the build-up of harmful gases (which may be poisonous and even explosive). Obviously bathroom salesmen are keen to cut down on internal clutter in order to sell their wares, but the ultimate say on removing the vent pipe will rest with the local-authority Building Control Officer, and you should seek his advice. He will want to check whether your neighbours still have sufficient roof-level vent pipes to keep the whole system safe.

CLEARING RAINWATER PIPES

Q I have a recurring problem with blocked plastic rainwater downpipes. I have resorted to a long ladder in the past, but with advancing years this is no longer possible. Is there such a thing as a 'rodding point' which could be inserted into the downpipe at ground level? A garden hose or spiral wire could then be used to safely clear the blockage from below.

A Blocked gutters and downpipes are a perennial problem and, if left blocked, can result in serious dampness problems and wood rot where the overflowing water soaks the walls below. There are various wire and plastic guards that can be fitted over the gutters, although in some cases these can clog up themselves and even make matters worse. Both Terrain and Polypipe make a small section of pipe incorporating an access door, which can be fitted to an existing downpipe, and used for rodding.

PLASTERING

The term plastering refers to spreading any wet material on to a wall. 'Plaster' can be lime, clay, chalk, cement or gypsum, used on their own, mixed with each other and/or with sand, earth, straw or lightweight aggregates.

Unfortunately, mention plaster to almost any modern builder in Britain and he will know only one type – pink gypsum, or calcium sulphate. This is a wonderful material which sets hard in ninety minutes and gives a smooth trowelled finish on plasterboard or dry internal cement-rendered brickwork. But expose it to any degree of long-term moisture and it starts to dissolve. Many of the so-called 'rising damp' problems in ground-floor flats in old Victorian properties are actually gypsum plaster efflorescence, caused by the combined influence of internal condensation, raised external ground levels and leaking window sills. The original lime-and-sand plaster coped with all this without a problem, but the gypsum can't.

To be fair to the gypsum plaster industry, they make a large variety of products for use in different circumstances. British Gypsum, for example, make and market thirteen types of plaster for the British building trade, including special formulations for application to plasterboard, brickwork and lightweight blockwork. But the average builders' merchants only stocks two – bonding backing coat and multi-finish skim coat – so these are the materials that jobbing builders use, to the exclusion of the more specialized products. British Gypsum have an excellent technical advice department and can arrange next-day deliveries to most parts of the UK, but most builders carry on regardless.

It is also a shame that British builders are afraid of using lime plaster. It is easy to use, and hydrated lime is available in bags at most builders' merchants. Mix it 1:4 with washed sharp sand, cover it with polythene sheeting and leave it to 'sweat' overnight, and it will match the lime plaster used on most Victorian houses. Any that is left over can be kept in buckets, with an inch of water on top, and it will stay usable for ever.

Animal hair reinforcement is also easily available from specialist suppliers, or 'Fibrin' polypropylene fibres are a useful modern equivalent [PLASTERING]. Builders have been persuaded that lime plaster 'won't work', probably by the propaganda of the cement industry. But its cause is not helped either by the 'lime loonies' – a group of mostly middle-class conservation enthusiasts who have discovered the joys of working with lime, but who insist that the only way to do it is to use traditional lime putty, preferably slaked in oak vats from quicklime fired in medieval kilns. This dotty purist approach makes real working builders very suspicious, and hardens their belief that the hydrated lime in bags from the builders' merchants is a 'different material', which will only work if mixed with cement. But I have been using hydrated lime and sand for fifteen years for bricklaying, pointing and plastering. It works fine.

STAINED PLASTERBOARD CEILINGS

Q Recent storms caused rainwater to come through my plasterboard ceiling. A builder has said that this will cause the plaster to crumble and the ceiling will have to be replaced. Is there a less expensive way of dealing with this, as the ceiling appears to be intact?

A Modern plasterboard with a gypsum plaster skim finish is not the best at coping with a soaking, but as long as the ceiling is still intact, and shows no signs of sagging, then it should dry out, and not need replacing. Even when there is serious water damage, it is usually possible to cut out and replace small damaged areas, and it is rarely necessary to replace a whole ceiling.

RESTORING AN OLD CROFT

Q I am bringing a derelict croft house back into use. All the internal cladding of the stone walls has fallen off and only traces of laths remain. My options seem to be rendering in cement, rendering in plaster or lining with heavy plasterboard on a wooden framework. Are there other options and have you an opinion on the best way forward?

A All these three suggestions would seem to me to be unwise. Applying modern materials to old buildings can often cause problems. You need to find out what type of internal plastering system was used originally, and try to replicate it as closely as possible. There is no reason why you shouldn't reinstate the original lath-and-plaster wall linings, perhaps with a breathable insulation material behind them to improve the thermal value of the walls. Contact the Society for the Protection of Ancient Buildings (SPAB) for more advice [CONSERVATION].

DURABILITY OF LIME RENDER

Q You often mention the advantage of using lime to repair render and brickwork on old houses. I have mixed and made sample patches of both lime render and cement render, and the lime render, whilst looking good, never appears to be particularly robust (e.g. when knocked by kids' bikes, etc.) Am I doing something wrong or is lime render a 'look-but-don't-touch' finish?

A Lime mortar and render hardens by carbonation (reacting with carbon dioxide from the atmosphere). So it takes many months, or even years, to reach the same hardness as cement render. This is why it is able to accommodate movement and moisture so well, and why it even retains the ability to 'self-heal' cracking for many years. If you want to speed up the hardening process then keep it moist with a light spray of water from a garden sprayer, especially in hot weather. In the winter, fresh lime render needs protecting from frost.

FINDING A LIME PLASTERER

Q I have tried to follow your advice about plastering (on my 1904 house), but I cannot get any plasterer to carry out lime plastering. They all wanted to skim it with 'Universal one-coat' or 'Thistle finish'. I mentioned possible damp problems, etc., but they all told me there wouldn't be a problem. I have since succumbed to pressure from the wife to finish the job, and have had it plastered with Thistle finish. Will this be OK in the future or should I persevere and try to find a lime plasterer for the other rooms?

A The problem with gypsum plasters is that they dissolve when they get wet, which is why they are unsuitable for the insides of solid exterior walls on old houses. Lime plastering is not difficult, but the current generation of plasterers have never been exposed to it, and so are afraid of the unknown. You could compromise by asking your plasterer to use Tarmac's 'Limelite' lightweight renovating plaster, which contains lime but also some cement [PLASTERING].

MATCHING OLD PLASTER

Q Our 1934 house was architect-designed and traditionally built, using lime plaster. We have cracks in some internal walls, due to cracked and leaking drains, which have been replaced or lined. The insurance company now want to have the cracks repaired and replastered using modern gypsum plaster. When I told them I thought they should use lime plaster, they replied that lime plaster 'was only used in the past because today's modern materials weren't available'. I maintain that it should be renovated to match the original. Do I have a case?

A Yes. You should always use plaster to match the original, otherwise cracks could open up between the old and new. Your insurers' statement about lime plaster reveals a worrying ignorance. It's a bit like saying you shouldn't go on holiday to Bournemouth, and that people only went there in the past because aeroplanes hadn't been invented! In any case, gypsum plaster is not a 'modern' material; it was known to the ancient Greeks and Romans. But lime plaster is better.

SAVING AN OLD CEILING

Q Our Victorian house has ornate plaster coving and ceiling roses in two downstairs rooms. Unfortunately the ceilings are not in good repair and we have been warned that they may fall down. Is there a way of repairing them without removing the plaster, or having the decorative elements removed and replaced? We are loath to just rip them down and lose the features.

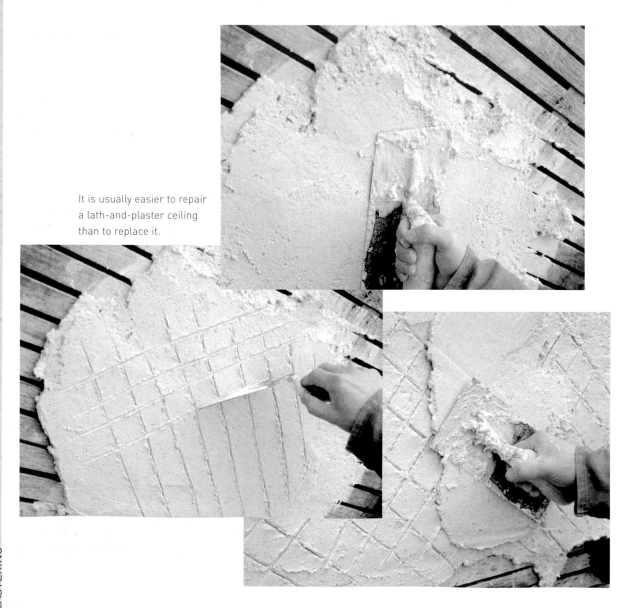

It is usually easier to repair a lath-and-plaster ceiling than to replace it.

A Old lath-and-plaster ceilings can usually be repaired and they are well worth keeping, as the dense lime plaster has much better sound-insulation qualities than modern plasterboard. The usual problem is that the plaster has lost its key with the laths. If the floorboards in the room above can be lifted, then the ceiling can be propped up from below, and a fresh coat of plaster spread on top, which will bond it back together. If the floor above is inaccessible, then the ceiling can be screwed up to the joists from below, using expanded metal lathing to reinforce any weak areas.

REPAIRING PEBBLE-DASH

Q Our external walls are part pebble-dashed, and I have noticed that there appears to be a blister in one area. I am concerned that it may split and fall off. Is there some way we could repair this area before it becomes a major job?

A If the house was pebble-dashed from new, then the blistered area is probably due to poor adhesion in that one spot, and it is not a fault that is likely to spread across the wall. If the house was originally built with face brickwork, however (check by looking at similar properties in the street), then the pebble-dash may have been applied later, to hide cracks or weathered bricks, and it is possible that other areas will delaminate in time. You could check by tapping gently with a hammer and listening for a hollow sound. Small isolated areas can be repaired, but if the damage is widespread then it would make more sense to hack it all off, fix expanded metal lathing to the wall, and re-render. Any experienced plasterer should be able to do pebble-dashing. It is basically two-coat render work, with the 'pebbles' (pea shingle) flicked into the top coat.

NAIL POPS

Q Our house was extended about seven years ago, with plasterboard nailed up to form the ceilings. Now in many places small discs of plaster are becoming detached from the nail heads, leaving holes for us to fill and paint over. Is this normal, and can we expect this to be a regular occurrence?

A These 'nail pops' can have a variety of causes. If they occur early in a building's life, it is often because the timber ceiling joists (or wall studs) are drying out and shrinking away from the plasterboard, leaving the nail heads protruding from the surface. The problem might also be that the plaster skim coat is too thin, and unable to withstand the normal slight thermal expansion and contraction of the nails. The worst-case scenario is when the ceiling joists are also floor joists for the room above, and are not substantial enough to withstand the loads imposed when people walk across the floor – the flexing of the joists can then cause the plasterboard nails to work loose. If this is the problem then the nail popping would usually be worse towards the centre of the room.

In all cases, the first step is to try fixing the plasterboard to the joists or wall studs using screws (preferred to nails for the last twenty years or so). Work out which way the joists are running using a battery-powered stud detector or by viewing the joists from above (either exposed in the roof space, or by the nail holes in the flooring of the room above). Drive 32mm plasterboard screws either side of the nail pop – the screw heads should sink slightly below the surface of the plasterboard but no deeper than a couple of millimetres. Then use a hammer and punch (or a stout nail) to drive the old nail completely through the plasterboard and into the joist. Then fill the hole and cover the screwheads with filler or pre-mixed drywall compound, such as Gyproc ready-mixed joint cement (from British Gypsum [PLASTERING]). Apply the compound as flat as possible with a scraper or filler knife, and sand it gently flat when dry.

PLASTERING – DRYING-OUT TIMES

Q How long should you have to wait for a plaster skim surface over plasterboard to dry out before painting? I have had different answers from different people and would like to know what your opinion is.

A You can give pink gypsum plaster a coat of thinned emulsion as soon as it is visibly dry. But be prepared for shrinkage cracks to open up at the joints, especially if they are smaller than the recommended 1 per cent of the total measurement in any direction. Most people expect to have to fill cracks and repaint after a year or two. For thicker plasterwork – say three-coat render and skim, or traditional lime-and-sand plastering, it is best to wait for a few weeks, to ensure that any shrinkage cracks have appeared. The cracks can then be filled and the surface decorated.

PAINTING & DECORATING

Most people who opt for so-called 'maintenance-free' PVC-U windows and roof-line products do so because they don't want the hassle of painting the existing woodwork. So, instead of paying someone else to do it (say £500 to £750 every five years to rub down and gloss an average terraced house) they would rather give £5000 to some cowboy trader to rip out all the existing windows and external woodwork and replace them with plastic of no known origin or specification, and uncertain longevity. The economics just don't add up. If these people made similar decisions at work, they'd have to justify themselves with cost/benefit analyses, and they'd realize it wasn't worth it. But because it's their home, they go into a blind panic, and believe what they read in the adverts. And because almost everybody else down the street has gone for plastic windows, they think they'd better get them as well. The replacement window and roof-line industry gets rich on this lemming-like behaviour.

This dislike of routine maintenance accounts also for the sale of so-called 'breathable' textured external wall coatings (they aren't breathable and they cost five times the price of getting the wall painted properly) and 'one-coat' paints, which a professional decorator described to me as a 'pudding-like' paint which never dries.

Given a modicum of care and attention, timber doors and windows will last for ever. This means a light sanding down, and touching-up or recoating on an occasional basis with proper spirit-based primer (on bare wood), undercoat and gloss. If you are not prepared to do it, or pay someone else to do it, then maybe you shouldn't have bought a house in the first place. If you've never tried it, then give it a go – it could change your life. Do bear in mind the toxicity of lead paint, though (see HAZARDS). This is one of the most toxic of building materials, is present in huge quantities in homes (it was used in Britain up to 1992), and is a known danger to children. The lack of both public awareness and government publicity about this problem is worrying.

External brickwork should not be painted; it traps the moisture. The only sympathetic coating on old houses is traditional limewash. Again, if you try it yourself you may get hooked – it's better value than watching the telly!

PEELING WINDOW SILLS

Q **I live in a large Victorian house. Every two or three years I have to have my window ledges repainted white since the paint seems to peel off and crack. The current painter says this is normal, particularly at the back where there is more sun. However, another friend told me that if the painter strips off all the paint back to the bare stonework, the paint should last for seven to ten years. The current painter says this is not so and it's not worth the extra effort.**

A External stone sills are subject to the extremes of the weather, but I would say that five years should be a reasonable life expectancy for a modern masonry paint. The peeling could be due to water penetration at the joint between the sill and the bottom rail of the timber window. But if it occurs over a wide area, it is more likely to be due to poor surface preparation or cheap paint.

If the paintwork is neglected, timber windows will soon decay.

It is probably not necessary to strip the paint right off, but it should certainly be sanded back hard to remove all loose or flaking areas, and then the whole surface should be given two coats of masonry stabilizing solution (a proprietary resin-based product, not to be confused with PVA adhesive). Then two coats of a quality smooth masonry paint, and application of an external-grade silicone sealant at the joint between sill and bottom rail.

PAINTING PUTTY

Q **We still have all the original windows (complete with 'ripply' glass) in our ninety-year-old house. However, I am fed up with linseed-oil putty. The back of the house, facing north, is not so much of a problem, but the windows in the front, which get the full hot/cold, wet/dry treatment, have to be resealed almost annually when the putty inevitably shrinks and cracks. Is there no end to this interminable chore? I have tried 'frame sealants' and, whilst they do not harden to the ceramic-like brittleness of old putty, I find their adhesion and consequent protection value questionable.**

A It sounds as though you are not protecting the putty with paint. Linseed-oil putty should remain moist and flexible for many years, but it does need to be protected; it's the paint that keeps it from drying out and cracking. The glazing rebate in the window should be primed first, to stop the wood drawing the oil out of the putty. And as soon as the putty has become firm (after a few days), it should be painted with an oil-based paint (an undercoat and two gloss coats). Try to let the paint flow slightly on to the glass, to seal the join between glass and putty.

SEALING SANDY WALL SURFACES

Q **We are about to re-wallpaper our interior walls but notice the plaster is very sandy and gritty. We have been advised to prime the walls with either a water-based stabilizing solution or an oil-based alkaline-resistant primer. From your experience do these actually work, or could you suggest an alternative?**

A Resin-based stabilizing solutions are generally used on exterior work. For inside walls, water-based PVA should be sufficient. Make up a weak solution in water and brush it on. When dry give it a light sanding, and if there are still any crumbly areas give them a further coating. Traditionally, decorators used rabbit-skin glue size for this purpose.

OILY DEPOSITS

Q The previous owners of our flat burnt incense sticks and oils in the living room, staining the walls and ceiling with a soot-like deposit. Both walls and ceiling are wallpapered and painted with matt emulsion. How can we clean the surfaces before freshening them up with more emulsion? We don't want to re-paper if it's avoidable.

A It is an interesting fact that condensation does not occur only with water vapour, but also with oils and fats. For example, the walls and ceilings of restaurant kitchens and fish-and-chip shops can become saturated right through with condensed oils, and will never take a water-based paint. With luck, your walls will not be that bad, and you may get away with washing them down with detergent and painting with vinyl emulsion. But if the paint won't take then you will have to strip off the lining paper, taking the oils with it. Any obviously stained areas of plaster should be sealed with Ratcliffe's Styptic or Polycell Stain Block before re-papering.

Chemical paint stripper can work well on mouldings and cornices.

PAINT STRIPPING

Q In my 1930s house we have panelled wooden doors, which originally had a dark varnish finish. They have been overpainted several times and are in generally good condition although the paint build-up is excessive on some mouldings. We would like to strip back to the wood before redecorating and have considered sending the doors to a company that uses a caustic soda bath. They have advised us that the doors should be left for a week before repainting. How do you rate caustic soda stripping against Nitromors or a hot-air gun?

A   Dipping in caustic soda is quick and easy, but it is not very good for old doors. It can make them shrink and warp, and some carpenters say that it damages the glued joints, causing them to fall apart. Blow lamps or hot-air guns are the traditional method, but unfortunately this exposes you to lead poisoning from the paint fumes. If you use this method wear a respirator, and do not allow children or pregnant women in the house. Chemical paint strippers are often the quickest and safest way of removing paint [PAINTING & DECORATING].

EXTERNAL WALL COATINGS

Q   I was given a demonstration by a company's sales manager of the way in which their coating keeps out moisture but still permits the wall to breathe. The demo consisted of a transparent cylindrical container. Halfway down was a segment of porous building block that had been covered by the wall-coating material. I was asked to fill the top of the container with water. There was no evidence of water passing through the block which remained dry. Then air was pumped into the bottom of the cylinder. Bubbles of air were seen to be emerging from the block of building material and coating. Pump air – bubbles. Cease pumping, no bubbles; no water passed from top to bottom. The work is also independently insured.

A   This is a demonstration that air under pressure passes through the coating, not that moisture vapour not under pressure would do so. So it does not mimic real conditions and sounds like a clever sales trick. The problem with these coatings is that if you get condensation forming within the depth of the wall – i.e. the wall becomes damp from within, with liquid moisture – then it will be unable to escape. As the demonstration shows, liquid moisture will be trapped within the wall.

TEXTURED COATINGS

Q   My elderly parents are considering having the pebble-dash exterior of their home treated by a company which specializes in 'an exterior protective and decorative coating which consists of modern synthetic resins noted for their ability to form strong and permanent films'. I am slightly apprehensive because their quote was reduced from an initial £11,000 to £4000. Do you know anything about this kind of product?

A   You are right to be apprehensive. Any building product that is sold by a salesman offering huge 'discounts' in order to get a signature on the contract is almost certainly bogus. Starting off with a very high price and then reducing it is, as they say, the oldest trick in the book. These exterior decorative wall coatings are not a good idea, as they can trap moisture behind them, stopping walls from 'breathing', and sometimes even creating dampness problems where none existed before. Several readers have written asking for advice on how to remove this stuff once it has been applied, and the chemical stripping methods involved can themselves prove to be very costly.

WALL COATINGS

Q   I have received an advert through the door for an 'exterior, long-life, waterproof, protective wall coating' which is claimed to be twenty times thicker than ordinary paint, and has a fifteen-year guarantee. I have asked builder friends whether they would recommend this type of coating, and their answer is, 'Well, that's up to you,' which isn't very helpful. My house is a 1935 semi, and I would like your advice on this. I normally have the walls painted with Snowcem every six years.

A The advertising leaflet you have sent me is typical of the kind of direct marketing tactics that readers should beware of. The leaflet states that the wall-coating company in question is 'looking for show homes in your area', and is offering 'substantial discounts for selected properties'. It goes on to state that this is a limited offer, and that you must reply within seven days to take advantage of it. These claims represent hard sales tactics of the most disreputable kind, and should make you immediately wary of both the product and the firm.

These wall coatings are, indeed, much thicker than ordinary external masonry paint, and the sellers' claims that they are 'microporous' or 'breathable' is not supported by any independent scientific evidence. The promise that they offer long-term waterproofing may sound attractive, but this is not actually desirable for external walls, especially solid brickwork as in the case of your 1930s semi. Many dampness problems are caused by moisture produced inside the house, and the coating will trap this moisture in the walls, leading to possible problems with condensation and mould growth. Readers buying these coatings also report being charged up to five times the cost of having a house painted properly, and say that, despite the advertising claims, the coatings can crack, allowing rainwater to penetrate, but preventing its evaporation. Needless to say, in such cases, the fifteen-year 'guarantees' often turn out to be useless, as the companies have ceased trading.

REMOVING TEXTURED COATINGS

Q Fifteen years ago we had our exterior walls treated with Protectawall wall coating. We have since had dampness problems, with water getting down behind the coating and then being unable to escape. The twenty-year guarantee is not worth invoking, as after fifteen years Protectawall say they are liable for only one quarter of the cost. We would really like to remove the coating altogether and go back to conventional masonry paint. But what sort of process is needed to remove it, and how would we find a reliable and competent contractor?

A The good news is that the textured coatings can be removed using chemical methods. There are two different types of coating that respond to different strippers. Both are painted on with a brush, and washed off with water. Strippers Paint Removers will provide you with a trial pack of both types for £12. When you have found which one works best, it will cost around £2 per square metre to treat the house [PAINTING & DECORATING].

REMOVING ARTEX

Q What is the most efficient way to remove Artex from my walls and ceilings?

A Artex and other textured paint finishes may contain asbestos fibres, and should be treated with care. Any potential danger comes from inhaling the dust, so it is best removed wet. The easiest method is to use a steam wallpaper stripper (about £30 from builders' merchants or DIY stores) and a scraper, and to seal the scrapings in plastic bin liner bags before they dry.

SURFACE PREPARATION

Q I've bought the paint for the front room of my Victorian basement flat, stripped the wallpaper, and found that the plaster underneath is uneven and cracked. I really don't want to put wallpaper back up, but if I just put paint on the walls they will look terrible. Is there anything I can do to make the surface any better?

A Yes. Wallpaper it. This kind of property was originally finished internally with lime-and-sand plaster. Lime plaster is a wonderful material, as it moves with the walls, and any severe movement is usually accommodated by a series of small cracks spread across the whole wall, rather than (as with hard, modern materials) one big crack down the middle. But the Victorians would not have dreamed of painting straight on to the plaster. They always lined the walls with thick lining paper, and this helps to iron out the cracks and absorb movement.

The correct way to deal with cracked lime plaster on old walls and ceilings is to rake out and fill any particularly wide cracks, and sandpaper when dry. Then apply one layer of heavy-grade (1000 gauge) lining paper, and a second layer of medium-grade (800 gauge) lining paper. The first layer should go horizontally ('cross-lining') and the second layer vertically. When dry, the newly papered surface will take emulsion paint and give a nice soft finish.

PAINTING TILES

Q Our bathroom tiles are over forty years old, very dingy white, and we would like advice on suitable treatment/paint for them. I understand that this painting may be a specialist job, following my viewing of a TV programme.

A I am not a big fan of painting ceramic tiles, as the effect can often look amateurish. But it can be done, as long as you are sure the tiles are still firmly fixed to the wall (check for loose ones by tapping and listening for a hollow noise). Use a special tile paint, and follow the manufacturer's instructions to the letter. For the best effect, rake out the old grout first using a proprietary raking-out tool, apply the paint finish, and then re-grout using a colour to contrast with the painted tile colour.

REMOVING GRAFFITI

Q Our front boundary brick wall has been covered with black spray-paint graffiti. We have approached the local authority, who boast that they are carrying out a campaign against graffiti and have a team to remove it, but they have quoted us a price of £15 per foot for removal. We have asked them if we can buy the gel they apparently use, to carry out the work ourselves, but they won't help us. Have you any advice on what to use and where to buy it?

A Removing graffiti is the same as removing paint from any other surface. Success depends upon identifying the type of paint used, and finding a chemical stripper that will not damage the surface, or result in permanent staining. For specialist advice call Strippers Paint Removers [PAINTING & DECORATING].

BLEEDING KNOTS

Q We have been renovating an old cottage. A number of the doors and windows had blisters caused by oozing from knots that had not been sealed. We have stripped off the paint down to bare wood and treated the knots with proprietary knotting sealer prior to repainting. Sadly, a few months later the knots are oozing once more. I deduce that whilst knotting compound works well on new wood, it will not properly seal old wood that has been painted. What is the secret?

A Knotting does not always work on new wood either. Some knots are very resinous, and will always bleed through. The staining is usually worse through water-based acrylic paint, but even with gloss the resin can dissolve the undercoat and form a blister. Next time try two coats of aluminium oxide primer.

REMOVING BLACK MOULD

Q The house we're buying has been empty for twelve months, with no heating or ventilation. Consequently, the walls have black mould on large areas. Have you any suggestions for removing it? I know we need to get it heated and the windows open, but we need also to decorate. Or, do you think we should leave the decorating alone until we get the house dried out and then remove the mould?

Wash it off with clean water containing a splash of bleach. Much cheaper and safer than proprietary fungicide solutions.

DECORATING DRYWALL

Q Having moved into a newly built house with plasterboard walls, I need to start redecorating. I have redecorated similar rooms at my children's homes with some difficulty, as the plasterboard is extremely absorbent and acts like blotting paper, even after several coats of emulsion. In my previous older properties I have not experienced this problem and new plaster has been decorated without difficulty. I am told that the up-to-date method of sealing such walls is by the use of a PVA adhesive solution. Could you please confirm that this is the preferred method?

A Many new homes these days are not plastered internally. The stud partition walls, and often the inner faces of the outside walls too, are lined with plasterboard, but this is not skimmed with plaster. Instead, the screw holes are filled, and the joints between the boards are covered with paper tape and filler (called jointing compound). The paper surface of the plasterboard is the only finish, and paint or wallpaper is applied directly to it.

Like many developments in modern building practice, this one comes from the USA, where plasterboard has always been known as 'Drywall', and is rarely given a protective coat of plaster. It is cheaper and more convenient for the developers, but not so good for homeowners. Several readers with recently built homes have complained that they have started to scrape off wallpaper, only to find that they are actually removing the paper surface of the plasterboard. And on walls that are painted, not papered, it is also necessary to take care when sanding the painted surfaces lest this, too, damages the plasterboard.

As you have discovered, plasterboard is very absorbent (so care should be taken not to get it too wet, lest it loses strength) and has to be sealed. Dilute PVA is one option, but it would be best to use one of the manufacturer's recommended products, such as British Gypsum's Gyproc Drywall Sealer. This seals the plasterboard before painting and if used prior to wallpapering it is also claimed to be resistant to subsequent steam wallpaper stripping [PLASTERING].

EMULSION ON BARE PLASTER

Q After painting several walls with emulsion, one of them shows signs of blistering. A professional painter has advised starting again and washing the wall with sugar soap first. Will this make a significant difference, and how does it differ from ordinary soap or detergent?

A Cleanliness is vital before painting – especially emulsion on old walls which have been decorated before. Sugar soap is a caustic alkaline solution, used chiefly for washing down woodwork before applying a fresh coat of oil-based paint. It can also help on plastered walls, especially if they have residual traces of oil paint, but usually a light sanding and washing down with clean water is all that is required. If you have stubborn patches that continue to blister, then the quickest solution is to undercoat them with Polycell Stain Block first.

BUBBLING EMULSION

Q I have been following with some interest your recent correspondence about bubbling emulsion paint on bare plaster. I have tried everything you suggest on the walls of my mid-Victorian terraced house – sanding down, washing with sugar soap, sealing with dilute PVA – but I still get patches where the emulsion bubbles or flakes off. The paint manufacturers seem to have no idea what causes this problem, and are unable to suggest a solution. Any further suggestions?

A Several readers have suggested that this problem lies with the incompatibility of modern poly-mer-bound emulsion paints with old lime plaster. In Victorian times, where lime plaster was painted, it was with limewash or distemper (basically chalk bound with animal glue size). There does seem to be a possibility that modern emulsion paint may be affected by the residual alkalinity still present in this old lime plaster. Lime plaster was traditionally lined with paper before being painted, and, in my opinion, this is still the best practice. Lining paper provides a nice soft surface, covers minor cracks and imperfections, and ensures that emulsion paint goes on uniformly.

PATTERN STAINING

Q I have lived in my 1978 bungalow for five years, at which time it was totally painted and decorated. Since I switched on the central heating last autumn I found black patches appearing on the Artexed ceiling. They are getting worse and a pattern is emerging, like stripes along the line of the ceiling joists (the loft above the ceiling is insulated). Gradually all the ceilings in the bungalow are being affected. What is the explanation for this, and how can I prevent it recurring after decorating?

A This sounds like pattern staining, due to the fact that the ceiling joists are at a different temperature from that of the insulated plasterboard areas between them. Slight condensation will be occurring along the lines of the joists, and the blackness will be due either to dust adhering to the damp surface or, more likely, to mould growth. It is likely that the loft insulation has been laid only between the joists, rather than being draped over the top of them. Applying an extra layer of insulation across the whole loft – covering the existing insulation and the joists – will probably make a big difference. But you will also need to tackle the source of the condensation by improving the background ventilation, keeping the bathroom and kitchen doors closed, and using an extractor fan and cooker hood whenever either of these rooms is in use.

CAUSTIC SODA DOOR STRIPPING

Q Five years ago we had all the internal panelled doors from our late-1920s house dipped, to strip seventy-plus years of accumulated layers of paint. It was summertime and they were dried outside in the sun for several days before being re-hung. We noticed that some parts were slow to dry, and it was suggested that this was sapwood holding the moisture, which could be driven off with careful (and tedious!) use of a hairdryer. This seemed to work reasonably well, and over the course of the next few months we repainted them all white. We noticed that in one or two places the moisture seemed to gradually return, especially in the more humid autumn days, and in subsequent years this cycle has continued, so that several now have brown drips in places, or exude brown liquid from the end-grain of parts of them; if this happens to be the bottom of the door, it is staining the carpet. We are becoming fairly desperate as things gradually get worse. Is the story about sapwood true, and is there anything we can do to remedy this, please?

A Dipping old doors in caustic soda may be a quick and easy way of removing the paint, but it is not good practice. Your 1920s doors were made from good-quality softwood, with plenty of resin-filled heartwood in the timber sections, and it is this which is now leaching through the new painted surface, not moisture from the sapwood. The early coats of paint would most likely have been lead-based, and although we now know this to be hazardous to health (so old painted woodwork should never be machine-sanded, nor stripped by burning-off), it was very effective at sealing the surfaces, and preventing resin-bleed. The dipping might also have removed the glue from the glued joints, further allowing resin to bleed from the exposed sections of end-grain.

The best way to seal the timber now would be to sand down the paintwork and apply two coats of aluminium oxide primer, followed by spirit-based undercoat and gloss. Unfortunately this may lead to a build-up of paint almost as thick as that which you had removed, but I'm afraid you were badly advised to have the doors dipped in the first place.

REMOVING WALLPAPER IN MODERN HOUSE

Q The previous owner of our ten-year-old property decorated all internal walls with a heavily embossed wallpaper finished with eggshell emulsion. I wish to remove this but have found on a test area that when I try to strip it off, the paper surface of the plasterboard comes away with it. I have also tried using two layers of lining paper over the existing embossed wallpaper, but the pattern still shows through. Do you have any suggestions?

A This is one of the big unspoken problems of modern house construction, due to the fact that internal partition walls (and the inner faces of many external walls too) are rarely plastered. Instead, the walls are 'dry lined' with plasterboard, and the wall covering is stuck directly on to this. Ideally, the plasterboard should have first been given a coat of acrylic primer/sealer, to enable wall coverings to be subsequently stripped off, but in many cases this has not been done.

I can only suggest that you try using a steam wallpaper stripper (about £30 from DIY shops). Work on small areas at a time, trying not to let the steam soften the plasterboard beneath. Try to peel the wallpaper off at a low angle, rather than pulling it straight out away from the wall, and if you use a scraper, then do so with great care. It is likely to be a slow, frustrating job, but once you have got the wall covering off, you can coat the plasterboard with a coat of primer/sealer, make good any small tears or gouges in the surface with filler, and sand it very lightly with a fine-grade sandpaper.

SPRAY PAINTING

Q My house has rendered walls which I paint every five years, using a paintbrush and ladder, but I would prefer an easier method. Is spraying the paint a good idea, and is there a cantilever type of scaffolding I can use? I have a lightweight scaffold tower but its use is limited on two walls due to a porch and extension.

A In my experience, spray painting doesn't save a lot of time on small domestic jobs. You spend more time masking the surrounding areas, and cleaning the equipment after use, than you save in the actual application. Try a roller with a telescopic extension pole; this might solve your scaffolding problem as well.

DAMPNESS

Questions about dampness constitute by far the largest proportion of my weekly postbag. Some of these concern genuine stories of water penetration (through roofs, walls and chimneys) which builders have been unable to stop. Many more describe black mould growth on walls, green mildew in wardrobes and water running down the insides of windowpanes, which are all symptoms of condensation (see CONDENSATION).

Condensation is the result of water vapour produced within the home by human activity, and which, as a result of inadequate heating and ventilation, is allowed to condense out as liquid water on and within the building structure. Condensation is easy to cure, but some people just refuse to open the windows.

But by far the largest number of queries concerns a dampness problem that does not actually exist. This is the notorious 'rising damp', which surveyors and damp-proofing company salesmen say they can detect using electrical meters. Selling damp-proofing to new homeowners on the basis of electrical meter readings must go down as one of the most successful confidence tricks in history. There is simply no independent scientific evidence to support the claim that British homes suffer from endemic rising dampness, and in every case that I have investigated the property was either bone dry, or else had obvious defects such as leaking gutters, raised outside ground levels, or condensation problems. But surveyors, estate agents and mortgage lenders all go along with the 'rising damp' myth, and so homeowners continue to fork out £200 million every year for this unnecessary and often damaging work.

Electrical moisture meters are calibrated for use on timber, not wallpaper or plaster. They will always give high readings on walls at low level in old houses because of condensation (warm air rises, cool air sinks, walls are colder at the bottom and so that's where the condensation is concentrated). The only really accurate way to measure the moisture content of masonry materials is the method described in Building Research Establishment Digest 245 [CONSTRUCTION LITERATURE/ DAMPNESS], which entails taking a drilled sample, weighing it, drying it in an oven and weighing it again; the difference between the wet and dry weights is the amount of water, which is recorded as a percentage of the wet weight. By placing the drilled sample in a 75 per cent relative humidity chamber, it is also possible to use this method to calculate its hygroscopicity, or salt contamination, and hence to distinguish between pure water (rainwater or condensation) and water from the ground or from plumbing leaks. This is a very simple method, which makes dampness diagnosis straightforward. It is a great shame that chartered surveyors do not make more use of it, as it is a very effective way of disproving the rising-damp myth.

But if rising damp is a myth, people ask, then why are damp-proof courses built into new buildings? The history of the damp-proof course is an interesting one and dates from the 1877 Building by-laws – themselves following the Public Health Act (1875) which was concerned mostly with drainage and sewage disposal. So the original idea seems to have been to stop sewage (which in those days was often still running down the streets) from soaking into walls. Water will not rise by capillary action in brickwork built with cement or strong lime mortars. Suffice it to say that in Holland, much of which is below sea level, DPCs are not used. Whatever, most British houses built post-1877 have DPCs built in (usually two courses of slate) and there is no evidence that they 'fail', or become porous over time, although most surveyors seem to accept these old wives' tales without question.

In any case, clay soils will always absorb water preferentially over brick walls (because the soil expands as it gets wet, creating a 'suction' effect), so there will only be free water available to soak into the wall once the soil has become saturated – in other words, in swamp conditions. And if your house is standing in a swamp, then you need land drainage anyway.

Oh, and by the way, if anyone tells you that your dampness problem is due to an 'underground stream', well, that's all part of the myth.

RISING DAMP?

Q I am in the process of selling my house. The buyer's mortgage lender insisted on a survey for rising damp, and the surveyor's report says that there is extensive damp in all walls. There is no evidence of damp, such as wallpaper lifting, and a recent TV programme concluded that treatment for rising damp is seldom justified. What is your advice about current practice?

A Rising damp is a myth. The 'surveyor', who says there is extensive dampness in all the walls is actually just a salesmen for chemical damp-proofing products. Tell your buyers that they need an independent dampness survey carried out to the standards described in Building Research Establishment Digest 245 [CONSTRUCTION LITERATURE/DAMPNESS], and under no circumstances should you allow them to deduct the cost of damp-proofing works from the asking price.

DAMP PATCHES ABOVE SKIRTINGS

Q My detached 1926 house is built with Accrington brick. There is a damp patch above the skirting board in one of the rooms which a local builder, using a moisture meter, 'diagnosed' as rising damp. You have expressed doubts about this kind of diagnosis on several occasions, but I have seen advertisements for the 'Shrijver' damp-proofing system, which they claim is new to this country. What is your opinion of this system?

Atmospheric syphon-type systems have never been independently proved to cure rising damp.

A   Electrical moisture meters cannot be used to diagnose the existence of rising damp, and the date of your house indicates that it will have been built with a damp-proof course, and so does not require any further form of damp proofing. The damp patch in the plaster must have some other source, such as a leaking gutter, cracked window sill or raised ground level. If your builder cannot locate the problem then you need an independent expert [DAMPNESS – Dampness & timber surveyors]. The Shrijver system is a version of the old (and discredited) Knapen tube system, which has never been shown to have any effect on the moisture content of walls.

  (Further investigation of this problem by Abbey Independent Surveys revealed that the house was built with cavity walls, and builders' debris had blocked the cavity, allowing ground water from outside to track across and produce a stain on the plaster. Removing a couple of bricks and cleaning the debris out of the cavity solved the problem.)

CONFLICTING DIAGNOSES

Q   I am buying a basement flat. Under 'essential repairs' the valuation survey report stated: 'You are advised to obtain a specialist rising-damp report from a member of the British Wood Preserving and Damp-proofing Association, and carry out their recommendations in full. Any treatment undertaken should form part of a long-term insurance-bonded guarantee.' On the strength of this the mortgage lender withheld some money and we have now had four quotes from BWPDA firms. All of them indicated different damp spots in different parts of the house, and their estimates ranged from £600 to £3750. Is there any reputable contractor you can recommend who provides an independent report on damp, preferably one whose views are respected by mortgage lenders?

A   Yes. Not a contractor but an independent surveyor [DAMPNESS – Dampness & timber surveyors]. In my experience, there's no such thing as a reputable 'contractor'. Almost all damp-proofing/timber treatment contractors make their money by offering free surveys and then saying you need work done. The unreliability of their diagnoses is underlined by the fact that, as in your case, different 'specialist' firms usually come up with different proposals.

DO I NEED A DPC?

Q   I am rebuilding an old house next door to my own in order to make the two into one. With the walls stripped of plaster, etc., I am now not sure what to do about a DPC. The bricks are very old and they are rock hard in the centre but soft on the outside, so if I drill them and try to inject damp-proof fluid it won't go anywhere. I have read your comments with great interest and would like to believe I don't need a DPC, but it is a lot of work if it all goes wrong. There are no obvious signs of dampness apart from one wall where the ground level outside is very high.

A   I think you should relax and stop worrying about something that hasn't happened yet. If the bricks are 'rock hard', then they won't allow moisture to pass through them, so there is no point damaging them by drilling, and then trying to inject a fluid that is not needed. If the ground level is high outside one wall, then you should lower it if at all possible.

DAMP WALLS CAUSE BY RAISED PATIO

Q   The damp-proof course of our 1917 house has been bridged by the patio laid against the external walls, in some areas up to 9in (225mm). The under-floor air vents are also below the patio level and fill with water in heavy rain. This has caused problems to decorations internally. Three solutions have been suggested: (1) to lift and relay the entire patio below the DPC (a large and expensive job); (2) to lift the patio stones adjacent to the wall, dig a trench out to below the

Chemical damp-proofing is usually unnecessary and rarely successful.

DPC, bitumen paint the walls and relay the patio stones; (3) to take an angle grinder and remove 4in (100mm) of stone around the walls, dig the trench out, bitumen paint the walls and fill the trench with pea shingle. Your recommendation please?

A No. 1 is the only option worth doing. The others will be throwing good money after bad. If your sub-floor vents are channelling surface water then you could soon have a rotten floor to cope with as well. The finished patio needs to be at least 150mm below DPC level, and sloping away from the walls. And definitely no bitumen paint anywhere, as it will simply trap moisture behind it.

DAMP WALLS CAUSED BY SOLID FLOORS

Q A few years ago a damp-proofing firm replaced my timber floor with a concrete one, and chemically treated the walls against damp. This has been unsuccessful and there is damp visible in the walls which they treated. They say that chemically retreating the walls would be the best solution. With the concrete floor and associated membrane, your previous comments would suggest this isn't a solution.

A Chemical damp-proofing is very rarely successful, and if it hasn't worked once, then there is very little point in repeating the process. It sounds as though removing the suspended timber floor with its sub-floor ventilation has upset the moisture equilibrium in the house and forced moisture up into the walls. No amount of chemical injection or replastering will deal with this; the only long-term solution would be to remove the concrete and reinstate the timber floor.

DAMP METER READINGS

Q I am buying a 300-year-old stone/flint cottage in Somerset. The property is very sound, but the surveyor says his damp meter 'went off the scale' and has advised we install a chemical damp-proof course. The ground floor is concrete laid, presumably over some sort of membrane, but one room is original flags on bare earth. There are no visible signs of damp in the house – no patches of mould or peeling plaster; the property doesn't smell damp or musty and feels warm and dry and we've heard that installing DPCs in properties of this type can result in more problems than it solves. Any advice?

A This sounds like another case where an old house is in an acceptably dry condition, but an ignorant surveyor has misused an electrical moisture meter to invent a problem that does not exist. And you are right – trying to 'damp-proof' an historic building like this can create problems. The most serious damage is usually caused by hacking off old lime plaster and replastering with a strong sand-and-cement mix. This should be avoided at all costs.

PENETRATING DAMPNESS: CAVITY WALL & CONSERVATORY

Q Our conservatory abuts the south–south-west-facing wall of our house, and during wet weather the bricks become saturated and water drips through above the opening between conservatory and house. I have been advised that repointing or a tile/slate hanging over the wet wall might be the answer.

A When cavity walls are saturated, water tends to run down the inside of the outer leaf until it meets an obstruction. In your case this is the lintel above the entrance to the conservatory. When an extension or conservatory abuts a cavity wall it requires the insertion of a cavity tray above the roof-line of the new addition, to throw water clear to the outside. This can be done from the outside by cutting out short sections of brickwork.

INSERTING CAVITY TRAY

Q You have described the need for cavity trays, which is exactly the problem with my 1920s house. It has had two bay windows extended, with much larger roofs. During south-westerly gales the ceiling leaks in the ground-floor rooms where the bays cut through the outside wall. But how do you retro-fit damp-proof trays in the cavity? Local builders don't know how!

A Cavity trays are needed wherever a bay, or extension, or conservatory, butts up to an external cavity wall. The fitting instructions are simple: (1) Remove two or three bricks. (2) Insert section of cavity tray. (3) Replace bricks. (4) Move along a bit and repeat steps 1 to 3. Where the extension has a pitched roof, the cavity tray has to be installed in stepped sections to follow the pitch.

Anyone who does not know how to perform this basic construction operation should not be describing themselves as a builder. Retro-fit cavity trays are available from several manufacturers [DAMPNESS].

DAMPNESS IN OLD FARM BUILDING

Q We live in an old farmhouse which was extended by the architect-owner by converting some single-storey farm buildings. Several areas of dampness have appeared on the walls; some cover many square feet whilst others appear as random isolated patches roughly circular in shape. We have sought advice from the local council, local builders and a reputable damp-proofing company. The latter advised us it was not rising damp, and that the wall is dry in depth. The external pointing is in good condition, and the roof and gutters are sound. Nobody can explain why the dampness has appeared or how to stop it.

A The damp patches could be due to salt contamination in the walls from animal urine, which is a common problem in converted farm buildings. The salts are hygroscopic, i.e. they attract moisture from the atmosphere. This can be easily tested for using the method described in Building Research Establishment Digest 245 [CONSTRUCTION LITERATURE]. If this proves to be the cause of the problem, then the salts can be drawn out by repeated application of a chalk poultice. Or, if you replaster using a breathable lime plaster, then they may crystallize out on the surface as efflorescence, and you can wash them off. Alternatively, you can line the walls with a drained, ventilated membrane system.

UNNECESSARY DAMP-PROOFING

Q We've just moved house, and it was recommended that we have damp-proofing done, which involves hacking off the plaster and replastering, etc. Our house was built in the 1930s and does have some wallpaper peeling off in corners near the floor on the external walls only, and not in every room. The only places it is happening is where the front doorstep joins the house, and at the back where the ground level has been raised by a layer of concrete. The problem is, it is written into our mortgage agreement that we have the damp-proofing work done.

A I would be surprised if your mortgage offer states that you 'have to have damp-proofing done'. It is more usual that you are asked to have further investigation of possible dampness undertaken. Your 1930s house cannot possibly need a new DPC as it was built with one in place. It may have minor condensation, leaking gutters, and the raised ground levels that you mention, but it does not need chemical damp-coursing or replastering. You should write to your mortgage lender saying that there is no evidence of rising damp (electrical meter readings are not evidence). If they insist then pay for an independent survey and report, which will stop you having to repeat the process when you come to sell.

ELECTRICAL DAMP-PROOFING

Q I have an old property – fifteenth-century in parts. The floor level in one of the rooms is 2ft (600mm) below the ground outside. At some time in its history somebody has put in a 'reverse osmosis damp course' from Rentokil. Was this a con, or could it really work? There is a plug behind one of the doors permanently switched on with a sign on it saying 'Under no circumstances to be switched off'!

A Several versions of these electrical damp-proofing systems have been produced over the years, all of which consist of wires inserted into holes or buried under the plaster. They have no effect, although some were installed with thirty-year 'guarantees'. Rentokil's was a 'passive' system, which did not use electrical power, so it sounds as though you may have two separate systems, the other being installed by Lectros. Rentokil insist that their system should work, even though this has never been independently proved.

COB HOUSE

Q We have just moved into a damp Devon farmhouse built of stone and cob. Broken gutters and downpipes, and built-up ground levels are obvious culprits for the damp, but the local conservation officer says that the modern cement render is exacerbating the problem. Three damp-proofing firms all say that cement render is fine, and they're also unanimous about injecting silicone damp-proof courses as part of the remedy. Who is right about the render? And is silicone damp-proofing suitable for thick cob walls?

A Your local-authority Building Conservation Officer is absolutely right. Cob, which is a mixture of local earth and straw, must be allowed to breathe. Plastering it internally with sand-and-cement render will cut down evaporation, and will actually make it wetter, rather than dryer. It should be plastered with a traditional lime mix, and any external decoration should be with limewash. Silicone injection damp-proofing is ineffective at the best of times, and it would be plain stupid to try to inject it into an earth building.

DRYING OUT AFTER LEAK

Q How long does it take wet walls to dry out? My dining room and hall wall were soaked from next door by a leaking hot water tank back in August (the house next door is unoccupied). My insurance company got involved, and the walls had the plaster stripped off them and were sand-and-cement rendered and replastered in mid-October. The decorating firm employed by the insurers wanted to decorate three weeks after this, which I felt was too soon. It is now six weeks after replastering and they are keen to get the job finished and off their books, but I am worried about two long cracks extending right across the new plaster in the hall, with some vertical offshoots. Do these matter? I have had many conflicting suggestions about the correct drying-out time.

A It is always a good idea to allow fresh plasterwork to dry out thoroughly before decorating, to allow for shrinkage cracks to develop and be filled. If the walls had been dry before they were plastered, then six weeks in dry weather, or in a heated house, would be a reasonable length of time to wait. Where a wall has been soaked by flooding or plumbing leaks, though, it should really have been allowed to dry out thoroughly before being replastered. The Building Research Establishment recommends one month drying time for every inch of thickness for a soaked solid brick wall. The best thing to do would be to allow the decorators to give the walls a coat of water-based emulsion now, and insist that they return in the spring to fill the cracks and apply the final decoration.

DAMP FLOORS

LEAKING PIPES UNDER FLOOR

Q I have a twenty-five-year-old detached house and the central heating pipes and water supply pipes are all embedded in the concrete flooring. I am confident that the damp-proof course is OK. However, there is very serious 'rising damp', which I assume must be from a leaking underground water pipe. Is there an easy way of determining this, or will it be necessary to dig up the floor to try to ascertain what is causing the problem?

A Concrete corrodes copper pipes. These days they have to be sheathed if they are buried, but many houses of your vintage had them just screeded over. Instead of digging them up, the easiest thing would be to cut them off and replace with new pipe runs in skirting ducts (floor ducts where they cross doorways).

FLOOR IN OLD COTTAGE

Q I have recently bought an old cottage. The ground-floor living room has damp, and it is proposed to have a concrete floor with a membrane for damp-proofing, with wooden sleepers and boards on top. There is no provision for airbricks, which I thought were necessary to preserve the timber. The contractors state that airbricks aren't needed. They propose to leave the concrete for ten weeks to dry out before putting in the flooring. Can you tell me if this is satisfactory?

A This sounds like a typical case of an old cottage being threatened by inexperienced builders using modern materials. If you want a wooden floor, then why not construct a proper suspended timber ground floor, ventilated underneath (with airbricks, as you suggest)? This will ensure that any moisture coming up out of the ground will be vented away, keeping both the floor and the walls dry. The contractor's plan for a damp-proof membrane covered with concrete will only trap moisture below it, and probably result in water being forced up into the walls.

DRYING OUT AFTER FLOOD

Q Our bath overflow pipe leaked and has caused every wall in our ground-floor flat to absorb water to about 1m high. There is no central heating. From what you've written, it would seem that anti-damp paint would just trap the moisture in the walls.

A Heating and ventilation are the accepted ways of drying things out. If you want to speed up the process then use a dehumidifier. These can be bought for around £200 or hired from a tool-hire shop.

DAMPNESS AFTER FLOODING

Q I am pretty convinced that my father's house does actually suffer from rising damp. He lives in a cottage that was built over 200 years ago and was recently flooded. After three weeks of drying time the house was redecorated, but the damp is now causing the paint to flake off the walls. Are there any DIY rising damp treatments that we can try?

A Flooding can take months to dry out. The place doesn't need damp-proofing, it needs drying. Try a dehumidifier.

COB HOUSE

Q We have recently bought a cottage in Dorset which is part-thatched and constructed with cob walls. Obviously it has no damp course, and is believed to be situated over or very near to underground springs, which can well up in winter when the underlying chalk becomes saturated! The floor is brick, probably laid straight on to earth. The Society for the Protection of Ancient Buildings, in its leaflets, advocates leaving things alone, saying that cob walls can disintegrate if dried out, and that plenty of ventilation and airflow should control the damp. We are thinking of digging out and laying a waterproof membrane over the whole floor area, and hoping that this will be sufficient to stop rising damp, and to leave the walls alone. Do you think that this is an advisable course of action, and do you have any alternative suggestions?

A I would think that SPAB have got it right. Who told you about the 'underground springs' – a damp-proofing salesman? It is quite true that cob walls need a certain moisture content to maintain their integrity. I cannot think of any reason to dig up a sound brick floor, and a membrane would be wholly inappropriate for a building of this type; it would upset the moisture equilibrium and possibly damage the walls by making them too wet. The floor needs to be allowed to breathe, and should not be covered with carpet or any other floor covering apart from loose sisal matting or similar. It sounds to me as though you might have bought this historic building without quite understanding the implications.

CONDENSATION

Condensation is one of the great banes of modern living. Energy-saving propaganda – much of it government sponsored – entreats us to insulate everywhere, draught-proof our doors and windows, fit double glazing and turn the heating down. All these measures increase the likelihood of condensation, which, when it occurs within the fabric of walls, floors and ceilings, lowers their insulation value and, paradoxically, allows more heat to escape than before.

All of the moisture that condenses out on windows and within walls is produced by the occupants. People may refer to their homes as being 'damp', but usually the property was dry until they came to live in it.

The most obvious symptom of condensation is misting on the windows, but if it is happening on the windows, then it is happening within the depth of the walls as well.

An example: 55 per cent relative humidity at a room temperature of 20°C is a perfectly normal, average sort of state in an occupied house. If you look up the tables, they will tell you that the dew point temperature in these conditions is about 10.5°C. In other words, if any surface falls to 10.5°C or lower, then condensation will form on it. So if you take a cold can of beer out of the fridge, it will soon be wet with condensation.

Now, if the outside temperature should fall to, say, 5°C, then there will be a temperature gradient through the wall, and where it falls to 10.5°C or below – just over halfway through the wall – the warm air passing through it from the room will be cooled enough to condense. If this condensed moisture is trapped in the wall by, for example, external paint or render, it will not be able to evaporate, and will stay in the wall and feed the black mould that grows on the wallpaper.

Black mould is a symptom of condensation.

Black mould is a prime symptom of condensation. Another is green mildew on leather goods in the wardrobe. The solution is to keep the bathroom and kitchen doors closed (to stop the moisture produced in these wet rooms from spreading through the rest of the house) and to open a few windows.

It is also important to keep the windows and walls above dew-point temperature, which means keeping the heating on in cold weather. The British habit of having the central heating on for two hours in the morning and four hours in the evening may sound sensible, but scientific analysis shows that it is not energy efficient. The condensation that occurs within the walls lowers their thermal insulation value and allows valuable heat to escape. In cold weather it is better to keep the heating on permanently, but to turn down the water temperature dial on the boiler, to provide a constant gentle heat.

CONDENSATION OR RISING DAMP?

Q Is there any way of distinguishing between condensation and a problem with the damp-proof course? When I bought my bungalow four years ago I paid £40 to take over a Certificate of Guarantee for a full damp course and woodworm treatment, valid for thirty years from 1995. I then discovered damp marks in the bedroom, so I called out the damp-proofing company. The man who came dismissed it as 'condensation'.

A Condensation occurs when warm, moist air from within the house meets cold surfaces – usually cold outside walls and window panes – and turns into liquid water. Rising dampness is very rare, and so called 'damp proofing' usually consists of little more than internal replastering. Unless your bungalow was built before 1877, it will have a damp-proof course built in, so it is unlikely to have needed damp proofing in the first place, and the 'guarantee' will be meaningless. The definitive way to distinguish between condensation and rising dampness is described in Building Research Establishment Digest 245 [CONSTRUCTION LITERATURE].

PASSIVE STACK VENTILATION

Q I am a council tenant, and I have been told that we are to have a 'stack' ventilation system fitted in the building. What does this mean, and do you think it is a good idea?

A Passive stack ventilation is basically a reinvention of the chimney. Victorian houses were often built with extra flues in the chimney breasts – some flues were to take smoke from the fireplaces, and others were to ventilate the rooms. The idea of the modern passive stack is that it will ventilate rooms without the need for electric power and so, with luck, there will be less resistance from council tenants to using it to keep their homes free from condensation.

The principles of passive stack ventilation, and details of how to construct a system using 100mm PVC-U waste pipe or flexible ducting are described in the Building Research Establishment Information Paper IP 13/94 [CONSTRUCTION LITERATURE].

MILDEW IN WARDROBE

Q We have lived in a detached bungalow for just over twelve months and have become concerned about dampness particularly in the main bedroom. The bungalow is double glazed and centrally heated. Over the winter months there have been signs of mildew on some of our shoes kept on shoe racks at low level in the wardrobes.

A Mildew will grow on leather at a relative humidity 72 per cent, so this is the level of moisture in your wardrobes. You need to provide extra heating and ventilation in the bedroom, and to stop water vapour entering from the kitchen and bathroom by keeping the doors closed.

BLACK MOULD IN THE WARDROBE

Q My daughter's house, which is over a hundred years old, has severe problems with black mould creeping up the walls from skirting-board level, wherever the wall is enclosed by cupboards or wardrobes. The house has a modern central-heating system and double glazing. The walls are solid brick. I am assured that there is a damp-proof course, and there is no evidence of damp on the outer wall. What is the prime cause of this and how can it be remedied?

A The black mould is caused by condensation. This occurs when moisture (produced by cooking, showering, drying clothes, etc.) meets the cold, unventilated surfaces at the back of the cupboards. The double glazing will not be helping, by cutting down on the natural ventilation, but the main problem is probably due to leaving the bathroom and kitchen doors open, thus allowing moist air to find its way into the other rooms.

BLACK MOULD GROWTH

Q My 1970s bungalow has one bedroom which has black mould growing in the two corners facing west, even with a window open permanently. I have cavity-wall insulation, but the problem does not occur in other parts of the bungalow. Have you any idea of the cause of this, and what needs to be done about it?

A Black mould growth in bedrooms, and in the corners of other habitable rooms, is often a sign of condensation. You are doing the right thing by having the window open, but the walls may also need extra heating, to keep them above dew-point temperature. However, there is also a possibility that condensation is not the cause, and that the cavity insulation is allowing rainwater through on the exposed west-facing walls. Cavity wall insulation is not suitable for houses in areas exposed to wind-driven rain for this very reason.

It should be relatively simple to diagnose the cause, since condensation will occur chiefly on the inside surface, whilst penetrating rain will soak the wall right through. An independent surveyor will be able to drill a hole from the inside, to test whether the wall is dry in depth, and to inspect the state of the cavity insulation using a boroscope. Try Abbey Independent Surveys, 01572 774398.

CONDENSATION IN ROOF SPACE

Q We had our roof retiled two years ago. The builder used a lightweight plastic type of felt under the tiles, which was different from the original heavy tarred hessian felt. In cold weather we now have condensation running down the inside of the felt and dripping on to the ceiling insulation. The builder suggested increasing the insulation from 4in to 8in (200mm) depth. We did this, but it didn't make any difference. The builder has now fitted some mushroom tile vents in the roof, but the problem continues. We have lived in the house for nearly forty years, always used the loft for storage and have never experienced condensation before.

A The condensation problem has been caused by the new plastic sarking felt, which has cut off all the natural ventilation to the roof space. The manufacturers claim that this stuff is 'breathable', but experience suggests otherwise. Warm, moist air from the house is finding its way up into the cold loft, is unable to be ventilated away and condenses out on the cold, impermeable surface of the plastic sarking felt. Your builder's suggestion to increase the thickness of loft insulation will have made matters worse, because, by keeping more heat in the rooms below, it will have made the roof space even colder. There is one simple, permanent solution to this problem, which is to go up into the loft with a Stanley knife and cut the sarking felt out from between the rafters. If this sounds too drastic for you, then some readers have suggested various Heath-Robinson methods for holding the overlapping layers of felt apart, to allow for a greater draught.

CONDENSATION IN BATHROOM

Q We have a big problem with condensation in the window area of our bathroom. It has rusted a venetian blind; it runs off the tiled window sill and wets the wall below, causing the paint to peel off; and there is black mould growing in the window recess. The window is already double glazed, and I wonder whether fitting secondary glazing would solve our problem – in effect creating a triple-glazed window. There is a fan vented to the outside but it seems quite ineffective.

A Adding an extra layer of glass is unlikely to solve a serious condensation problem. What is needed is better ventilation, to get rid of moist air before it has a chance to condense out on the cold surfaces. The double-glazed window should have a permanent trickle vent at the top, and after bathing or showering you should leave the fan running, or the window open, until the surfaces are dry. Most bathrooms also need permanent heating, to keep the surfaces above dew-point temperature. An electric towel rail or tubular electric heater below the window may be all that is needed. A 120-watt heater uses only as much electricity as a couple of light bulbs, and will pay for itself by saving money spent on repairs and redecorating.

CONDENSATION CAUSED BY CAVITY INSULATION

Q Some six or seven years ago the cavity walls of our house were insulated. Since then, in colder weather, condensation on the windows has got progressively worse. We do not have or want double glazing. Is there any remedy?

A The cavity-wall insulation will be keeping your home warmer, so the air is capable of holding more water vapour than before. But at the same time, it will be keeping the inner surfaces of your walls warmer as well, so that condensation does not occur on them. The result is to concentrate the condensation effect on the remaining cold surfaces – the window panes. The solution is better ventilation, so that the moist air is removed to the outside of the house before it has a chance to condense on the windows. It is especially important to keep your kitchen and bathroom doors closed and to use the cooker hood and extractor fans whenever these rooms are in use. You should also open a few windows and give the house a good airing at least once every day.

CONDENSATION ON WC CISTERN

Q I get condensation running down my toilet cistern all winter. I have tried lots of things to prevent it. The latest is to put in an airbrick. This did not work, so now my wife is fed up with me not solving the problem. Can you help?

A The first thing is to make sure the cistern is fed from the cold-water tank in the loft, rather than direct from the mains. The tank water will be slightly warmer, and so will allow a higher relative humidity before attracting condensation. The second is to fit an electric extractor fan in place of the airbrick and to use it whenever the bathroom is used. Most bathrooms would also benefit from permanent heating from, for example, a 120-watt tubular electric heater. Readers have also suggested drip trays clipped to the flush pipe (although these are no longer made commercially) and lining the inside of the cistern with 10mm polystyrene (such as ceiling tiles) to keep the surface above dew-point temperature. One exasperated reader has even plumbed his cistern to fill from the hot-water system. If all else fails, install a dehumidifier.

Condensation occurs when warm, moist air meets a cold surface.

DEHUMIDIFIERS & HUMIDISTAT FANS

Q We have a serious condensation problem in our bathroom and a friend has suggested fitting a humidistat-operated fan. Do you think this will be effective, or should we be looking at other solutions, such as a dehumidifier?

A Most humidistat-switched extractor fans are factory pre-set to start running when the relative humidity reaches 60 per cent. This is not usually low enough to stop condensation occurring, and in any case the setting soon changes, due to a process called electronic drift. I have tried several brands and models, and none has worked satisfactorily for more than a couple of months. The most reliable solution is to have a fan with a manual switch or pull-cord, and to use it religiously whenever the bathroom is in use. Permanent heating also helps, in the form of an electric towel rail or low-wattage tubular heater.

Dehumidifiers are a good, efficient way of controlling moisture levels, regardless of the weather conditions, and are especially useful in homes where the windows are kept closed for security purposes, or where washing is regularly dried indoors. They work by passing air over a cooled element, where it condenses and drips into a container. The container must be emptied when it gets full, but most models can also be permanently piped to the existing drainage system.

WHAT HUMIDITY?

Q What is the optimum level of humidity for a house – I cannot find the information in the book accompanying my dehumidifier. Obviously 100 per cent is rain and 0 per cent a bit drastic – what should I aim for?

A Opinions vary about this. Owners of antique furniture and musical instruments are often critical of dehumidifiers, as too dry an atmosphere can cause shrinkage and splitting, especially in thin timbers. A 'normal' relative humidity on a dry summer day in Britain will be around 55 per cent; most people will find this comfortable, and it is too low for moulds and mildew to grow. Humidistat-switched bathroom extractor fans are usually set to come on at 60 per cent. So the optimum level is probably between 55 and 65 per cent. The difficulty comes when you try to measure this, as the humidistats on dehumidifiers and extractor fans are notoriously unreliable, as are the dial-type hygrometers which some people have on their walls, and the 'sling hygrometers' used by some surveyors. A truly accurate electronic hygrometer will cost upwards of £200, and need annual recalibration.

CONDENSATION REDUCED BY PERMANENT HEATING

Q For forty years I have had our boiler on for four hours in the morning and six hours or so in the evening. You now advise leaving the boiler on continuously (though reducing the boiler stat at night). Would this not increase the fuel bill to a great extent?

A The idea is to keep the walls above dew-point temperature, and so stop condensation forming either on them or inside them. The problem with the typical British 'morning and evening' heating practice is that between times the walls cool down and condensation occurs. Then when the heating is switched on again half the energy is used to evaporate the condensed moisture (known scientifically as the 'latent heat of vaporization'). If the room thermostat is left on 15°C and the boiler thermostat is turned down to '1' or 'Min', rather than turning the heating off completely, this problem should be avoided. Readers who have followed this advice usually report that their fuel bills go down, not up.

Q Following your advice on permanent low-level heating, would mean, in my case, turning the boiler thermostat well down from its usual setting. Would this not mean that the boiler would switch on and off far more often in an attempt to achieve the temperature required by the room thermostat? I would have thought this would mean uneconomic use of the boiler.

A No. The boiler does not run continuously anyway, whatever the water temperature. Once the water has reached the temperature set by the boiler thermostat, then the boiler modulates, firing up and running for a few minutes at a time to keep the temperature at that level. Running it at a lower temperature will not alter this pattern.

HEATING ON OR OFF?

Q My system has thermostatic valves on every radiator instead of a central room thermostat. If I turn the boiler down at night and leave the pump on, surely as the temperature drops in a room the thermostatic valve will call for more heat from the radiator, which means more hot water from the boiler, and it will simply remain fired up all the time to meet the demand. It is impractical to turn every valve (some twenty) down individually and so twenty-four-hour gas usage must be more expensive than say eight-hour usage.

A The idea is to keep a flow of warm water going round the whole system in very cold weather, so as to prevent the wall temperature falling below dew point. To this end, your TRVs should be kept open, not closed down. You should turn down the water temperature on the boiler. I should add that TRVs should not be seen as a substitute for a room thermostat, and you should consider having one of these fitted. Preventing condensation and keeping the walls dry should improve the thermal insulation of your home and so save energy.

CONDENSATION ON DOUBLE-GLAZED WINDOWS (1)

Q I have had new PVC-U double-glazed windows fitted, and am shocked to find that they are now streaming with condensation. I was led to believe that double glazing would be a cure for the condensation, but it seems I have just wasted thousands of pounds. Or might there be a fault with the windows?

A This is a common question from readers who have bought double-glazed replacement windows in the belief that they are a 'cure' for condensation. However, if the internal humidity is high, and the glass falls below dew-point temperature, then condensation will still occur. The prevention of condensation requires ventilation, to get rid of moist internal air to the outside of the building – and heating, to keep surfaces (not just windows, but walls and fabrics too) above dew-point temperature. This principle applies equally to single-glazed and double-glazed windows.

CONDENSATION ON DOUBLE-GLAZED WINDOWS (2)

Q Have you any idea why our replacement double glazing would get condensation on the *outside* glass? It looks strange as it forms perfectly to fill each window apart from a gap of about 2–3cm around each frame.

A Condensation on the outsides of windows is simply dew. We are used to seeing it on our car windows on cold mornings, but house windows are usually warmed above dew-point temperature by heat coming from inside. Double-glazed windows are better insulators, so their outer panes are cooler, and dew is more likely to form on them. The clear gaps at the edges are because the frame is not as thermally insulating as the glass. I'm guessing you have PVC-U frames, and this material is actually a poor insulator, made even poorer by the steel or alloy inserts inside the PVC-U extrusions needed to stop them from collapsing. So the heat inside your house is being conducted out through the window frames, and then transferred to the edges of the outer panes of glass, thus keeping this area above dew-point temperature.

CONDENSATION CAUSED BY GAS FIRE & DOUBLE GLAZING

Q My 1930s house has solid brick walls. In 1999 I had all the original timber windows replaced by similarly styled double-glazed PVC-U units. At the same time I had a new gas fire fitted in the lounge. Now, when I use the fire, the walls below the windows become soaking wet and the wallpaper is starting to peel. I have tried leaving the windows ajar, to no avail. The gas fire has a balanced flue and provides the only heating in the room. Is there anything I can do to remedy the situation?

A The wet walls are clearly a result of condensation. It sounds as though your previous gas fire had a conventional flue, and this would have drawn its combustion air into the room through gaps around the doors and the old timber windows. The new fire takes its combustion air directly through the balanced flue, and thus does not have the same ventilating effect. The replacement PVC-U windows will probably also be airtight. The solution is permanent extra ventilation in the form of airbricks in the outside walls and trickle vents in the PVC-U window frames (although these should have been fitted from new).

WOODWORM & WOOD ROT

Regular news reports about the health problems suffered by Gulf War and Balkans War veterans are timely reminders of the dangers posed by exposure to toxic chemicals. Years after the events, there is disagreement over the causes of ill health suffered by returning troops, but the finger of suspicion points at the many chemicals encountered in the course of modern warfare. Unfortunately, some of those chemicals are used by the building trade as well.

Worryingly, chemicals in the house can pose risks even greater than when they are encountered on the battlefield. For one thing, their effects can be longer-lasting because they are trapped within the building, and for another, occupants can be exposed to them for longer periods. Young children and retired older people especially can be at high risk, as they often spend eighteen hours or more per day indoors.

But perhaps the most significant finding of the research into so-called Gulf War syndrome is the fact that combinations of two or more chemicals can be more damaging to health than the sum of each individual substance. For example, one researcher fed chickens with 'safe' doses of the insecticide permethrin (used to de-louse Iraqi prisoners) and the common insect repellent DEET (diethyl toluamide), and found that they became ill and died. Each chemical on its own had no significant impact; it was the cocktail effect that did the damage.

These findings deserve wider publicity, because permethrin has been sprayed in millions of British homes as a woodworm treatment, and it is also present in new clothes, carpets and soft

These old woodworm holes are only in the sap-wood at one corner of the joist.
They have not weakened the timber and do not need any treatment.

furnishings, to prevent moth damage. Meanwhile, DEET is the active ingredient in insect repellents sold over the counter in pharmacies. So anyone using an insect repellent and living in a house sprayed with permethrin timber treatment could be exposing themselves to the same chemical combination as the Gulf War veterans. Not to mention those unfortunate chickens.

The timber treatment industry has put much effort into persuading the public that its products are risk-free. It defended its use of the deadly organochlorines DDT and dieldrin until they were finally banned in the 1980s, and then continued to spray homes with the organochlorine lindane until it, too, was withdrawn from use. It then put its weight behind permethrin, and I was even told on an industry training course in 1994 that it was quite safe to drink a pint glass of this stuff. Strange, then, if it is so safe, that the industry is now moving away from permethrin and switching to boron, the latest 'safe' pesticide.

But like its predecessors, boron is a poison. If it wasn't, then it would not be used to kill insects and fungi. And, like its predecessors, boron has never been tested for the effects it has on health when it is combined with other chemicals. So if you buy a house that has been previously sprayed with permethrin, and your surveyor advises you to have the empty woodworm holes sprayed again with boron, what effects will this chemical combination have on your health? Nobody knows, because the research has never been done.

In any case, most woodworm holes are the harmless relics of insects who departed many years earlier, and spraying them is unnecessary. And when scientific research has suggested that Parkinson's disease may be linked to a cocktail of two readily available gardening pesticides, isn't it time for some serious research on the combination effects of all these common chemicals?

WOODWORM

Q I have bought a house where the survey revealed woodworm in the floorboards and in the attic. Are there specific questions that I should ask the woodworm treatment companies when they come to look at the property to quote for the work? I am also wondering if you know if some woodworm chemicals are safer than others.

A The first point to bear in mind is that your survey did not 'reveal' woodworm. What your surveyor may have noted is the presence of holes in the timber, which are the flight holes left by the departing beetles. In most houses these holes are many years old, and often occurred soon after the house was built, when the timber still had enough sap in it to support insect life. As the wood dried out, it will have become less attractive to wood-boring insects, and it is unlikely that there is a current infestation. It is also quite probable that the empty woodworm holes in the timbers of your house have already been sprayed with insecticides in the past, so there will be no justification for repeating this exercise.

If you do still want to get a further investigation of the woodworm holes, then get this done by an independent specialist, and not one who offers a 'free survey' and then tells you that your old woodworm holes need spraying with a chemical timber treatment. There is no such thing as a 'safe' insecticide; they are all poisons.

HEALTH DANGERS

Q Can you suggest any safe woodworm fluid for an attic which has worm holes? We would be concerned for our children's health particularly. We have installed modern Velux windows and need to protect these from any live woodworm. What would you suggest?

A I cannot recommend any woodworm fluids. They are all nerve poisons (see HAZARDS chapter). Your worm holes are probably many years old. They are actually 'flight holes' of the adult beetles leaving the wood. There is no justification for using insecticides unless you have definitive evidence that there is a continuing active infestation, and that this cannot be dealt with by normal construction methods, i.e. central heating and ventilation. Your new Velux windows are unlikely to be affected by wood-boring insects – the timber in them is kiln-dried and sealed with a water-based varnish.

Q I have discovered old woodworm holes in my bathroom floorboards after removing old lino tiles. Since the boards have been exposed to air this last week, new holes have appeared, with fresh sawdust around them. How can I get rid of these myself without the deadly sprays the companies use?

A You don't have to do anything to get rid of them, because they have already gone. Your lifting of the lino has coincided with the spring flight season. It is quite likely that the lino tiles were trapping moisture and keeping the floorboards damp. Now that they have been lifted, and as long as your house is properly heated and ventilated, the timber will probably dry down to below the 11 per cent moisture needed to support wood-boring insects. If you are really worried, then boiled linseed oil is a safe natural insecticide.

DEATH-WATCH BEETLE?

Q I have found that my 100-year-old Victorian terraced house has death-watch beetle, judging from the ticking coming from different locations in its pitch-pine timberwork. I'd greatly value your advice.

A Death-watch beetle prefer hardwoods, especially oak, so it would be unusual to find them in pitch pine. Are you sure it couldn't be expansion/contraction noises you are hearing?

TIMBER TREATMENT – SAFE IN KITCHEN?

Q I need woodworm treatment for a kitchen. Can you suggest a treatment that is safe to use in a kitchen environment? I have been told that certain products are not allowed where there is food preparation.

A In my opinion no insecticide could be regarded as 'safe'. If you really have active woodworm in your kitchen (and not just old flight holes in the floorboards), then the way to get rid of it is by normal heating and ventilation. If wood is dry then nothing can live in it. An additional measure is to use an ultraviolet 'Insect-o-cutor' to kill any adult beetles that emerge in the spring. This is a useful device to have in a kitchen anyway.

WOODWORM IN OLD FURNITURE

Q I have noticed that an antique beechwood chair which I bought a few years ago has active woodworm – i.e. sawdust sort of dust coming out of new-looking holes. I treated the whole chair with an anti-woodworm treatment. Now I am wondering whether I need to treat the house timber (house built in 1880s) and the other furniture (mainly oak). I would hate to do that, partly because of the pollution, partly because I am asthmatic and just doing the one chair affected my breathing for a few days. On the other hand, everyone tells me that eventually the worms will eat half my house! I take great comfort from what you say about the worms preferring sapwood, but do wonder why they invaded the chair in the first place – it is definitely not a new chair. I note that I live in an area where there are lots of garden trees, and the window is often open, so any beetle wanting sapwood would have no trouble finding it.

A Woodworm is not infectious, and there is no reason why it would spread from one piece of furniture to another or to house timbers. Each infestation results from the female adult beetle laying eggs in an environment that she thinks will be suitable for her offspring, i.e. moist, nutritious wood. If you have moist, nutritious wood anywhere in your house then adult female beetles –

which are flying around everywhere between April and July – will lay eggs in it. If the wood is dry, as it will be if you live in a normal heated and ventilated house, then they won't. The infestation in the beech chair probably happened five years ago when it was stored in damp conditions. Three to five years is the life cycle of the insects. Once this generation has hatched out and flown then that will probably be the end of it, regardless of how many chemicals you spray around the place.

DRY-ROT DIAGNOSIS

Q I have recently discovered that I have dry rot in my house, and I am ready to invite some-one into my house to give me a quote for sorting out this problem – but who? Where do I start? Carpenter, plasterer, general builder, dry-rot specialist? Who would you suggest as the best starting place?

A The first step is to ensure that the diagnosis of dry rot is accurate. There is nothing 'dry' about dry rot. This is a fungus that will only live on very wet wood, and in very humid conditions. If you have come across some decayed timber which is now dry, then it was probably left by a previous case of wet rot, caused by a water leak that has now been repaired. If you really have dry rot in the house, then it must be caused by a rainwater or plumbing leak, and the correct course of action is to locate the leak and have it repaired, by a builder or plumber as appropriate. A 'dry-rot specialist' will usually be a commission-paid salesman from a company that sells chemical timber treatments and he will therefore specify chemical treatment. For independent, non-chemical advice see Useful Contacts [DAMPNESS – Dampness & timber surveyors].

Dry rot only lives on wet wood. Removing the source of the moisture, and increasing the ventilation, will get rid of it.

DRY ROT IN BRICKWORK?

Q I have what a few builders call 'a serious problem, mate'. The problem is I have dry rot on one of my walls (outside wall with a gully). The rot has eaten away my stairs and strands appear to be coming from between the brickwork (I hacked off all the old plaster and mortar) over a certain area. I have taken away all the damaged wood and believe that I have found where the damp is coming from. My problem now is what to do with the wall; should I plasterboard it up or get it rendered and plastered?

A   The key things are to stop the source of moisture ingress (which you appear to have done) and allow the affected area to dry out and 'breathe'. To this end cement-and-sand renders are usually a bad idea, especially if the house is old and the original plaster was lime-and-sand. Similarly, plasterboarding the area would be a bad idea, as any future problems would be hidden from view. The ideal would be lime plaster to match the original, but if you can't find anyone to do traditional lime-and-sand plastering then something like Tarmac's Limelite is a good second choice. Avoid gypsum finishing plasters as they do not perform well in damp conditions.

DRY-ROT TREATMENT

Q   My local wood treatment company have told me that even though my windows are to be replaced with a set of PVC-U French doors, and the house has a concrete floor, it will still be necessary to treat and replaster the surrounding walls as the dry-rot fungus can live in them and spread throughout my house. (The walls are cavity brickwork construction.) Can dry rot live in mortar?

A   Dry rot is a fungus that lives on wet wood. If you remove the source of any moisture, and if (as in your case) you have very little wood in the house, then there will be nothing for it to live on. Irrigating brickwork with fungicidal chemicals is an expensive process that involves removal of the existing plaster and subsequent replastering. It is a trick that timber treatment companies have been using for years to extract the maximum amount of money from their customers, but it has no scientific basis, and is a complete waste of money and effort.

REPAIRING ROT IN ROOF

Q   Can you advise me on how to treat dry rot in the roof of an old house, without using 'specialists'. The roof has been repaired and there is no more ingress of water.

A   It would be unusual to find dry rot in a roof space, since it needs a large amount of water and high humidity in unventilated conditions. Roof spaces are usually too warm and draughty for it. The damage was probably wet rot, caused by the leaks. If these have been fixed, and there is good ventilation, then nothing further should need to be done.

INSULATION

Insulation – if applied correctly – is a good way of cutting heating costs and energy waste. Houses constructed before 1945 often had minimal insulation, and thus took a lot of energy to heat. As fuel costs rose in the 1960s, householders were encouraged to put 50mm of fluffy quilt in their lofts, and after the oil crisis of 1973 this was raised to 100mm. We are now encouraged to have at least 250mm (10in) of insulation above our bedroom ceilings, which, if carried out, would make it impossible to board-out the loft space for storage use. Since many British town houses already have inadequate storage space, this is an additional restriction that many readers find baffling.

The 1970s also saw cavity-wall insulation introduced for new buildings; first 25mm, then 50mm, and now 75mm. The trouble with this approach is that successive thickening of insulation does not necessarily result in corresponding savings in energy. The law of diminishing returns applies. So if your uninsulated home costs £1000 per year to heat, then wrapping it in the latest specified thickness of fluffy stuff may well reduce that outlay to £500, but doubling the thickness will not reduce the heating costs to zero. Homes in northern Europe will always need a source of internal heat, although the current government obsession with insulation encourages people to believe otherwise, and this can have unfortunate consequences.

The chief problem with a spartan fuel regime is an increased risk of condensation. Some pensioners and other low-income families have annual fuel bills of less than £150, and they achieve this by keeping their windows permanently closed, taking the fuses out of mechanical extractor fans, and blocking up air vents. The inevitable result is black mould growth on ceilings and walls, and green mildew on shoes and clothes in the wardrobe. Local-authority tenants on income support are especially likely to live in such conditions, and there is usually a friendly local damp-proofing company on hand to persuade them that they are victims of 'damp', and to encourage them to sue their landlords to have their homes 'damp proofed'. Many cash-strapped local authorities waste millions of pounds of council taxpayers' money every year on this sort of nonsense.

Every new version of Part L of the Building Regulations seems to produce yet another increase in the thickness of wall and loft insulation, and new homes are also soon to be subject to airtightness tests, which will ensure that ventilation is kept to a minimum.

Building Research Establishment Report

Thermal insulation: avoiding risks

bre BUILDING RESEARCH ESTABLISHMENT

8

rising main within heated space

loft insulation turned up

insulate pipework in roof void

loft insulation draped over overflow not underneath

cold water storage

heat rising from below prevents freezing

This all means that new houses are set to become hermetically sealed boxes, full of chemical timber preservatives, mineral wool fibres and formaldehyde emissions from plastics and adhesives. Condensation will be a major problem, but will probably be dwarfed by the epidemic of asthma and other allergic reactions which will affect the children brought up in these ghastly buildings.

Cavity-wall insulation is being heavily promoted, and in some cases – if installed to a high professional standard – it can work well and reduce fuel bills. But in many cases it is installed quickly and cheaply, and can create serious dampness problems. The worst complaints involve blown mineral wool fibre, which, when investigated, is often found to lie in damp lumps in the cavity, providing little insulation value, and increasing the likelihood of water crossing the cavity. Yet, despite frequent horror stories, the industry refuses to admit to any problems.

If you are thinking of improving your home's insulation, then before you do anything you should get hold of a copy of the BRE booklet 'Thermal Insulation – avoiding risks' [CONSTRUCTION LITERATURE].

CAVITY-WALL INSULATION (1)

Q I (and, I believe, other elderly people) am being pressed to have cavity-wall insulation fitted, with a promise of a government or local-authority grant to cover part of the cost. My house, built in 1962, has its inner walls made of Thermalite blocks, and we were assured at the time that this would provide excellent insulation. If I were to have cavity insulation installed, would it actually reduce the heat loss by a significant amount, or would it be equivalent to a person putting on a scarf when they are already wearing a thick coat and several woolly jumpers? The tone of the literature I have received so far seems to infer that if people fail to take advantage of these offers, they will have only themselves to blame if their fuel bills go sky high. I suspect pressure is on the government from interested industries. What are your views?

A I have written about the perils of cavity-wall insulation many times, but I still get a regular stream of readers' letters on the subject, due to relentless marketing pressure from the companies, the government and the green lobby. Cavity walls were built to provide a barrier, to prevent wind-driven rainwater from crossing to the interior decorative surfaces. Filling the cavity compromises this barrier, and also increases the risks of condensation forming on unfilled 'cold spots', caused by uneven filling, or by settlement of mineral wool-fibre insulation after filling.

You are right to suspect vested interests; the trade body representing mineral wool fibre manufacturers has been highly active in promoting the supposed benefits of cavity-wall insulation, and has even contributed to the writing of the relevant Building Regulations. However, there is no proof that cavity-wall insulation actually saves heat or money, or prevents carbon emissions or climate change. *Sunday Telegraph* reader Peter Luker, a qualified engineer, has investigated this issue in depth, and has requested figures from the government to support their claims, but none has been forthcoming.

It may sound intuitively sensible that filling cavities with insulating material must save on heating bills but, amazingly, the government has been unable to provide any independent research to support this hypothesis. Mr Luker's analysis of his own home heating costs before and after having his cavity walls insulated show no discernible benefits. And anecdotal evidence from the building trade is that when insulated cavity walls are opened up – for example when window and door openings are altered, or when new boiler flues are inserted – blown mineral-wool fibre insulation is often found to be wet and uneven, and therefore of doubtful insulation value.

There is also the risk of rain penetration and internal condensation causing decorative damage, that might cost more to rectify than any projected energy savings. So my advice remains that filling existing cavity walls with mineral-wool fibre insulation is a bad idea. Readers who are determined to have their cavity walls insulated should consider foam or bonded polystyrene beads, but these materials are not always supported by government or local-authority 'grants'.

Thermal image of a house with cavity wall insulation. The red 'hot spots' show where it has not been properly installed.

CAVITY-WALL INSULATION (2)

Q Our 1950s bungalow has polystyrene bead cavity-wall insulation, installed some years ago by the previous owners. The polystyrene beads are falling down and blocking the airbricks that are supposed to ventilate below the suspended timber ground floor, and are also spilling out through the holes in the inner leaf of the cavity wall. We have tried clearing the beads away from the airbricks and openings, but more beads then fall down from higher up the cavity. We have considered inserting some kind of ducting into the cavity behind the airbricks, to keep the airways open – is there a product on the market for this purpose, and where would I find a stockist?

A Your story illustrates a common problem with cavity-wall insulation; it is often carelessly installed. In the first place, the installers should have inspected the cavity to check that the structure was suitable, and that openings such as those around airbricks were properly lined. Instead they have just pumped the insulation into the cavity, thus blocking off the sub-floor ventilation, which could lead to problems with dampness and wood rot. The other problem is that polystyrene bead insulation is supposed to be bonded with an adhesive, to hold it together. The fact that the beads are loose is a sign that this was not done properly by the installers.

You can cut out the airbricks and insert clay or plastic cavity liners, which should be stocked by your local builders' merchants. You will then need to find an installer to fill the gaps in the insulation which, if left unfilled, could lead to localized condensation problems on the inside wall surfaces.

CAVITY-WALL INSULATION – INSPECTIONS

Q You recently wrote that before cavity walls are insulated, the installers should check them for suitability. How should an installer go about this? We had cavity insulation installed eighteen months ago, and all the surveyor did was drill into one of the walls and tell me the cavity width.

A The most important thing is to check that the outer leaf of brickwork is properly built, with full mortar joints and no cracking. This is especially important in areas of high exposure to wind-driven rain, as water that finds its way through defects in the outer leaf may be able to track across the filled cavity. This will require internal inspection of the cavity, either by using a boroscope, or by removing one or more bricks at the corners. At the same time, the surveyor should be looking for debris that might prevent the insulation from filling the cavity properly – especially mortar sticking out of joints, and mortar that has fallen and lodged on the wall ties, or obstructed the cavity above damp-proof course level. All such obstructions should be cleared before the cavity is filled. In addition, in an older house, or one built between 1964 and 1981, the wall ties should be inspected for corrosion by cutting out bricks and exposing at least two ties on each elevation. If the ties should have to be replaced after the cavity has been filled, there is no satisfactory way of making good the holes in the insulation. Needless to say, there are few, if any, installers who carry out these inspections properly.

The British Standard wind-driven rain index is also reproduced in various Building Research Establishment publications, including 'Thermal insulation: avoiding risks', and 'Good building guide 44: Insulating masonry cavity walls'.

It is also in Building Regulations Approved Document C [CONSTRUCTION LITERATURE].

CAVITY-WALL INSULATION REMOVAL (1)

Q **I am considering having my polystyrene cavity-wall insulation removed. The polystyrene beads were not bonded together when they were installed, and consequently they are constantly 'leaking'. As the extraction operation will require the removal of a few bricks, I am worried that this will leave the walls looking unsightly. Can you please advise whether it is possible to remove and replace the bricks without leaving the walls looking as though they have been tampered with?**

A There are several reasons why bricks in cavity walls might need to be cut out and replaced – to replace corroded wall ties, to clean out debris, or remove troublesome cavity insulation. Any good professional bricklayer will pride himself on being able to do this and leave the wall looking as though it has never been touched. Surprisingly, the most important factor is not matching the bricks – slight variations in colour are often not noticeable – but in matching the mortar. Minor differences in colour or texture of the mortar can stand out like the proverbial sore thumb. An experienced local bricklayer will know which combination of sand, lime and/or cement to use, and how to reproduce the profile of the mortar joint, whilst a less skilled general builder might not.

CAVITY-WALL INSULATION REMOVAL (2)

Q **I have had my cavity walls insulated with mineral wool, and now damp patches have appeared on the inside walls. Is it possible to have the insulation removed? It was blown in, so could it possibly be sucked out?**

A Several readers have reported problems with penetrating dampness since having cavity-wall insulation installed. The British Board of Agrément approval for these products clearly states that they are unsuitable for areas of high exposure to wind-driven rain, and that a thorough inspection of the walls should be undertaken first, to check for watertightness. Needless to say, these requirements are often ignored.

All cavity insulation can be removed. Mineral fibre can be vacuumed or blown out, whilst bonded polystyrene beads and solid foam insulation must be manually broken up and scraped out. In both cases, bricks will have to be removed at various points around the building, and it is important that these holes are made good by a skilled bricklayer, using bricks and mortar to match the original.

Removing damp mineral-wool fibre cavity insulation.

CAVITY-WALL INSULATION CAUSING DAMPNESS

Q Our 1970s semi-detached house was fitted with replacement PVC-U double glazing about ten years ago. Two years ago we had cavity-wall insulation installed and the depth of insulation in the loft was increased to the latest recommended depth. Now we find that the wall reveals on each side of the master bedroom window are almost always damp during the winter. Sometimes it's possible to actually wipe moisture from the walls. Might the problem be the double glazing? We always sleep with one window open, leaving it open during the day too. What remedies are available to deal with the damp and the damage it causes to the wallpaper, apart from redecorating frequently?

A It sounds as though your dampness problem did not occur during the previous ten years, despite the installation of the double glazing. So the main suspect has to be the cavity-wall insulation. The manufacturers and installers – and the government-funded Energy Savings Trust – all deny that cavity insulation can allow moisture to cross cavities and penetrate to the inside surfaces, but many readers report that this has happened to their properties. If you have access to the roof space, and the cavities are open at the top, you might be able to feel down to check whether the insulation is damp. Otherwise you will have to drill a hole in the wall and try to fish some out with a length of wire. Or engage a chartered surveyor to visually inspect the cavities using a boroscope. If the cavity insulation is the problem, then the only real solution will be to have it removed.

Should the cavity insulation be dry, however, then the finger of suspicion will shift to condensation, for which the cure is increased ventilation and heating.

SOLID WALLS

Q We are all being urged to insulate our cavity walls, but I have heard stories about this causing dampness problems. It seems to me to be more logical to insulate walls on the inside, thus maintaining a clear cavity. This is also the only option for buildings with solid walls and no cavities. What materials are available on a DIY basis to insulate the insides of the walls?

A The best way to insulate any wall – either solid or cavity – is on the outside, but most UK houses have face brickwork on the outside, so external insulation is not usually an option. Internal insulation is easy to fit, although it does necessitate redecoration, and some repositioning of light switches and power sockets. The most efficient material is rigid foam-board insulation (Celotex or Kingspan) which is available in 25mm-thick sheets, equivalent to 50mm of glassfibre or mineral-wool fibre [INSULATION]. The usual method is to fit a framework of timber battens to the wall – such as 25mm x 38mm roofing battens – cut the boards to fit between them, and finish with plasterboard or wood panelling.

Ideally, you are supposed to fit a polythene vapour barrier on the 'warm' side of the insulation, i.e. between the insulation and the plasterboard. This is to prevent water vapour finding its way from the room through to the 'cold' side of the insulation, and condensing out in the depth of the wall.

If your DIY skills are not up to plaster skimming over the plasterboard, you might consider 'dry lining', i.e. taping the joints between the boards and covering them with jointing compound. The plasterboard can then be papered or painted in the normal way. (Technical advice is available from British Gypsum [PLASTERING].)

EXTERNAL WALL INSULATION

Q I am having the 1950s extension of my eighteenth-century stone cottage re-roofed. At the same time, I would like to improve the insulation in the walls. To avoid disturbing the interior fittings, an architect friend has suggested using insulating panels on the outside of the walls. I gather these are quite new, and they certainly seem to be new to the builders who are quoting. Also, I am slightly worried that adding a layer on the outside could trap moisture and so cause damp, or perhaps just not work.

A External insulation is almost always a good idea, as it keeps the walls warm and thus helps prevent condensation. It can be applied to most types of houses, apart from those with face brickwork. There are two main systems: one consists of fixing insulation boards to the walls and rendering over them; the other uses a lightweight insulating aggregate in the render. The insulation is stopped above DPC level, and window sills may have to be extended to cope with the extra wall thickness. For details of specialist companies call the Insulated Render and Cladding Association [PLASTERING].

INSULATION IN BOARDED LOFT

Q I have recently moved into a 1990-built house and wish to extend the boarding in the loft, as it has just an island around the access trap. At present the insulation is 100mm-thick fibreglass laid between the 100 x 50mm ceiling joists. I hear that insulation standards have recently been increased; can you tell me what is the new standard for existing dwellings, and what should be done to upgrade the existing insulation prior to extending the boarding?

A There is no 'new standard' for thermal insulation in existing dwellings; 100mm fibreglass covered with close boarding will provide a good level of insulation, and any extra thickness is unlikely to have any noticeable effect on comfort or heating bills. If you really wanted to, you could remove all the fibreglass and replace it with 100mm rigid polyurethane board insulation cut to fit between the joists, or – by sacrificing some headroom in the loft – you could leave the fibreglass in place, lay rigid extruded polystyrene board insulation across the top of the joists (e.g. Marmox construction boards [INSULATION]), with timber boarding on top of this. Again, the benefits are likely to be marginal, and it is questionable whether any small savings in your heating bill would justify the cost or effort.

INSULATION BETWEEN RAFTERS

Q **I have a timber house, finished internally with lath-and-plaster. The original part is Tudor. It was completely renovated in 2000 but wasn't insulated. We have put loads of insulation down in the flat part of the loft but there is none between the roof tiles and internal sloping ceilings at the edges. I would like to fill the gaps between the internal plaster and roof, and the internal plaster and outer walls with Micafil because I cannot believe that insulating this gap won't make the house warmer. You have warned against the dangers of cavity-wall insulation, and I wonder if you think what we want to do is pointless, or indeed likely to cause problems.**

A You should take great care insulating such a historic property, as any mistakes leading to dampness problems could be very costly. Your first call should be to your local-authority Building Conservation Officer, who will have experience of similar properties in the area, and will be able to advise on the best solution. I would think it unlikely that he would recommend cavity-wall insulation, because of the risks to the timber frame, and the most sympathetic option is likely to involve insulating on the insides of the lath-and-plaster walls.

Regarding the roof space ventilation, ideally you need to keep a clear 50mm ventilated gap between the insulation and the roof covering, which is not possible with loose-fill products such as Micafil (granular vermiculite). If you can access the space from the loft, you may be able to push stiff 50mm or 75mm mineral-wool batts down from above. Again, the Building Conservation Officer should be able to advise on the best procedure.

INSULATION IN ROOF SPACE

Q **I am concerned that I am wasting heat though the loft/roof of my ten-year-old house because the ventilation is so effective. There are vents in the soffits between every joist, and also 6in (150mm) diameter vent holes drilled into the masonry of each gable end of the loft. Not surprisingly, the ambient temperature in the loft is that of the outside and I was wondering if I could block these vents off in order to conserve heating costs. My neighbour has done this already but I am worried about attracting moisture/rot in the future. At present the house becomes very cold only half an hour after switching the heating off and I think this may be the main reason.**

A The level of insulation above the top-floor ceilings in a modern house is now so high that very little heat escapes through it, meaning that the loft space remains cold in winter. Because of this, there is a danger of condensation occurring when warm, moist air from the house finds its way into the cold loft area, and it is important that there is adequate ventilation to expel this moist air to the outside. If you restrict the ventilation, then you would really need to add extra insulation at the very top of the structure, i.e. under the tiles and between the rafters, in order to raise the loft temperature and prevent condensation occurring on cold surfaces.

In any case, it is unlikely that the loft ventilation is causing your house to cool down. The most likely reason is that the house is built with a timber frame (or some other form of modern lightweight construction) and so, unlike a traditional brick-built house, does not have sufficient thermal mass to store heat for more than half an hour. The only way to keep such a house warm at night is to keep the heating on.

INSULATING FLAT ROOF

Q **We have a two-storey Edwardian (approx. 1908) mid-terrace house with a flat roof. Is there a method, or is it necessary, to have some form of insulation?**

A Roof insulation is always a good idea, because hot air rises, and the roof is the most significant part of the building for heat loss. Homeowners are often put off the idea of insulating flat roofs because of the difficulty of inserting insulation above the ceiling and between the joists. But actually the best way to insulate is to leave the ceiling and roof structure undisturbed, and put slabs of extruded polystyrene (such as Dow's 'Roofmate') on top of the existing waterproofing layer. This creates a 'warm roof' – sometimes known as an 'upside-down roof' – where the whole of the roof structure reaches internal room temperature, and does not have to be ventilated to prevent condensation forming within it. The insulation slabs can be mechanically fixed, or else weighted down with ballast or paving slabs to form a roof terrace. It is important that you first have the flat roof thoroughly inspected to ensure that it is sound, laid to the correct gradient to shed rainwater, and able to withstand the extra loading of the insulation and ballast. (For more information call Dow on 0208 917 5050 or visit www.styrofoameurope.com).

LOFT INSULATION COVERING CABLES

Q **I know that we have insufficient insulation in the loft of our bungalow and I am considering adding more. However, there are many cables and wires running along the beams. Can I just lay new insulation over these, making a note of what is where as I go?**

A The government is very keen for us all to increase the depth of our loft insulation, but this needs to be done with care, otherwise it can cause problems. One of these is that if electrical cables are covered by insulation they can overheat. This may cause damage to the cable sheathing and adjacent materials, and lead to a reduction in the service life of cables.

Ideally cables should be lifted above the insulation, preferably stapled to rafters or purlins. This is not just to avoid overheating, but also to make sure the cables can be easily found and identified during future electrical work, and to reduce the possibility of accidental damage to hidden cabling. In many cases, unfortunately, cables have been installed with insufficient slack to allow this.

In practice, however, most of the cables running above top-floor ceilings will be to domestic lighting circuits rated at 6 amps, and these are unlikely to experience a problem, since the thinnest cable used (1 sq mm) already has a current-carrying capacity well above that which is needed. Some bungalows might have cables for power circuits running in the loft space, however, especially if they have solid concrete ground floors. And houses might have power cables running to electric showers or shower pumps in upstairs bathrooms. If these cables are covered with insulation, they should be 'derated', meaning that they should not be required to carry their maximum designed loading. For power circuits buried under the current recommended insulation depth of 270mm of mineral-wool fibre, the circuits may have to be derated by a factor of up to 50 per cent, and should carry only that proportion of their designed current.

The worst situation occurs where cables are already lying on top of the existing loft insulation and extra insulation is laid across the top of them, effectively making them the filling in the sandwich. It is better to reposition the cables below the existing insulation, laying them flat against the plasterboard surface of the ceiling, which will conduct some of the heat away from them. If in any doubt, consult a qualified electrician [ELECTRICS].

For maximum benefit, loft insulation should be draped across the joists, rather than in between them (not possible if you wish to have a boarded floor), but there should be no insulation beneath water tanks – these need warmth from the rooms below to prevent freezing, and should be securely lagged around the sides and over the top. And don't forget to lag any exposed water pipes.

INSULATION GRANULES

Q My loft floor is insulated with granules – I do not know what they are made of. Now an insulation firm has told me that polystyrene granules rot electricity cables. This is alarming, but is it true? And how can I tell whether my granules are polystyrene?

A Most loose-fill loft insulation is expanded vermiculite, made by heating a naturally occurring mineral. It has a grey, flaky, slightly reflective appearance. Slightly less common is expanded perlite, also made by heating a mineral, which has the form of small white beads. Perlite looks similar to expanded polystyrene, but it is hard when pressed between finger and thumb.

Expanded polystyrene beads are a familiar material, used in a bonded form to make the packaging for electrical goods, etc. If you can squash the individual beads in your fingers then they could well be polystyrene. It is true that polystyrene reacts with the PVC sheathing on electrical cables to make a sticky mess on the surface. The cable manufacturers say that this should not represent a fire risk, but should be avoided nevertheless. In loft spaces insulated with loose polystyrene fill, the lighting cables should be protected with conduit.

If you suspect you have loose polystyrene fill in contact with your cables then the simplest way to check is to inspect the cables themselves, and see if any of the granules have stuck to the cable sheathing. For safety, you should turn off the electricity at the consumer unit before handling the cables.

BELOW GROUND FLOOR

Q My house has wooden floors and copious amounts of airbricks. Whilst I am aware of the importance of the airbricks, there is a definite chill around the ankles in icy and windy weather so I wonder whether it would be practical to install baffles, around 2in (50mm) larger than the airbricks, to stop the wind blowing directly into them. Does that sound like a good or bad idea to you?

A Bad idea. Any sort of obstruction will impede the air flow below the floor and could lead to a build-up of moisture. If you are troubled by draughts into the ground-floor rooms, then draught-proof the gap between floor and skirting. But the best thing would be to insulate the ground floor by lifting the floorboards, draping an insulating membrane across the joists, and fitting insulation slabs between the joists, before refixing the boards. If you don't want to lift all the boards, you may be able to get away with lifting every sixth one, or so, and pushing stiff mineral-wool batts (as used to insulate new cavity walls) into place, supported on battens nailed to the sides of the joists). That way, you will have a warm floor, but preserve the ventilating effects of the air flow below it.

SOUND-PROOFING

According to a report from the World Health Organization, noise is the most widespread pollutant on the planet, presenting a significant threat to health, well-being and quality of life. And figures from the UK's Chartered Institute of Environmental Health show a consistent year-on-year rise in noise complaints to local authorities.

With noisy neighbours, the Institute recommends communicating with them as the most effective way of dealing with the problem. This is often easier said than done. As I write this I am trying to ignore my neighbour's dog which barks from eight in the morning till ten at night. When I first politely drew this to the neighbour's attention she told me that it was natural for dogs to bark. On the second occasion she accused me of harassment and said she would call the police if I complained again. The local Environmental Health Department say that barking dogs do not constitute a 'statutory nuisance' under the Environmental Protection Act (1990), and that they are unable to take action.

So, since we now live with so much noise – traffic, dogs, television, amplified music – and since the legislation is so useless, it may be easier to soundproof our homes than to deal with the noise at source.

Noise from outside, such as traffic and barking dogs, should first be approached by draught-proofing around doors and windows and fitting secondary glazing. Secondary glazing is not to be confused with double glazing, which has a small sealed gap – around 15mm – between the two sheets of glass, and is good for thermal insulation. Secondary glazing creates a bigger air gap between itself and existing windows – 100–200mm – and this is better for reducing noise. Fitting secondary glazing is cheaper than complete replacement double glazing, and offers the advantage of retaining the original fenestration pattern in older houses.

Noise from immediate neighbours, whether through walls or floors, enters in two ways: impact sound and airborne sound. Impact sound is most likely to be the footsteps of the people in the flat above, and becomes worse when they follow the latest trend for taking up the carpets and having bare wooden

Secondary glazing cuts down road noise and preserves the original windows.

floors. The solution involves physically separating the floor and ceiling, so breaking the path of the vibrations. The best way to do this is to construct a new floor above, with joists between, but not touching, the original ceiling joists below. This will raise the floor level slightly, and doors will have to be trimmed to fit. Alternative, but less effective, solutions are to re-lay the existing floor so that it 'floats' on acoustic rubber strips, or to construct an insulated false ceiling in the downstairs flat.

Older houses converted into flats during the last ten years should have a fair measure of soundproofing, supervised by the local-authority Building Control Officer, but earlier conversions may have escaped their attentions, as might buildings where planning relaxations were granted – to preserve ornate Victorian ceilings, for example.

Airborne sound, if loud enough, can make the walls and windows vibrate as well, but its usual entry route is via gaps. If you can smell your neighbours' cooking or cigarette smoke, then you will probably also be able to hear their noises, travelling along the same paths. In terraced houses, a common route is through the cracks that open up between front walls and party walls; locating these gaps and sealing them with a flexible filler can sometimes achieve good results. Chimney breasts in party walls are also a route for sounds and smells, when the internal brick lining of the flues may have broken down.

More serious soundproofing of a party wall involves constructing a new timber stud wall close to, but not touching, the original brickwork, filling the space with sound insulation quilt, and finishing with high-density plasterboard or plaster on metal lathing. Proprietary plasterboard sheets with soundproofing quilt already attached, such as British Gypsum's Triline system, can be fixed straight on to the existing wall with dabs of adhesive [PLASTERING].

Readers can obtain a free leaflet, 'Improving sound insulation in homes', from the Building Research Establishment website [SOUNDPROOFING].

BRE — Improving sound insulation in homes

Many people are bothered by neighbour noise. The problem can occur in any type of attached house, flat or bungalow but most commonly in flats that have been converted from large houses. You may be bothered by your neighbour's noise because:

- you are unusually sensitive to noise
- your neighbour behaves unreasonably
- the sound insulation between your homes is poor

While everybody sometimes hears some noise such as raised voices, laughter or occasional loud music, you should not be able to hear your neighbour's normal conversation or television. You can look for a legal or DIY solution to the problem. This document outlines some of the DIY measures possible.

First of all you have to decide how the sound is travelling into your home. It may be coming directly through the party wall or floor or it may be coming along another route called a flanking path. The most common such path is the inner leaf of an external cavity wall. Some examples of flanking paths are shown in Figure 1.

Paths of type 1 are direct paths
Paths of type 2 are flanking paths

Figure 1. Transmission paths for airborne sound through rooms in a pair of flats separated by a timber floor

It is essential to determine the path of the sound so that the remedial treatment can be chosen correctly. *Some information on how to diagnose the sound path is contained in leaflet XL4¹.*

The unwanted noise travelling along direct and flanking paths makes the structure vibrate and this causes the sound to radiate into your room. A solution is to build another wall or ceiling beside the original, but not connected to it. In flats converted before June 1992 there may have been little or no sound insulation improvement undertaken on the floor. If this is the case, upgrading the floor is almost certain to be effective.

Remedial Treatment: Walls
The following steps for construction are suggested, see Figure 2:

- build a studwork frame, attached to the ceiling and floor but not fixed to the original wall
- hang mineral wool inside the cavity, and tack between the studs or to a batten on the wall
- line the studwork with two layers of plasterboard, making sure the joints between the sheets in the first and second layer do not coincide
- seal perimeter and all other sound paths with flexible sealant

Figure 2. Wall improvement layout of studwork and plasterboard

---

NOISE THROUGH PLASTERBOARD WALLS

Q My house is built to 'modern standards', and the walls of the bedrooms surrounding the bathroom transmit all sounds with embarrassing clarity. I am erecting fitted wardrobes down the bedroom walls and I wondered if there is a soundproofing sheet which I could fit to reduce noise transmission?

A You can fit a special plasterboard sheet with soundproofing quilt attached, such as British Gypsum's Triline system. Better still, construct a separate stud wall with 50mm x 50mm timber with a 50mm gap between this and the original wall. Fill between the studs with 100mm soundproofing quilt and finish with two layers of 12.5mm plasterboard with staggered joints.

NOISE THROUGH FLOORS (1)

Q My problem is with airborne sound – television, music, loud conversation (occasional bedroom noise!) – from the flat below. Whilst not deafening, it is irritating. I live in a top-floor conversion flat of a large Edwardian terrace (conversion pre-building regulations of the early 1990s). An architect friend has suggested laying a product called Fermacell (a sandwich of dense fibreboard and insulation material) on the floorboards. This, however, will raise the floor level 30mm and will involve lifting skirting boards and, possibly, the fireplace. It is also expensive – £1500 for just one room plus the cost of redecorating and re-laying carpets. As my problem is not severe, merely irritating, can you suggest cheaper solutions?

A Airborne sound travels through gaps, so you could try sealing the gaps between your floorboards by lining the floor with hardboard, which would be a lot cheaper than the Fermacell and is only 3mm thick. Before you fix the hardboard (with serrated 20mm hardboard nails every 150mm) you might as well lift a few floorboards and put some glassfibre or mineral-wool quilt between the joists. Be careful not to bury any power cables under the quilt, but let them sit on top of it, otherwise they may overheat. After the hardboard is fitted (rough side up), seal the junction between the floor and skirting board with decorator's flexible filler applied with a mastic gun.

But before you do anything, why not see if you can get your neighbours to contribute to any proposed works. After all, I'm sure they can hear you too, and it is in both your interests to upgrade the soundproofing of your properties.

NOISE THROUGH FLOORS (2)

Q I have recently bought a rather nice flat, rebuilt from a burnt-out hotel *c*.1947. The problem is that I can hear my neighbours above change their minds. They are aware of the problem (noise goes both ways) and have had two layers of rock wool 800mm deep put between the joists underneath their floorboards and above our main bedroom ceiling. This has made a big difference and now all we can hear is their boards creaking (a bit) and their loo flushing.

Now we would like to do our bit. What can we do to insulate our ceilings without spoiling the decor? We don't mind losing a bit of height (say 200mm) and re-coving. If we are shown to be doing our bit then I think we could persuade them to do the rock-wool treatment over the remaining rooms.

Another potential problem is that they are talking of putting down a hardwood floor. That would seem to nullify all the insulation efforts. We will have to try and persuade them otherwise. Local builders don't seem to have much of a clue.

A If your upstairs neighbours are going to spend money on a new floor then this would seem like an ideal opportunity to effect a complete acoustic break, so that they put in new floor joists between your ceiling joists. You could offer to contribute to the cost, and keep your existing ceiling intact. Alternatively, they could lift their existing floorboards and lay the new ones on acoustic rubber damping strips on top of the existing joists – not as effective, though. (Details in the BRE leaflet [SOUNDPROOFING].)

FALSE CEILING

Q My builder has just attempted to improve sound-proofing in my bedroom (because of noise from the flat above). He was going to rip down the ceiling and start again with fibreglass insulation followed by a double thickness of plasterboard hung from metal strips. However, when he started to pull down the old ceiling he found, to his surprise, that it was already stuffed with fibreglass insulation. So he left the ceiling as it was and simply hung more plasterboard from metal strips, then plastered it. It hasn't made that much difference.

A The trouble with suspended ceilings is that they are hanging from the joists above, and so can act as a sounding board for transmitted sound. They only really work with new joists spanning the whole room. And whilst false ceilings can help in stopping airborne sound from the bottom flat going upwards, they are less useful the other way round. There is a lot of ignorance in the building trade about this. Extra insulation on top of the new plasterboard may have helped, but it sounds as if it's too late now.

SOUNDPROOFING AN EXISTING ROOM

new ceiling – 2 layers plasterboard / original ceiling

100mm insulation

stud wall

2 layers plasterboard

original floor

18mm chipboard

25mm rockwool

100mm insulation

10mm plasterboard

POLISHED FLOORBOARDS

Q I have bought a two-bed top-floor flat in a Victorian conversion, and I want to strip the floors, polish them and put rugs down. However, the lease states 'to cover and keep covered with carpet and underlay all floors except kitchens and bathrooms'.

Has anyone come up with a system of insulation that has an effect equal to carpet and underlay? As this is apparently a standard clause, do people either ignore the clause completely and just strip the floors, or respect it totally and stick to carpet? The sanding hire people say most people ignore it, but I do not want to upset the people downstairs.

A You are right to consider the result of your actions on your downstairs neighbours, as stripped wooden floors are a major source of irritation, and can lead to serious disputes. In your case, your lease clearly states that the floor must be carpeted, and this provision may have been imposed by the local authority when they gave planning consent and Building Regulations approval for the conversion of the property into separate flats. If you ignore this then you could find yourself on the wrong end of legal action from the neighbours and the freeholder.

There are various ways of installing soundproofing divisions between flats, but they are a lot more complicated than the scheme you describe, and are not guaranteed to be 100 per cent effective. The effect of heels on a polished timber floor can be like drumsticks on a drum, and it might be heard not just downstairs, but next door too. My advice is to accept that your flat is not suitable for bare floors, and to stick with the carpet. Console yourself with the thought that polished wood floors are a fad, and they will not always be as fashionable as they are now.

BRICK WALL

Q My neighbour proposes to have built a 6ft (1800mm) high brick wall to cut down the traffic noise. Her house is only some 20ft (6m) from her boundary with a pavement and busy road. She would ideally like to sit in her garden in the lee of the wall in some peace, but I am not sure the wall will give her the relief she expects from such a large outlay. Also, would she need permission for the wall?

A Boundary walls under 2m high (1m if within 1m of highway) do not need planning consent unless you are in a conservation area. Solid brickwork is a good direct sound blocker, although there will still be airborne sound refracted around the sides and over the top. But in general, if the wall blocks the view of the traffic then it will also block its noise. It may be possible to construct a quiet corner by returning the wall down one or both sides of the garden, as well as just along the front. Brickwork is expensive, but if built to a high standard, with an attractive facing brick, then a garden wall of this nature will also add to the value of the property.

NOISY DOOR CLOSERS

Q I live in a small block of twelve flats. The front door of the building, the doors along the passageways, and the front doors to the individual flats all have springs to close them, and the sound is like a pistol shot. Is it obligatory to have such a loud bang when a fire door shuts? We also have springs on all the internal doors. I find the kitchen door annoying and sometimes dangerous, when I have to leave the kitchen with my hands full, holding the door open with my foot. Are these also obligatory?

A Self-closing fire doors are certainly compulsory in apartment buildings, and in new houses over two storeys high, as they are designed to stop fire spreading and protect escape routes. There is a wide choice of door-closing devices, however, and unfortunately many developers opt for the cheapest ones, comprising a simple spring that accelerates the door closed until it slams. More sophisticated models have hydraulic dampers, and are adjustable, so that they close doors quietly and gently [SOUNDPROOFING]. Regarding your own internal doors, there is nothing to stop you propping them open, or even removing the door-closers. You would be well advised to keep the kitchen door closed whenever possible, however.

LAMINATE FLOORS

Q What are the current regulations regarding the installation of laminate flooring to the upper floors of blocks of flats? I live on the ground floor and the owner of the flat immediately above has installed a laminate floor. As a result all contact noises, including footsteps, are accentuated to a level which I, as an octogenarian, find disturbing. I had thought that laminate was not allowed, but I can find nothing in the leasehold agreement to back this up.

A There are no regulations covering alterations to existing dwellings, I'm afraid, unless there is a covenant in the lease. However, there is an increasing backlash against the noise problems caused by uncarpeted timber floors in apartment buildings and converted flats, and some insurers are even raising the premiums for dwellings with timber floors. Your first call should be to your local-authority Environmental Health Officer.

NEW HOUSES

Q **Our eight-year-old house has a sound-insulation problem. Over our living room are three loos in bathrooms and every sound from above is transmitted down to those sitting round the dining table or relaxing on the sofa. We have had the ceiling boards out and additional insulation put in but it has not made much difference. Have you any suggestions as to how we can resolve this embarrassing problem of the tinkle factor?**

A Unfortunately, most developer-built houses constructed in recent years have the same poor levels of sound insulation, due to the lightweight nature of the materials used. Sad to say, there is very little that can be done to rectify the situation without extensive (and expensive) building work. Stuffing mineral-wool insulation between the floor joists will have very little effect, as noise is absorbed best by dense, heavy materials, not light fluffy ones. For the same reason, a new false ceiling suspended below the existing one is unlikely to have any appreciable effect.

There are various acoustic quilt materials on the market, developed for use in recording studios and the like, and these can be effective at reducing the passage of airborne sound sideways through lightweight partition walls. But the type of noise that concerns you is largely impact sound, not airborne. The WCs upstairs are fixed directly to the floor, so the noises are transmitted as vibration through the floor joists, which are also the ceiling joists for the living room below. The plasterboard ceiling can even act as a sounding board, amplifying the noise.

The only real solution would be to create a complete acoustic break, by taking up the upstairs flooring, and inserting extra floor joists between but not touching – and slightly higher than – the existing joists. New floorboards should be laid on top of these, on acoustic rubber damping strips. Even better would be pre-cast concrete joists and a concrete slab floor. This work will be expensive and disruptive, and will necessitate complete refitting of the bathrooms, with WCs, baths and showers all taken out and re-installed on top of the new floor finish. There will also be a step-up into the bathroom where the floor changes level. It might be cheaper and easier to sell the house and buy a pre-1939 one.

CONSERVATORIES

Adding a conservatory is one of the most popular of home improvements, and the off-the-shelf conservatory industry is experiencing an unprecedented boom. In terms of adding value, however, conservatories are not always the good investment that some people assume. Estate agents and valuers report that a conservatory – even one costing many thousands of pounds – might add little or nothing to the actual sales value of a house.

Many readers have also discovered that their conservatories are too hot in the summer and too cool in the winter. The main problem is over-heating – or 'solar gain' – caused by too much sun shining on too big an area of glass. The extent of this problem can be gauged by the fact that the number of adverts for conservatories in the glossy magazines is almost equalled by those for conservatory sun blinds and air-conditioning systems. I must say that building a conservatory as a suntrap, and then paying money and using energy to cool it, has always struck me as one of the greater absurdities of the home-improvement game, but this is what many people end up doing.

The 'too much sun' part of the equation comes about through building a conservatory in the wrong place. For most houses, there is little choice about this, and the conservatory is plonked down outside the back door, whichever direction it faces. When there is a choice, many people assume that a south-facing aspect will be preferable. But researchers at Cranfield University have found that over the course of a year, a southerly orientation actually provides fewer hours of comfortable occupation than one facing north. They also found that the higher the thermal value

Fully glazed conservatories are often too hot or too cold.

of the glazing, the lower the number of comfortable hours. In other words, single glazing is better than double.

The 'too big an area of glass' is partly a design problem and partly due to the Building Regulations. Conservatories get hot because of the greenhouse effect: the sun's heat is able to pass in through the glass but, after being reflected off internal objects, has a different wavelength, and is unable to get out again. Only a small area of glass roof is required for this build-up of heat to become excessive, but in order to stop a conservatory being classed as an extension, and thus becoming liable to building control, at least 75 per cent of the roof must be glazed. So most conservatory firms, to avoid the hassle of applying for Building Regulations approval, and of having their work inspected by the Building Control Officer, do not offer any alternative to the completely glazed roof.

Another situation where the Building Control Officer should be involved, but often is not, is when a conservatory is connected to the house by means of a permanent opening, rather than a closable door. This effectively makes the conservatory part of the habitable space, and therefore, for energy-conservation reasons, imposes restrictions on the area of glass, which is limited to around one-quarter of the floor area of the whole house. In this situation, all the glass also has to conform to the latest thermal insulation standards (i.e. double-glazed with low-E glass), whereas a conservatory separated by a closing door can still be single-glazed.

The best way to keep a conservatory from overheating is ventilation. This requires vents at both low and high level, to allow a through convection current to flow. Many owners are persuaded to buy internal sun blinds, but are not told that these are ineffective without through ventilation, and can, in fact, sometimes make things worse by exacerbating the greenhouse effect described above.

Another serious problem with conservatories is that they can sometimes compromise fire-safety regulations. Even though it might not require an application for Building Regulations approval, any new conservatory added to an existing house has to be built in such a way that it does not worsen the existing fire-safety situation, specifically the means of escape, and this is the area that is causing concern. For many years now, houses have had to be built so that every bedroom has a special 'escape window' of sufficient size and shape that an adult can climb out through it, and this window is supposed to be accessible by ladder from ground level outside. Building a conservatory below one of these windows can prevent a ladder being used to access it, meaning that the room in question is effectively deprived of its emergency escape route. If you already have a conservatory beneath one of your bedroom windows, try it yourself and see. Of course, you might think that in an emergency, you could always climb out on to the roof of the conservatory, and thence make your way down to the ground. But before you try it, remember that glass or plastic conservatory roofs are themselves exempt from Building Regulations approval, and therefore unlikely to take your weight. (Further details in the 'Building Regulations Explanatory Booklet' [CONSTRUCTION LITERATURE]).

Anything else? Oh yes, it is rumoured that only 30 per cent of the price of a PVC-U conservatory covers the cost of the thing – the rest is profit and salesmen's commission. You see, the sun always shines for someone.

MISTING IN POLYCARBONATE ROOF

Q **I have condensation within the layers of my five-layer polycarbonate conservatory roof. The roofer has carried out resealing, but the problem persists.**

A This type of sheeting does not include a desiccant material, so it must be allowed to breathe. Sealing the edges will only trap moisture between the layers. All the interstices must be drained and ventilated at both ends.

CONSERVATORY TOO HOT

Q I have a modern traditional-type conservatory with a glazed pitched roof fitted with metal glazing bars. With hindsight, this should have been built as a sunroom, as it is too hot and bright in the summer and too cold in the winter. Could you recommend a form of solid roofing in place of the glass which would fit into the glazing bars and give insulation in both directions to solve the problem?

A Many readers have reported buying conservatories that turn out to be too hot or too cold to use for much of the year. The salesmen often describe a conservatory as a 'room in the garden', giving the impression that it will be habitable, but this is rarely the case. In the British climate a fully glazed conservatory is unlikely to provide more than two hours of comfortable temperature per day.

Internal sun blinds can stop the glare, but they do not reduce the 'greenhouse effect' which causes overheating, as once the sun's rays have passed through the glass, the heat is inside, and it makes no difference whether this is absorbed and re-emitted by the blinds or by the floor and furniture. The only sensible way to keep a conservatory cool in summer is to have permanent vents at low and high level, to allow a through-flow of air. As to winter usage, you should understand that the insulation value of glass is very low, and it will take a large expenditure on (mostly wasted) heating energy to make it comfortable.

Fitting a solid roof would certainly make a conservatory more usable, and you may be able to fit lightweight insulated 'sandwich' panels, some of which even have an imitation tile pattern on the top. It is unlikely that they would fit into the existing glazing bars, but would need to be mounted on their own metal purlin system (e.g. Kingspan Panels [INSULATION]). The problem with this, however, is that when your conservatory was built, it was exempt from building-control approval, and by adding a solid roof, you will technically be converting it into an extension, which *does* require building control. The first step should be to consult your local-authority Building Control Department to see what they will allow.

Conservatory sun blinds stop glare, but will not prevent overheating.

OVERHEATING

Q We have a south-facing conservatory which gets much too hot to use in summer despite having roof blinds and front blinds inside the glass. We can open the door, windows and rooflights but these really need to be closed if we go out. Would air conditioning be a solution?

A Conservatories are often too hot for comfort. Internal sun blinds are ineffective without through ventilation. The problem is that once the sun's rays have passed through the glass, then the heat is inside, and it makes no difference to the internal temperature whether this is absorbed and re-emitted by the blinds, or by the floor and furniture.

I suggest you try to get permanent low-level vents fitted in the walls and/or doors and investigate the possibility of locking the rooflights in an open position, so that you can leave them open when you go out. Of course, the advisability of this would depend on whether you have a lockable door between the conservatory and the house, otherwise you could compromise your insurance cover.

The idea of building a conservatory as a sun-trap and then installing air conditioning to cool it has always struck me as slightly crazy.

ROOF LEAKING

Q I have a largish conservatory. It is well constructed with sealed double-glazed units set in wooden frames, but the roof leaks. The glass roof panels have been put in traditional glazing bars on a putty bed and then fastened in with wooden strips also bedded in putty and then painted. I have in mind to fix some sort of a covering strip spanning the wooden glazing bar and lapping the glass on each side, but can't find anything suitable.

A I am afraid your conservatory has been completely wrongly glazed. Whatever you cover the joints with, water will still find its way down the sides of the sealed glazed units (SGUs) and, worse, will be trapped there, leading to premature internal misting. The only worthwhile solution would be to take the glass out, scrape away the old putty, and re-bed the glass on load-bearing glazing tape, leaving drainage channels between the edges of the glass and the glazing bars. The timber beading should also be fixed to the glazing bars using the tape (which is sticky on both sides). That way, air will be able to circulate all round the edges of the SGUs, and any water that does get in will be able to drain out without attacking the seals.

CONSERVATORY TOO COLD

Q Heating our new conservatory during the winter months seems difficult beyond belief. It's 4 metres square, has a glass roof and is north facing. A radiator has been fitted running off the main central-heating system, but that does no more than take the chill off. Do you have any suggestions? We want to be able to use the conservatory all year round.

A A conservatory is basically a glass box, which is largely transparent to transmitted heat. So it will warm up rapidly when the sun shines and cool down just as rapidly when it doesn't. The insulation value of glass is very low, and if you want to heat your conservatory during the winter months, then you will waste a lot of energy and money. In the British climate, a conservatory is unlikely to provide more than two hours of comfortable temperature per day, and using it as a habitable space will require a large expenditure on either air cooling or heating.

HARDWOOD ROT

Q In 1994 I had a conservatory supplied and erected by Wickes. It was described in the brochure as being made of hardwood. I have followed all the maintenance suggestions given by the company, and treated the timber regularly with Wickes' own branded product, as originally supplied by the installers. Recently I had to have five of the twelve double-glazed window units replaced because of misting. However, the removal of the old units revealed severe and widespread rot in the timber which could not be seen until then.

I complained to Wickes and their reply was that the five-year guarantee had expired, and they could assist me in no way at all. The local tradesman who replaced the windows and drew my attention to the rotten wood said that the original windows had been fitted in an odd way using rubber flaps rather than sealant. It seems odd to me that Wickes can, in effect, say that a building can fall down five years after they put it up and they can wash their hands of it. Plus, what is 'hardwood' supposed to mean? I had hardwood on my boat, both above and below the water-line, and it was as good as new when I sold it at getting on for twenty-five years old.

A There is nothing intrinsic in 'hardwood' that means it won't rot if it gets wet. Hardwood is really a botanical term, for timber from deciduous trees, to distinguish it from 'softwood' which comes from coniferous trees. Balsa wood – as used to make model aircraft – is classified as a hardwood, for example, as is Meranti – a red tropical hardwood widely used for building products, but which is chosen for its appearance rather than its durability. Good-quality resinous pine (a 'softwood') will usually withstand moisture attack much better. I have spoken to Wickes and the company says that it markets its conservatories as being made of hardwood only as a factual description, not to imply any superior performance characteristics.

The fact that your conservatory windows have suffered premature internal misting would suggest that it was probably poorly glazed, using methods that do not comply with British Standard BS6262. However, there is no obligation on suppliers to conform to British Standards unless they were part of any contract or documentation at the time. I would have thought it unlikely that you have any legal case, and Wickes insists that it has done nothing wrong in declining to replace or repair a product beyond its five-year guarantee period. However, the company says that in this case it is prepared to see what it can do to help you.

CONSERVATORIES

DRIVES, PATIOS & OUTSIDE JOBS

Having a drive in front of your house can be a great boon, and most motorists who live in terraced town houses would love to have the private off-street parking that a drive represents. However, a drive is like a small private road, and like a road it needs a certain amount of maintenance – cleaning and occasional resurfacing. All drive surfaces need diligent below-ground preparation if they are to last and cracking, crumbling concrete or tarmac is often a symptom of shoddy construction.

Of the various choices of surfaces, gravel is the most luxurious, but also the most expensive, and requires annual raking and weed-killing. Concrete is probably the hardest wearing and lowest maintenance. A good professionally laid concrete drive could easily last for fifty years. Shame it looks so ugly.

Pattern-imprinted concrete needs cleaning and resealing every few years. Tarmac is the most likely to be installed by cowboys and anyway, like tarmac roads, after a few years it breaks up and has to be resurfaced. Brick and concrete block paving looks nice, and is easy to dig up and re-lay damaged areas, but it can be slippery when wet, and weeds grow in the joints.

Mosses and lichens will grow on all surfaces, especially badly drained ones (i.e. those with an insufficient slope for surface water to run off) and in shaded locations. If they bother you, then scrub them off with a stiff yard broom, or commit yourself to a lifetime of applying proprietary path and patio cleaner-type herbicidal chemicals. I don't fancy them myself.

New homes are now having to be built with smaller areas of hard paving – to limit the surface water run-off going into the main drains – and grass block paving (where grass grows in gaps in plastic or concrete pavers) looks set to be a big seller. Maintenance is as easy as mowing the lawn.

So you pay your money and take your choice. But if you're getting a new drive installed, then the most important things to look out for are proper sub-surface preparation and attention to drainage. Rather than answer a newspaper advert by a nationwide drive company (which will only pass your details on to a regional franchisee), you would be better contacting local groundwork contractors through the Yellow Pages. Get them to give you a detailed written specification of what they propose to do.

Drives are like icebergs. The most important part is below the surface.

WHICH DRIVE SURFACE?

Q I have been given conflicting advice regarding my drive, which has quite a steep slope down to the garage. One contractor (who does either tarmac or block paving) recommended the tarmac, as it would give better grip during icy weather, but the second contractor (who only does block paving) disagreed, saying he thought the opposite was the case.

A And if you asked a contractor who did gravel drives, no doubt he would recommend his product as being better. Actually, he might have a case, although from the sound of it, you might have to keep sweeping the gravel out of your garage. A fourth possibility is perforated plastic 'grass blocks', which you back-fill with soil and plant with grass seed. If icy weather conditions are really a big problem in your area, then this may be a solution. But otherwise, I think you should decide which surface you prefer, in terms of appearance and cost, and keep a bag of road salt in the garage for those few days every winter when it might be needed.

PATTERN-IMPRINTED CONCRETE

Q Our front garden is covered with compressed smooth concrete, indented to resemble cobbles. Alas, the colour (black) was not incorporated in the concrete but sprayed on afterwards. This peeled off and subsequent repainting with aggregated exterior floor paint is wearing off under traffic. As it is pointless to repaint flaky paint, could the very smooth concrete be roughened to hold paint, or is there any other suitable treatment?

A This type of patterned driveway is made from fibre-reinforced aerated concrete, with an impression of bricks or cobbles being rolled into the top as it hardens. The surface colouring is usually trowelled into the top, so that two-tone effects can be achieved, but also because colouring the concrete right through would be expensive. Once the top wearing surface has been worn away, there is really nothing that can be done to patch it up. As you have discovered, paint or any other surface coating will simply wear away or flake off. Thousands of people have had these drives installed, often under the impression that they would be 'maintenance free', and were not told that they would need to have the surface resealed every three to five years (at a cost of £600 to £800) to prevent the colour wearing off. Your options are to have the damaged areas repaired by a specialist contractor, or to cut your losses and have it dug up and replaced with a more perma-nent surface, such as block paving.

BLOCK-PAVED DRIVE

Q **Two years ago I had my drive block paved. The builder raised the drive level to within one brick of the damp-proof course. Am I likely to have problems later?**

A External ground surfaces are supposed to be kept at least 150mm (6ins – or two brick courses) below damp-proof course (DPC) level in order to stop rain splashing off the ground and wetting the wall above the DPC. As long as your drive surface is still one brick course below DPC, and if the front wall is reasonably sheltered from driving rain, then this is unlikely to give you any imme-diate problems. Unfortunately, it does not say a great deal about the knowledge or workmanship of the 'builder' who did the work. The first step in constructing any drive or path should be to remove the existing surface and excavate down to a suitable level to receive a new sub-base. Laying block paving on top of an existing surface is very poor practice.

RAISING GROUND LEVEL WITH DRIVE

Q **We are planning on having our crumbling driveway and soggy front lawn replaced with imprinted concrete to make a much larger drive and parking area. We live in a 1930s bunga-low with a double row of blue bricks as the damp-proof course. The upper row was drilled and injected to improve damp proofing on the recommendation of the building society's surveyor before we moved in. The salesman suggested that the slope on the lawn, which is towards the bungalow, could be reduced a little if the surface of the concrete was raised. This would bring it up to the level of our porch and to the lower edge of the double blue bricks of the damp-proof course. Drainage would still be needed and this is proposed to be along the front wall (and around the bay windows). At the moment all paths, garden, etc., are 6ins (150mm) below the blue bricks. Is having the concrete this high a good idea?**

A On no account should you allow anyone to raise your exter-nal ground levels. This will result in nothing but problems (see DAMPNESS). You have already been ripped off once by paying for an unnecessary DPC injection – there is no way that a double course of Staffordshire Blue engineering bricks could allow dampness to rise and, equally, they could not possibly be 'improved' by chemical injection.

Raising ground levels with a drive or patio can lead to dampness problems inside.

GRAVEL DRIVES

Q **Have you any advice on creating a gravel drive? Gravel is all the rage round us, but my neighbours' drives seem to be just piles of shingle tipped out over their existing driveways. Every time they move their cars pebbles spill out over the road, creating a hazard to the windscreens of passing vehicles. How should one lay a gravel drive to avoid this?**

A A properly constructed gravel drive is like an iceberg, in that 90 per cent of it is out of sight below the surface. The top layer should be only two layers of gravel thick, stuck into bitumen, and none of it should be finding its way on to the public highway. The preparatory work should be the same as for any drive – excavate 250mm of soil, line with a geotextile, roll in 150mm of Type 1 road-stone and 75mm of Type 2 hoggin, each of which has to be carefully compacted with a vibrating roller. Then comes the hot bitumen and the final gravel surfacing.

Unfortunately, as you say, many people's idea of making a gravel drive is to order a truckload of pea shingle and spread it over an existing drive. This might look good for a few weeks, but will quickly disintegrate as the stones are either pushed down into the soil, or scattered around the garden by spinning car wheels. Like many other construction operations, finished appearances can be deceptive, and mask a lot of preparation work. A gravel drive is not a DIY job, and specifications and quotes should be obtained from experienced groundwork contractors. The cost, for a straight single drive, will be in the region of £50 per square metre, so a simple straight run up to the house, twice the length of your car, might set you back around £1000.

GEOTEXTILES

Q **You have referred to the use of a geotextile (e.g. for lining drives and soakaways). Is this a heavy-duty plastic membrane which is porous to water transfer, such as those sold in garden centres which suppress weeds and roots? I would like to know a little more about this product and who manufactures or supplies it.**

A 'Geotextile' is a fairly loose term which covers a number of different products. The ones I have referred to are used to line excavations for drives or other below-ground installations, with the purpose of allowing water to escape downwards, but preventing soil and silt from percolating upwards. Geotextiles can also be used to strengthen weak soils, and stabilize steep slopes, such as those at the sides of road embankments. And yes, there are also versions used to suppress weed growth and allow young hedge plants to get a head start. For further details call Geosynthetics [PAVING].

TARMAC

Q **Some time ago, together with several neighbours, I had my drive surfaced with tarmac by a company no longer in business. At the time we were all happy with the result. However, the surface of the tarmac now appears to be crumbling where the edge meets the pavement. Is there a product available on the market that can be applied to seal the surface, or have we all been caught out and bought an inferior product?**

A 'Tarmac' is a name that is somewhat loosely applied to a number of bituminous surfacing materials. The quality and grade vary hugely, as do the skill and diligence with which they are applied. The preparatory work should be the same as for any drive, and the tarmac finish should comprise two layers with a total thickness of at least 50mm, applied hot, and rolled in with a heavy roller.

Cowboy firms often just spread a thin layer over hardcore, or on top of the existing surface, and don't roll it hard enough. Then it can start to break up after the first winter's frosts. There is not much point trying to stick it back down with anything if the foundation is inadequate, although some readers have recommended sealing crumbling tarmac with resin, a process which is apparently used in tennis-court construction.

SECTION THROUGH A DRIVE

tarmac

hoggin

road stone

geotexttile

GRASS PAVING BLOCKS

Q I have been trying to trace a supply of perforated blocks which have grass growing out of the holes, but which allow cars to be driven across them. The local garden centres and builders' merchants have not heard of them despite the local council using something similar on road verges. Where can I find these elusive blocks please?

A There are several types of grass-paving systems, which allow cars to be driven across or parked on grassy areas without sinking. Councils often use perforated concrete blocks, but the new plastic versions are lighter, easier to lay, and accommodate a larger area of grass. Grass-paving systems are likely to become more widely used as regulations require new homes to have more car-parking spaces, and the environmental rules on surface drainage are tightened up. Two suppliers are Hoofmark Ltd and Hauraton [PAVING].

Note, however, that none of these systems produces a really satisfactory grass surface. The perforated concrete blocks seem to dry the ground out, so that the grass turns brown quickly in dry weather, and the plastic paving systems hold the water, leading to moss growth.

CONVERTING FRONT GARDEN

Q I am thinking about using my front garden as a car-parking space. What are the legal requirements for doing this?

A You will have to consult your local-authority highways department. On minor roads there is usually no problem, as long as traffic will not be emerging on to the road in an area of restricted visibility. However, on a 'classified' road – a principal road or bus route – planning permission may be needed. You will then have to pay the local authority to drop the kerb and rebuild the footpath as a ramp, and you will be liable for any costs incurred by the utilities companies for re-routing or ducting service pipes or cables. The total cost could reach several hundred pounds, although some local authorities offer special deals, usually when they are resurfacing the road.

WASHED-OUT GROUT

Q I have used a power washer to remove the accumulated grime from our patio paving slabs, and this has flushed out some of the mortar from between the slabs as well. Is there an easy way of replacing this – can a suitable mix be brushed dry into the gaps and then wetted with a watering can, or must I go back to a more tiring pre-mixing of the mortar and subsequent hands-and-knees job with a small trowel? And what is the best mix to use?

A Power washers are useful tools, but care is needed when using them on building materials, as the destructive effect of the water jet can be surprisingly large. They can easily blast mortar away, take the faces off soft red bricks, and even damage PVC-U door and window frames. If you want to make a mortar that will withstand future pressure washing, you will need to use a strong (3:1) sand/cement mix, applied wet, and compacted firmly into the joints. A brushed-in dry mix will never set as hard. But the easiest solution would be simply to brush in dry sand, and to go easy on the pressure washing.

CONCRETE PATIO BREAKING UP

Q Last spring we laid a new patio which was constructed in two sections, laid on hardcore and finished with ready-mixed concrete. Our problem now is that one half is perfect but the other has completely broken up and appears to have reverted to ballast. The weather conditions were dry at the time and the sections were laid within a few days of each other. The builder considers that the concrete supplied by the ready-mix supplier was at fault. I would be most grateful for your comments.

A I am interested in your observation that the weather conditions were dry at the time the concrete was laid, and that it was poured on top of hardcore. Fresh concrete needs to be kept wet for at least a week (and preferably for twenty-eight days) in order to achieve full strength, which results from a chemical reaction between the cement and the water. The correct procedure is to cover the hardcore base with a 2-inch layer of sand blinding, and spread a polyethylene sheet membrane on top of this. The concrete is placed on top of the polyethylene, and in dry weather it should be covered with hessian and sprayed with water. Sandwiched between the membrane and the damp hessian, the concrete will be able to cure properly. Without either, it will probably have dried out before curing could occur. If your builder still thinks the ready-mix concrete suppliers are at fault, then there is a British Standard test that can be used to determine the mix proportions.

RUST MARKS ON PATIO

Q My cast-iron patio furniture has stained the paving slabs. I've cured the source of the problem by painting the feet of the table and chairs with a bitumen-based product but the rust marks have defied all attempts to remove them.

A You could try brick-cleaning acid if it really bothers you, but it seems a bit drastic and you may end up with clean patches that stand out as much as the rust stains!

CAST-IRON RAILINGS

Q I have bought some old Victorian railings to fix on top of my front garden wall, to restore it to its original style. I note that the original railings (presumably removed during the Second World War metal-salvage campaign) appear to have been bedded in some sort of lead or metal compound. My builder seems to think this is old fashioned and unnecessary, and that he can fix the railings into drilled holes and fill the holes with cement. Other people say this will lead to corrosion. What is the correct method, and who can I engage to do the work properly?

A Old cast-iron (or modern steel) railings should be set in lead, for two reasons. One is that the lead helps stops the iron from rusting. The other is that the lead is soft, and helps to absorb thermal expansion movement, which might otherwise crack the wall which the railings are set into. Melting and pouring lead is not difficult, and you – or your builder – should be able to find a local roofer or metalworker who has the necessary gas burner and crucible.

BRICK PAVING

Q We have a small patio and are considering replacing the boring concrete slabs with brick. To help give a more mature look we would like to use reclaimed bricks, but I am wondering if they would be satisfactory for that purpose, in terms of both wear and safety when wet. I would also like to know whether bedding in sand only would work, as seems to be used for what I believe are called paviours.

A Reclaimed bricks can look great as a surface for paths and patios. House bricks vary enormously in strength and frost resistance, depending on the type of clay and the firing temperature, and the best thing to do would be to ask advice from a good demolition yard. I have used red Victorian wire-cuts for a variety of garden projects in the past, and they have performed very well. Bedding paving bricks on coarse sharp sand rather than concrete or mortar is good practice, as it allows water to drain away without the need for dedicated gulleys or drain runs.

TREES & PLANTS

Buildings and trees have an interesting relationship. On the one hand, most people like seeing mature trees, as they have a softening impact on the urban landscape, and are homes for insect and bird life. On the other, trees have recently become demonized by insurance societies following a series of expensive subsidence claims. As a result, surveyors are now very quick to recommend 'further investigation' of trees near houses, and some arboriculturists (tree surgeons) are quick to recommend felling. The surveyors' and insurers' main fear is that

Ivy can cause serious damage to buildings.

as a tree grows, its roots will extract increasing quantities of water from the soil, causing drying shrinkage and subsidence. In reality, subsidence and cracking that can be directly attributed to the presence of a tree is extremely rare. There is always seasonal drying and shrinkage in soils, anyway, but trees seem to get the blame for this whether they are guilty or not. And there are many cases where trees have stood for a century or more within touching distance of a house without causing any damage at all.

Decisions on whether mature trees should be removed or left standing should be taken only after joint consultation between an arboricultural consultant and a structural engineer – the one to assess the condition of the tree and its roots, and the other to look at how these factors are likely to affect the building. If a mature tree has historic or landscape value, then there are simple steps that can be taken to prevent its roots from damaging a building, and keeping the tree may actually add more to the value of the property than removing it. For further advice call The Tree Care Company [TREES].

SURVEYOR SAYS CUT IT DOWN

Q **The surveyor's report on my London house drew attention to a sycamore tree in the garden, and recommended that it should be felled. But there are no signs of cracking in the property and I am reluctant to cut down a beautiful mature tree, which also shades the garden from the southern sun. Is there any evidence that trees actually damage buildings?**

A The idea that trees and buildings don't go together is greatly overstated, but surveyors are paranoid about being sued for negligence, so they prefer to recommend their removal. The fear comes from the idea that tree roots extract water from the subsoil, and where this is shrinkable clay – i.e. in London and most of southern England – then it can result in shrinkage, foundation movement, and subsidence. In reality, more subsidence is caused by leaking drains making the subsoil wet and plastic, but since this is happening out of sight below ground it generally gets overlooked. Trees are a more obvious target. Local authorities often prune or pollard trees because of their supposed threat to buildings, but some experts say that this is pointless, and just makes the tree grow faster and extract more ground water in order to recover.

If your house has shallow foundations, and is sited on genuine shrinkable clay, then there is a possibility that it might contribute to drying and shrinkage of the ground. But then again, there are many situations where mature trees are growing close to buildings, and causing no apparent problems at all. Ironically, cutting down a mature tree on a shrinkable clay subsoil can sometimes even cause cracking where none existed before. This is because the tree, the soil and the house are existing in equilibrium, but when the tree is removed, the excess water causes the subsoil to expand, pushing the foundations upwards. And even when a tree *is* found to be contributing to soil movement, there might be ways of lessening the damage without cutting down the tree – for example by reinforcing the foundations and/or inserting root barriers.

So every case has to be investigated individually, with a trained arboriculturist acting, where necessary, in tandem with a structural engineer to assess likely damage to the building.

Trees and buildings can co-exist happily together.

Condemned – another tree takes the blame.

DAMAGE FROM ROOTS

Q Surface roots from a neighbour's tree are damaging the surface of my drive. Is the neighbour liable for this damage? Would I need their permission to root prune?

A You are free to prune whatever grows on your side of the fence – as is the case with overhanging foliage – as long as the tree is not protected by a tree-preservation order. But it would be a shame if your pruning damaged the tree or made it fall over. Younger trees have more chance of recovery following root pruning than mature ones. If the roots are really causing damage to a particular structure, then the best bet would be to dig a narrow trench next to the building, cutting through the roots, as deep as you can manage, and drop a sheet of thick polythene down it. Tree roots grow towards moisture, so they'll turn back when they hit an impermeable barrier.

VIRGINIA CREEPER

Q Our 1958 house has a large Virginia creeper covering the front and side walls up to roof level. I am concerned that this plant may cause damage to the mortar between the bricks, although I have seen no evidence of this so far. In general, is it a good idea to have such a plant attaching itself to the walls or would I be better advised to remove it?

181

A The term 'Virginia creeper' can apply to more than one species. But in general this type of plant does not damage masonry, unlike ivy, which roots in the mortar joints.

NEW TREES & NEW HOUSE

Q I have bought a house on a new development that has a small paved and planted front garden containing three wild cherry trees, each about 3–4m tall, some 1.5–3m from the house front wall. As the trees develop will they pose a threat to the house foundations?

A Modern houses are built with deep concrete foundations, which are often supported by piles, and are most unlikely to be affected by trees. Count yourself lucky to have a new home with established trees already in place.

THREAT FROM NEW TREES

Q Some years ago the roots from a neighbour's willow tree travelled about 50 feet under my garage floor and into my main drain, resulting in a lot of damage and expense. I am now having trouble convincing my local council that the twenty willow trees they have planted on a bank about 15 feet from my front door are likely to cause similar trouble. I have had a letter from the council assuring me I have nothing to worry about. I would like to confront them with written evidence from an expert, but my problem is where to find one.

A There is a high level of ignorance about the relationship between trees and buildings. On the one hand, many homeowners and surveyors wrongly believe that all trees cause soil shrinkage and subsidence damage; on the other, genuine problems caused by fast-growing species such as willow and poplar are often ignored in the belief that all trees are beneficial. The fact is that every situation needs to assessed individually by a trained arboriculturist, acting, where necessary, in tandem with a structural engineer. For advice contact The Tree Care Company [TREES].

OAK ON CLAY SOIL

Q My bungalow is built on clay subsoil, and I am worried about trees drying out the clay and causing subsidence. I have a large oak some 20 yards from my property, and have now instructed a 'tree doctor', who tells me he will prune it by some 20 per cent. Will this have the desired effect of reducing the amount of water consumed by the oak?

A Pruning or pollarding trees has very little effect on the amount of water they consume. Some experts say that the tree responds to the shock of pruning by actually growing faster in order to recover. Oak trees do present a greater risk than some other species, but 20 yards (18 metres) would seem to be a fair distance away, and at the limit of the likely zone of influence. Tables for the preferred distances away from buildings for different tree species are given in BRE Digest 298 [CONSTRUCTION LITERATURE].

MODERN HOUSES & SELF-BUILD

We are accustomed to the fact that as the years go by, things get better. Health care, transport, communications – all these have improved ten-fold over the last hundred years. So it is only natural to expect that the homes built today will, similarly, be superior to those built in the Victorian and Edwardian eras. Sadly, this is not the case. The reasons for this are complex, but the underlying problem is that whilst a particular model of car, say, undergoes a constant process of year-on-year refinement, each individual car is only expected to last for five to seven years. So the manufacturer knows that if he is to achieve brand loyalty, and persuade satisfied customers to come back for more of the same, then he had better provide good after-sales care, and make sure that next year's model is better than last year's. Homes are not like that. They are expected to last for at least forty years, or a lifetime, whichever is the longer. And nobody buys a house because of the name of the builder – they buy it because of its location. So the builder knows that no matter how well he builds a property, he is never going to achieve brand loyalty or get customers coming back for another one in a few years' time. So he might as well build it as cheaply as possible and maximize his profits.

This philosophy is reinforced by the Building Regulations which govern new construction work. The Building Regulations lay down a set of minimum standards, but since modern speculative house-builders build to the minimum anyway, they build to the requirements of the Building Regulations and not a jot more. Which is why modern houses are often flimsy, noisy and hard to heat. This often comes as a shock to people whose lifetime dream has been to buy a wonderful new house, which needs no repairs and minimal maintenance. What they often get is cracking

Most modern houses are built to the minimum possible standards.

plasterboard walls and ceilings, creaking floors and second-rate plumbing. And a builder or developer who has no interest in coming back to repair faults.

Many new homeowners are provided with a ten-year warranty from the National House-Building Council (NHBC), and are disappointed when they discover that its long-term cover is only for structural defects, and not internal cracks, binding doors or constantly blocking waste pipes. The NHBC warranty is somewhat unique in that it is an insurance policy taken out by the builder, but paid for by the customer as part of the house price. If owners had to take out the policy themselves, then they might take more care to read the small print first, but then that's probably why it is done that way.

On the other hand, for those prepared to build their own homes, and who will not be trying to cut corners, modern techniques and materials mean that a very high-quality product can be built for the same or lower cost than the price of an off-the-shelf house from a speculative builder. The self-build home market in Britain is growing every year, and it has never been easier for ordinary people to build a real dream home.

LEAKY WALLS

Q My house is two years old and very well constructed to the latest standards (I assume!) except that where the plasterboard dry lining is punctured, e.g. by pipes coming through the wall under the bath, there is a tremendous draught. Surely this is not correct. On the outside wall there are narrow vertical plastic vents at first-floor level; my neighbour believes these are vents into the void between the inner wall and the liner, but if that is correct then any wind will penetrate into the house via areas like the bathroom?

A The extent of the problem depends upon whether it is a timber-framed house, or just plasterboard stuck on to the inner block leaf of a conventional cavity wall. The vents are weep holes, situated along the top of the cavity-tray lintels. They are not there to ventilate the cavity. The draught is clearly due to some very poor construction quality, and the first thing you should do is give the builder the opportunity to rectify it. You need to engage an independent professional to make sure the work is done properly, though. You don't just want a dollop of foam gunned in to fill the gaps.

NHBC PROBLEMS

Q In my nine-year-old house the connection from a washbasin has been plumbed in downstream of a WC and protrudes about 70mm into the 100-mm soil pipe. This causes frequent blockages and build-up of sewage. The builders and the National House-Building Council have declined to take any action to correct the faulty plumbing. Can you suggest any way in which I can get some action from the builders or the NHBC?

A After an initial two-year 'snagging' period, the NHBC ten-year Buildmark warranty covers only structural faults. And new houses are not even covered by the normal legal protection of the Sale of Goods Acts. If you buy a car or a stereo system then you would be protected by statutory rights, but, unbelievably, property – the biggest single investment most of us ever make – is not covered by the Act. The NHBC trumpets its warranty as being some kind of wonderful consumer protection but it is in fact a simple insurance policy, taken out by the builder but passed on to (and paid for by) the customer. And what many homebuyers fail to appreciate is that it is really only an insurance against the builder ceasing to trade. As long as the builder is still trading, you have to take up the problems with him, and try to persuade him to rectify them. Only if he ceases trading, or steadfastly refuses to act, will the NHBC warranty come into effect. And, like all insurance policies, the decision on what to pay out for in claims is determined solely by the insurer. Your problem is not untypical.

A big problem is that chartered surveyors often advise purchasers that the existence of an NHBC warranty means that a full building survey will not be needed. This can be a big mistake.

SELF-BUILD

Q **I'd like to build my own house (or more accurately contract a builder to do it) but have no real idea where to start. Can you offer any advice?**

A Building your own house is a great idea. It is the norm in many European countries, unlike in Britain where the market is dominated by volume house-builders. You can engage an architect to design it and run the operation for you or, if you want to save some money and have a more hands-on experience, there are three monthly self-build magazines – *SelfBuild*, *Build It*, and *Home Building & Renovating* – an annual show, and a host of self-help books. Some of these are heavily slanted towards timber-frame construction, and it is important to realize that this is still unproven technology in the British climate. Other trendy self-build systems include hay bales, rammed earth, and pouring concrete into pre-formed polystyrene formwork. Remember, however, that traditional brick-and-block construction is tried-and-tested, and well understood by builders. It can provide just as much insulation value as any other method, with the added advantage of good thermal mass.

Start your research by reading *Building Your Own Home* [CONSTRUCTION LITERATURE].

SELF BUILD: TIMBER FRAME

Q **I am considering buying a piece of land to build my own house on. Whilst staying with friends over in the States I have been very impressed with their timber-framed houses. A big plus is they seem to be relatively easy to erect. What are the downsides and are there any reputable UK suppliers, or do I have to import direct from USA?**

A There are lots of 'kit' houses available from British and European suppliers for self-builders. Most of them are timber-framed, which is OK as long as they are assembled to a very high standard, but remember, a timber-framed house that performs well in Scandinavia, Germany or North America may not do as well in the damp, temperate British climate. Cold climates are dry climates; the UK climate is moderate, maritime and comparatively damp.

TIMBER-FRAMED HOUSES

Q **We are constantly being told that timber-framed houses are superior to (i.e. better insulated than) brick houses. If this is the case, why do we not see them being built everywhere?**

A A significant proportion of new houses being built are timber-framed, but developers do not seem keen to advertise the fact, because of problems that have been associated with this method of construction in the past. They are mostly clad on the outside with brickwork, and many owners are under the impression that they have bought a brick house.

The insulation is right on the inside, next to the living space. This allows them to warm up quicker and makes them appear better insulated than masonry construction. Unfortunately, the part of the frame on the cold side of the insulation stays cold, and is therefore prone to condensation. It is therefore vital that there is a perfectly installed vapour barrier on the warm side of the insulation, to stop water vapour produced by the occupants from crossing to the cold side and condensing, where it could cause the frame to rot. Very often the vapour barrier is inexpertly installed, or punctured by electricians and plumbers, who do not understand its importance. It is essential that the building contractor understands these principles and supervises the work accordingly.

The thermal insulation quality of timber-framed houses is not so much a product of the frame itself, as of the thickness of insulation built into it. New brick-and-block houses can conform to exactly the same thermal insulation standards, and also have greater thermal mass, meaning that they do not cool down so quickly when the heating is turned off, and are not so prone to overheating in the summer. They are likely to have better structural and sound insulation qualities as well.

The really big controversy with timber frame, however, concerns fires. Timber-frame aficionados point out that all houses have timber floors and roofs, and that house fires can occur in any type of construction. But a timber-frame house is only fire-safe when the last piece of the frame has been encased with plasterboard. Until this is done, and whenever the frame is opened up in the course of renovation or alteration work, it is much more of a fire hazard than a brick-and-block house will ever be.

Timber frame fire on a building site in east London.

HOW TO IDENTIFY TIMBER-FRAMED HOUSES

Q If I was looking around a house with a view to buying it, is there any easy way to determine if the property is in fact timber-framed? I could of course ask the vendor, but they might not wish to tell me.

A They might not know, either. One survey revealed that over 70 per cent of owners of timber-framed homes had no idea of the fact. Because they are usually clad externally with brickwork, most owners assume that they are living in a brick house.

In a timber-framed house, all the internal wall surfaces are lined with plasterboard, and sound hollow when tapped. Some brick-and-block houses are also lined with plasterboard ('dry lining') but this doesn't sound quite so hollow, and is sometimes only done on visible surfaces, not in the backs of airing cupboards, behind kitchen units, etc. The sure-fire way is to look in the roof space – in brick-and-block houses the gable walls will be bare blockwork; in timber-frame they will be plasterboard.

OUTSIDE TAP IN TIMBER FRAME HOUSE

Q I wish to install an outside tap – teed off from an internal pipe – in a timber-framed house. I have been told that this is not recommended as it will perforate the membrane.

A Modern timber-framed houses should not be confused with traditional oak-framed English vernacular buildings (such as the famous 'black and white' Herefordshire cottages). Modern houses often have a brick outer leaf built in front of a 100mm x 50mm timber stud wall, lined internally with plasterboard. In order to stop condensation occurring in the cold space between the brick wall and the timber, and causing wood rot in the frame, it is important that there is a continuous, uninterrupted vapour barrier below the surface of the plasterboard. This is usually a sheet of polyethylene, and it has to be carefully sealed around the edges of anything that punctures it, such as electrical wiring or plumbing pipes.

TIMBER-FRAMED WALL

(labels: stud wall; plasterboard; vapour barrier; insulation; plywood sheathing; DPM; wall ties; brick outer leaf; foundations)

STEEL-FRAMED HOUSE

Q I am buying a 1960s holiday bungalow, and the survey has revealed it to be built with a steel frame. The mortgage lender describes this as 'non-traditional construction' and it sounds doubtful whether they will lend money on it. I like the position of the property, but would it be too much of a risk to buy?

A Most steel-framed houses have actually performed well, and have a good reputation with engineers. Larger mortgage lenders are often suspicious of non-traditional (i.e. non-brick) houses, but if you shop around, you will probably find a building society prepared to consider it. You may need to commission a building survey from a specialist Building Engineer or Chartered Building Surveyor who is familiar with this type of construction in the area.

WALL FIXINGS FOR PLASTERBOARD

Q My son has moved into a five-year-old house and although the external walls feel solid when tapped, the internal walls sound hollow, as though they are constructed of little more than plasterboard. Apart from having a sinking feeling that corners have been cut in the construction process, I would like to know how to hang a heavy mirror without bringing the wall down.

A British houses have always been built with timber stud partitions. Pre-1939 they were clad with timber laths and plastered with thick lime-and-sand plaster, which gave them a more solid feel.

Post-war, plasterboard has generally been used. Although they sound flimsy when tapped, plasterboard walls can take surprisingly large weights if the load is spread and the right fixings are used. Self-drilling nylon or alloy plasterboard fixings are designed to hold mirrors and large pictures.

NEW SWITCH & SOCKET POSITION

Q The power sockets on the walls of our new house are quite high up – about 450mm from the floor – and the light switches are approximately in the middle of the door height. We were told that there is now a European law which says this is the requirement, in case the occupant is disabled. Is this true?

A There is no 'European law' about this, but the latest Building Regulations require all new homes to be accessible for wheelchair users and other disabled people (and remember that most of us experience a disability or immobility problems at some time in our lives). If you really don't like the position of the switches and sockets, then you can get them relocated after you have bought the house, or add additional switches and sockets at your preferred height.

SOUNDPROOFING

Q My husband and I have moved into a block of retirement flats built four years ago by a reputable builder. We are pleased with the size of the rooms, apart from the pokey kitchen. However, we were a bit miffed, to say the least, to find that the internal walls of the flats are made of hollow plasterboard, even the wall between our living room and that of our very deaf neighbour. Is this acceptable building practice these days, and is there anything we can do to improve the sound insulation?

A Many new houses and flats are now being built with a timber-frame construction, and this often extends to the party walls between dwellings. Apart from the noise problem, this can also present a security risk, as a burglar in one property only has to kick through two sheets of plasterboard to get through to next door. The government had promised to clamp down on the sound-insulation problem by introducing compulsory random testing, but they back-tracked on this two years ago under pressure from the developers, and left it up to the builders to use 'robust standard details' to prevent the transmission of sound. The Building Research Establishment produce a leaflet on remedial measures that can be taken to soundproof existing homes [SOUNDPROOFING].

BUILDERS

Probably the most frequently asked readers' question is, 'How can I find a good builder?' The answer is that there is no foolproof way. There is one professional body – the Chartered Institute of Building (CIOB) – that represents degree-level construction professionals who, in the main, work for reputable contractors. Unfortunately for the readers of this book, these contractors work mostly on large commercial and industrial developments, and are not interested in small domestic repair and maintenance work, even though this accounts for around 50 per cent of the total market. However, the CIOB do operate a scheme called the Chartered Building Company Scheme, to put householders in touch with small- to medium-sized construction companies, and there have been recent moves to expand and promote this [BUILDING ORGANIZATIONS].

From there on down we are talking about trade associations. These generally claim to check members' financial standing and professional repute, but this is often perfunctory and does not confer any legal protection upon verbal agreements entered into with its members. Always bear in mind the old saying about trade associations – that they exist to protect their members from the public.

The best way to protect yourself against shoddy workmanship is to have a signed contract with your builder, and then you are both covered by civil law. There is a simple Joint Contracts Tribunal (JCT) document called 'Building contract for a homeowner/occupier' which can be bought from the Construction Confederation for £10.99 (and is also promoted by the National Federation of Builders – see below). But in my experience, most homeowners are too timid to suggest it to their builders, and most builders are too scared to sign it. Both sides need educating. If both client and builder became more accustomed to contractual agreements then the work would get done better and faster, and builders would get paid on time.

The most influential trade association, which covers medium-sized construction companies, is the National Federation of Builders. They are keen to present their members as the reputable side of the domestic sector and they are probably right. Members offer customers a building insurance guarantee scheme (Benchmark Plan), for an extra payment, which means that most customers refuse it.

Successive governments have refused to implement a compulsory registration scheme for builders, and a recent attempt at voluntary registration, the Quality Mark, was always doomed to failure, since it asked reputable builders – who already have far more work than they can handle – to pay to join the scheme, whilst doing nothing to legislate against the cowboy operators. The latest government effort is the TrustMark [sic], which is little more than a loose affiliation of trade associations.

HOW TO FIND A BUILDER

Q We need a few simple repairs doing to our flat – moving a radiator, putting up some shelves, plastering a ceiling, etc. We have called seven separate builders, of whom only two came round to look at the work, and neither of them has ever called us back. How on earth can we find a decent builder to do this work?

Some builders prefer big sites to domestic repair and maintenance work.

A There are no easy answers to this one. There are plenty of good builders around, but they are usually booked up for months, if not years, in advance, and can afford to be choosy about which jobs they take on.

Builders who do work in the domestic sector are there for a variety of reasons: they may prefer the relative peace and quiet away from the big sites and the ability to choose their own hours; or they may really like the conservation aspect of restoring old houses; or it may be because they are complete cowboys who wouldn't last five minutes on a proper site and only work for cash because they are claiming benefits, avoiding paying tax, or have been made bankrupt.

The usual advice is to use a builder recommended by friends or relatives. This may or may not work. It is likely to put you in touch with someone who is polite, turns up on time and feeds the cat when you're away, but is no guarantee of their construction skills or knowledge.

Another suggestion is to use a builder who is a member of a trade association. This is no guarantee at all, as trade associations exist largely to protect their members from the public. (The Federation of Master Builders, for example, whilst it claims to check applicants' accounts and credit worthiness, does not require any evidence of construction training or qualifications.) Two exceptions to this are CORGI (Council for Registered Gas Installers) and the NICEIC (National Inspection Council for Electrical Installation Contracting), which have rigorous checking and monitoring procedures and can initiate legal action against interlopers.

Most builders on big sites are now obliged to carry a card from the Construction Skills Certification Scheme (CSCS), which shows their qualifications, and confirms that they have recently passed a written health-and-safety test. But it is unlikely that the builder who works on your house will have one. Even if he does, it will not necessarily prove anything; for example, my CSCS card shows that I am a trained bricklayer, but when I am doing small jobs in people's homes I might also be called upon to do plastering, plumbing, carpentry and roofing, with varying degrees of expertise. So rather than inquiring about qualifications, it might be better to ask to see a copy of your builder's Public Liability insurance.

At present the best advice is to have your building work organized by a registered Architect or Building Surveyor. There is a common misconception that architects' and surveyors' fees are an expensive addition to the costs of repairing or altering a building. But if you are not in a position to specify and supervise building works yourself, then you may well end up paying builders for unnecessary or sub-standard work. A good local Architect or Surveyor will specify building works, employ contractors, and supervise the whole operation, and should be able to save you a sum well in excess of his fees, whatever the value of the property.

HOW TO ENGAGE A BUILDER

Q We have found a local builder through recommendations. He came round twice, once to see what we wanted and another time to measure up. He's provided a single-page typed estimate saying not much more than the external size of the proposed extension, that the price includes supply of plans and seeking planning approval, and allows for external rendering to match existing. No painting is included in the estimate. That's all it says. Estimate is £31,200 plus VAT.

Is this usual? I am very uneasy about commissioning work on such a flimsy estimate, but everybody speaks highly of the man and his work seems to be of a high standard. How should I take things forward? Is there a standard form of contract that should be drawn up when employing builders?

A I would say that for a project of this size it would be unwise to engage a builder who you know only by word of mouth on an imprecise design-and-build contract (which is what you have described). Your builder may well be totally trustworthy, trained and experienced, but it would still be as well to have an independent construction professional supervising operations and acting as your middleman [ARCHITECTS, SURVEYORS & ENGINEERS].

CASH JOB

Q I've recently had a lot of different building jobs done. Each time the materials were needed, the builder asked me to make out a cheque for the suppliers. When all the jobs were done, he asked if I would pay his bill (the labour) in cash. This is obviously to avoid tax, or he may even be bankrupt and can't put any money in his bank account. It doesn't bother me how I pay him, but could I be considered to be a party to him avoiding tax?

A The Inland Revenue has recently tightened up the rules with regard to construction site work, and trade employers have to be careful to make due deductions or to collect exemption certificates from subcontractors. But as a private householder this is not your concern. Whether you pay by cash or cheque, it is up to your builder to declare his profits to the taxman and has nothing to do with you. However, you would be wise to get an invoice or receipt for work done, in case problems arise later. And the best thing is always to have a written contract with a builder before work starts, such as the JCT Building contract for a homeowner/occupier [CONSTRUCTION LITERATURE].

PAYING BUILDERS

Q **I have recently accepted a quote of £6000 for a new patio and other work. The tradesman is a local landscape gardener who has not done work for me before but I have reason to believe that he has been around for a number of years. I was a little surprised to be asked for £3000 in advance of any work. Should I have been surprised? I would appreciate your guidance.**

A This is a perennial thorny issue when dealing with small builders. In general, I would advise readers never to pay money up front for any kind of building work. Before agreeing to a price, you should have a written contract, including materials specifications and drawings if applicable. The contract should include start and finish dates and details of stage payments. Of course, we all know that when dealing with a small builder, things aren't always that simple. One advantage is that the price should be cheaper because he doesn't have office staff and other overheads to support. A disadvantage might be that his administration and paperwork will be minimal or even non-existent. And, from the builder's point of view, there is always the fear that you might turn out to be a 'cowboy client', who gets him to do the work and then finds an excuse not to pay. Also, let's face it, with a job this size, neither of you is likely to think it worth taking the other to court, should things go badly wrong.

Rather than paying him half the money before work starts, I suggest it would be reasonable for you to pay him the costs of the materials once these have been delivered to site (and therefore legally become your property), and thereafter two further stage payments – say, the second after completion of the excavations or groundworks and the third at the end of the whole job.

TRADE ASSOCIATIONS

Q We have had three quotes for damp-proofing our 1920s terraced house. One for £550, one for £2,300, and one for £7,875. The last is from a member of the British Wood Preserving and Damp-proofing Association, and my husband thinks that they must know what they are talking about. But how can there be such a difference in the three prices?

A In the first place, it is highly unlikely that your 1920s house needs damp-proofing, since it will have been built with an integral damp-proof course, which will still be doing its job (see DAMPNESS).

The British Wood Preserving and Damp-proofing Association is a trade association, not an officially sanctioned professional body. Its members like to boast that they are more highly trained than non-members, and might use this to justify higher prices and more extensive works. But in my experience members of this association are just as likely as non-members to misdiagnose problems, and specify unnecessary treatment.

INSURANCE

Q I am about to have an extension built by a small-sized local building company. Should I tell my buildings insurer, and is there any insurance I should take out during the work for damage against the main house? Also is there an insurance that gives me legal protection should I encounter any difficulties?

A You should give full details to your insurers. This is because the finished work will increase the rebuilding costs of the property, and you may find yourself under-insured in the event of making a claim. There is also the question of increased security risks whilst the building work is taking place (scaffolding, temporary window and door openings, etc.) – your insurers are unlikely to raise your premiums for this, but again, there could be a problem if you made a claim and you hadn't told them. Damage to the main house whilst the extension is being built should be covered by your builder's public liability insurance, so make sure that he is adequately covered.

Regarding your relationship with your builder, you will be legally covered during the course of the work provided you have signed a suitable contract, and you can cover yourself against possible future defects by entering into a warranty scheme, which is usually available for around 1 per cent of the contract price.

STANDARDS OF WORKMANSHIP

Q We are having a kitchen fitted by a national company. In one place where the worktops have to join, there is a gap and they are not at the same height. The carpenter says this will be solved with a joining strip. The worktop also stops short of the wall, but the carpenter tells me not to worry as the tiling will cover this up. But the gap is big enough for a tile to slip through. Are these acceptable degrees of error, or a bad job which I should ask to be rectified?

A It's entirely up to you. There are no British Standards for fitting kitchen worktops, but I would have thought you could reasonably expect them to be level all round, and fitted to a tolerance of 5mm. So, if you are not happy with the standard of work, then complain. But to whom? The carpenter is probably not employed directly by the 'national company' but is a jobbing builder doing the job for a fixed price. His margins are tight, and he doesn't have time to do things twice. The salesman who sold you the kitchen is the one making the big money, so stop the payments and get him round to explain himself.

LATE BUILDERS

Q **Why aren't house builders subject to 'penalty clauses' for delays, in the same way that road builders are? Our new house is now ten weeks late.**

A If the builders were working directly for you, then you could have incorporated a penalty clause for late completion into the contract. But if you are buying your new house from a developer, no such contract will apply. In fact, you will find that you have very little legal protection at all, as property is not even covered by the Sale of Goods Act. You actually have more consumer rights when you buy a tin of baked beans than when you buy a new house.

SUPERVISING BUILDERS

Q **I intend to buy a new timber-framed house later this year and hope to be able to visit the site frequently but unobtrusively (i.e. without being a nuisance). Though I have faith in the developer, he is a busy person and I am concerned to ensure that those he employs keep to the standards set. In particular, a sentence from the Scottish Consumer Council's briefing paper on the new house building market in Scotland has imprinted itself in my mind: 'New-built homes are exempt from the protection provided by the Sale of Goods Act 1979, so effectively the consumer has more statutory rights when buying a loaf of bread ... and the common-law rule of *caveat emptor* has always applied.' How can I satisfy myself, without being unnecessarily awkward and obtrusive, and whilst maintaining a good working relationship with the contractor and his employees, that the work is being carried out to the highest possible standards?**

A You are right to be wary about buying a new developer-built house. As you have already discovered, new homes are not covered by the Sale of Goods Act, and many readers have been disappointed by the quality of their newly built houses. The employment structure of the construction industry means that the work will most probably be done by subcontractors working to the lowest price, some of whose workers might be unskilled or casual labour. The quality of the finished house will therefore depend on how rigorously the developer supervises the work.

Supervision of the construction of timber-framed houses is especially critical, as the fire safety depends on the correct fitting of fire stops within the cavity. Also, to avoid risks of condensation within the timber frame, it is vital that a vapour barrier is installed in all the external walls, floors and ceilings, and sealed perfectly wherever it is punctured by pipes and cables. This requires that subcontract electricians and plumbers understand the principles of timber-frame construction and are strictly supervised.

The best thing you can do to ensure good standards or workmanship, whilst maintaining a good relationship with the developer, is to employ a Chartered Building Surveyor to inspect the construction on your behalf. He will be conversant with the latest Building Regulations, and aware of the construction quality needed [ARCHITECTS, SURVEYORS & ENGINEERS].

BUILDERS

PROJECT MANAGEMENT

Q I am about to have an extension built. It comprises an extra bedroom, a new dining room, an extension to the existing lounge and a study and utility room from the current dining room. The work will be done by a local building firm. Do I need an independent project manager? One quote I have had is for 5 per cent of the total building cost. What would you advise?

A The answer to this depends on how much you know about the building process and how prepared you are to get involved in managing the contractor, with all the stress and headaches that this might potentially produce. In general, I would always advise an inexperienced home-owner to engage a project manager, both for their expertise and because they form a vital zone of separation between the client and the builder. In the unfortunate event that disputes might occur, you will not have the problem of dealing personally with the builders and risking falling out with them.

Five per cent sounds like a reasonable figure for a qualified construction professional, and the extra expenditure might well pay for itself if it helps to avoid errors, disputes or cost over-runs. However, most professionals would prefer to be involved at a very early stage in the design and planning process, and also be involved in finding and engaging the contractor. If you have already given the job to a local building firm, then you might have to tread gently, lest they feel that you have suddenly decided to engage someone to 'check up on them'.

A project manager might be a Registered Architect, a Chartered Building Surveyor, or a Chartered Builder, all of whom will have Professional Indemnity insurance cover and member-ship of a professional body with an established complaints procedure. But you should take care to choose one with experience of supervising this type of work in your area, and with whom both you and the builder can have a good personal rapport [ARCHITECTS, SURVEYORS & ENGINEERS].

HEALTH & SAFETY – WORKING OFF A LADDER

Q Recent heavy rain revealed a leak from a joint in my plastic guttering, which was efficiently repaired by a local man. He reported, however, that the gutter was sagging, so that the water was unable to flow to the downspout, and that it needed replacing. I asked him to estimate for this work, but he says he is unable to do so as HSE rules will not let him work off a ladder above 15 feet, and the cost of scaffolding is prohibitive. He did the repair job off a ladder, with me standing at the bottom, but it seems that this was illegal. Your advice about these legalities would be much appreciated.

A It is not 'illegal' to work off a ladder, neither is it prohibited by the Health and Safety Executive (HSE), although it is obviously uncomfortable, inefficient and can be scary. HSE advice is that wherever possible, building work should be carried out from a 'safe working platform', but that inspections, small jobs and emergency repairs can be carried out from a ladder as long as no undue risk is involved, and if erecting scaffolding would be unreasonably difficult or costly.

The easiest, safest and cheapest way to repair or renew guttering is to hire a tower scaffold with wheels, or to employ a builder who has his own.

SURVEYORS

If you have bought a home that is older than you are, then your mortgage-valuation survey may well have recommended further investigation by 'specialists' for timber and dampness defects, drains, cracks, heating system and electrics. Even if you thought to avoid these nasty-sounding problems by buying a recently built property, there may still have been some bad news in the Surveyor's report, such as a recommendation for further investigation of the state of your cavity-wall ties.

For many people, especially first-time buyers, this turn of events can be confusing, because, having commissioned a survey and report from a chartered surveyor, they thought they had already paid for an authoritative investigation. The last thing they expected was a list of other people they should consult because the surveyor did not wish to express an opinion.

For, sadly, when you engage a chartered surveyor, you are not necessarily employing an experienced construction professional. More often than not you are getting someone who got an A-level in geography, spent three years in the classroom at a 'new university', and then got a job in a surveying practice. There, they will have been taken under the wing of a slightly older surveyor, who probably advised them to 'forget everything you learned at college' (no big problem), and took them out to do a couple of mortgage-valuation surveys. These entail filling in the blank spaces on a printed form, such as, 'State whether main water, drainage, electricity and gas are connected', an acceptable reply to which will be, 'All mains services appear to be connected but have not been tested.' You could do better yourself.

A clue to the limited nature of surveyors' investigations can be had from the clothes they wear to work. Most chartered surveyors turn up in their best suits, hardly well equipped for climbing up into the loft or having a poke round in the gutters. They won't even want to get down on one knee for fear of dirtying their trousers, which rules out looking at the drains or even lifting the edge of a carpet. In fact, the standard Homebuyer Valuation includes the stock phrase, 'Furniture, wall

Surveyors can only look: they can't touch.

hangings, floor coverings, insulation material and stored goods have not been moved.' So if you are selling a house and you don't want the buyer's surveyor to notice some particularly dodgy detail just hide it with a few tea chests or a bit of carpet. I once looked at a place where a huge crack between the main house and the kitchen addition was covered with a calendar of pastoral scenes. The surveyor had missed it completely.

Even when they do try to 'investigate' a bit deeper, most surveyors manage to give the impression of being totally ignorant. In one study, 93 per cent of surveyors questioned did not know how to use an electrical moisture meter correctly to diagnose dampness problems in walls. The result is that, rather than risk making mistakes and laying themselves open to future compensation claims for negligence, surveyors always recommend 'further investigation' by others of tricky subjects like dampness. So their reports give *carte blanche* to cowboys to come in with estimates for thousands of pounds' worth of unnecessary work, all sanctioned by the surveyors and, therefore, by the mortgage lenders.

But why get a survey done at all if it is likely to be so inadequate? The answer lies in the Building Societies Act (1986), which requires a written valuation report to be obtained on the occasion of each advance. Since demutualization, most of the building societies are now actually banks, and are not governed by this rule. But old habits die hard. As Adam Smith pointed out, all professions are a conspiracy against the public.

TYPES OF SURVEY

Q **We are always told that we should not rely on the mortgage valuation, but should pay extra for a more detailed survey. But having done just this during the recent purchase of my terraced house, I feel that it didn't tell me any more than I could see for myself. Should I have paid even more for a full survey? What exactly are the advantages and disadvantages of the different types of survey?**

A Good question. The basic valuation (£250 to £350) is carried out on behalf of the mortgage lender, for them to judge whether the property has sufficient collateral for them to lend money against it. Even though the buyer pays for the valuation, in law the documentation belongs to the lender. So if the surveyor fails to spot a costly defect, you might have trouble suing them afterwards.

With the Homebuyer Survey and Valuation (£350 to £450) you are engaging the surveyor to work for you directly, so if he fails to spot a defect then you may be able to sue him. But obviously surveyors are aware of this, which is why they hedge the wording of their reports so carefully. Hence the prevalence of phrases such as, '... xyz *appears* to be in good order,' and '... floor coverings and furniture have not been moved,' because surveyors know that in order to be found guilty of negligence in court, it is not enough to prove that they have missed something – it must be shown that the defect was clearly visible or that they should have been able to infer its presence from symptoms visible to them at the time of the inspection. This accounts for surveyors' use of electrical moisture meters on walls, even though they should know that the readings are meaningless. Ever since a judge in a noted court case ruled that a surveyor would have been able to spot some hidden dry rot if he had used a moisture meter on the wall nearby, surveyors have always recommended further investigation by damp-proofing and timber-treatment companies.

The wording on the Homebuyer Survey and Valuation report form is set by the Royal Institution of Chartered Surveyors (RICS), although some firms of surveyors amend the wording in their own versions of the form. Also, the quality of the survey varies according to the type of surveyor. Most Homebuyer Surveys are carried out by General Practice (or GP) members of the RICS, who are often little more than estate agents or valuers. A more specialized surveyor will belong to the Building Surveying division of the RICS, and may also have engineering experience or qualifications, in which case he may be more knowledgeable about building construction, and more confident about making judgements about the state of a house.

The more expensive Building Survey (£500 to £800) should be a much more thorough investigation, carried out by a Building Surveying RICS member, or a structural engineer. You would expect anyone undertaking a Building Survey to wear overalls and to bring a set of ladders so that they can access the roof space (although they are still unlikely to go up on to the roof, and will state in their report that they have not done so). They should lift manhole covers to inspect the drains, and may use tools to lift carpets and floorboards (although this may not be done if the sellers are still in occupation, and do not give their permission).

TYPES OF SURVEYOR

Q When we moved house four years ago I was very disappointed by the performance of the surveyor, who I felt did very little for his fee, landed us with a huge bill for damp-proofing (which turned out to be unnecessary) and failed to point out the things that we really should have spent our money on, like the leaking roof. We are planning to move again in the next couple of years and would like a better service. Can we get a survey from a different kind of professional (an engineer, perhaps) and would this be acceptable to the building society?

A The RICS has a near monopoly on simple mortgage valuations, because of the 'panel' system operated by the major chains of estate agents. But Homebuyer Surveys and Building Surveys (which can include valuations) are carried out by professionals who belong to other organizations as well, including the Chartered Institute of Building (CIOB), the Association of Building Engineers (ABE) and the Institution of Civil Engineers (ICE). Finding someone who is going to provide you with the quality of survey that you expect is a matter of contacting members of these bodies, finding out if they do domestic survey work, and quizzing them with regard to their experience and attitude. Valuations from members of these professional bodies should all be acceptable to mortgage lenders.

HOMEBUYER SURVEY

Q I am hoping to move house but the survey has concerned me. I have had the 'expert' builders' quotations – on the advice of the surveyor – and the roof is apparently 'shot to pieces'. I also need a damp course to the ground floor, etc., etc., etc. I really don't know whether to go ahead with the purchase now or not. One quote yesterday came to £14,000! Apparently I need a whole new set of PVC-U windows, as well as fascias, soffits, etc., which are rotten. I made the mistake of asking the various builders to quote for points marked in the survey and they really have gone to town. Where can I obtain honest advice? My mortgage lender (on the basis of the survey) is withholding money until the damp/timber treatment is carried out to the surveyor's satisfaction, so I need to make up the shortfall *and* pay for the work.

I don't really trust any of the opinions given. The surveyors are so careful about protecting themselves that apparently nearly everything 'probably' needs replacing.

A In general I advise against damp-proofing, timber treatment, PVC-U windows and PVC-U fascias, as these items are usually (a) unnecessary, (b) damaging to the house and (c) damaging to the environment. The roof may or may not need repairing, depending upon age, type, etc. 'Shot to pieces' seems to imply some kind of war damage which, as far as I am aware, is uncommon in present-day mainland Britain. It sounds to me as though you need independent advice, rather than asking contractors to quote for specific items. When builders are called in to quote for work on newly purchased homes they tend to smell mortgage money and worried new owners, and react accordingly.

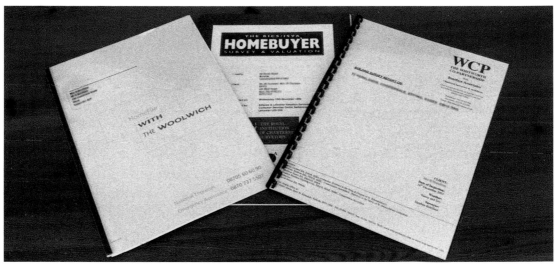

Mortgage valuation, Homebuyer survey and Building survey.

PARTY-WALL PROBLEMS

Q We have recently had plans drawn up to add a single-storey extension across the whole of the back of the house, and these have been passed by the council. I have read in a book that cognizance has to be taken of the Party Wall Act (1966). The architect is very sanguine and says just go and chat to the neighbours, but my understanding is that we need written permission from the neighbours on both sides. Both are elderly and I cannot find a specimen consent letter not written in intimidatory legalese. Do I really need written consent?

A You should seek expert advice from a surveyor experienced in party-wall legislation. You will have to pay a professional fee for this, but it could save you a lot of trouble in the future [ARCHITECTS, SURVEYORS & ENGINEERS].

DODGY SURVEY (1)

Q I bought an Edwardian ground-floor flat a year ago and was ordered by the surveyor to have a new damp-proof course injected into the external walls. I got this done and thought that damp would never be a problem. Then I read your article stating that 'rising damp' is a myth, and also found that in two rooms that were treated there is a serious damp problem caused by condensation. I've paid £300 plus VAT for completely pointless work. Do I have any comeback?

A It depends what you mean by 'ordered by the surveyor', and the wording of his report. You could try suing for negligence and damages, but your costs may come to more than the £352.50. The Royal Institution of Chartered Surveyors (RICS) have an arbitration system for disputes with their members, and this may be the best first step. In any event, you should first contact the surveyor in writing and make your feelings known, and see what the response is.

DODGY SURVEY (2)

Q I am selling a house that has just had a complete renovation throughout the interior, including a loft conversion. A buyer recently pulled out of the sale because her surveyor put in her Homebuyer's report that there was no damp-proof course, and mentioned that wall ties may be a problem. Now the estate agent is saying I should reduce my asking price by £5000 as the building

199

has problems. The house was built in 1930, is a typical semi-detached, and has no damp or signs of wall-tie decay. What can I do?

A This is the kind of question that makes me despair of the surveying and estate-agency professions. Of course your 1930s semi has got a damp-proof course. All houses constructed in Britain since 1887 have been built with DPCs. Your buyer's surveyor has clearly been taken-in by the propaganda of the damp-proofing industry, that all homes must be suspected of being damp unless they have a certificate showing that they have been 'treated' against it. Similarly, the potential of wall-tie corrosion is often mentioned by surveyors in Homebuyer survey reports, even when there is no evidence of it, and it is no coincidence that the firms that advertise themselves to be specialists in wall-tie replacement are often 'specialists' in damp-proofing and chemical timber treatment as well. I can only suggest that you move your custom to a more reputable estate agent – one who is prepared to represent your best interests, rather than accept the opinions of an obviously incompetent surveyor.

SURVEYORS: WHAT ARE THEY FOR?

Q Why do I have to pay for a survey before I can buy a house? The things that the surveyor comes up with are laughable. What I want to know are the things I can't see for myself, i.e. structural deficiencies, etc., but I have to seek further professional advice on such matters because 'fixed floor coverings have not been lifted', etc. However, it is very helpful to be told that 'the interior decoration requires some attention' and 'the kitchen units would benefit from some updating'. Having average eyesight I can spot that for myself!

A It's all to do with the Building Societies Acts (of Parliament). Building societies, unlike banks, were bound by these acts to commission independent valuation surveys before lending money against a property. Now that most building societies have been demutualized – i.e. they are effectively the same as banks – there is no legal reason why this charade should continue. But the whole property industry is hamstrung by inertia and complacency, and it is difficult to see the surveying profession changing practices that it has been doing for years. It's a bit like the First World War soldiers' lament: 'We're here because we're here, because we're here because we're here…'

HOUSE LOG BOOK

Q We have heard a lot about a proposed 'house log book'. I have made enquiries in various bookshops but to no avail. I am wondering if you can give me any guidance as to how I might obtain such a book in which to record bills, location of taps and other useful information for a prospective purchaser.

A I think the house log was just somebody's bright idea, and doesn't exist in the real world. In my view it would be totally impractical, and lead to pre-emptive disinformation, much like the Government's Home Information Packs intend to do.

HAZARDS

The history of construction is littered with materials which, in their day, were thought to be the answer to every problem, and which later turned out to be damaging to health. The most notorious of these is asbestos, which was widely used as a fireproof lagging material and is now known to cause cancer and respiratory illness. But hot on its heels comes lead, used for water pipes and in paint, and now associated with nervous disorders, reduced intelligence, hyperactivity and behavioural problems, especially in children. Although it was banned in Australia in 1906 and the USA in 1978, lead paint continued to be used in Britain until 1992.

Formaldehyde adhesives, used to bind together the particles in many types of building board, are a known respiratory hazard, and their use is strictly controlled in a number of American states. But they remain in widespread general use in the UK.

The most toxic substances in construction are pesticides. Concerns have been expressed about the safety of these chemicals for more than thirty years, but in the UK many of them continue to be licensed as 'safe' by the Health and Safety Executive (HSE), and they are routinely sprayed in thousands of homes every week, usually as a precaution against imaginary problems. Among the letters in this section are some from readers whose health has been ruined by exposure to these supposedly safe treatments.

ASBESTOS

Q We bought our thirty-year-old council flat a few years ago and had central heating fitted. The council are now installing heating in the remaining tenant-occupied flats and replacing their asbestos water tanks with plastic. Our tank is tucked away on top of the airing cupboard and seems perfectly sound. In view of the asbestos scare do you think the tank is a health hazard?

A The main dangers come from the brown and blue varieties of asbestos, which were used mainly for insulation and pipe lagging and these should always be removed by specialist contractors when found. Water tanks, wall panels and corrugated roofing sheets were usually made from the less dangerous white asbestos, mixed with cement. Asbestos is only dangerous when the fibres get into the air and are inhaled, so if your asbestos-cement tank is in good condition, then it should not represent any problem, and the safest option is to leave it undisturbed.

ASBESTOLUX GARAGE CEILING

Q I am concerned about the ceiling of my garage. The house was built in 1974 and has an attached garage which backs on to the kitchen. The ceiling is covered in 'asbestolux' boarding and is there, I understand, for fire safety reasons. Is it asbestos? Is it dangerous? It is attached by nails and there is a broken piece at one end. Are we likely to find surveyors insisting the broken sheet, or the whole lot, should be removed or replaced if we came to sell the property?

A Asbestolux does contain white asbestos. It is safe as long as you don't disturb it and inhale the fibres, so the best thing is probably to leave it alone for now. If you decide to remove it, then you should contact your local authority Environmental Health Department for advice about disposal, or for details of local approved removal contractors.

ASBESTOS IN STORAGE HEATER?

Q I recently had cause to remove the front of my Creda bathroom storage heater, which was fitted in 1984. I was surprised to find what I thought was an asbestos-type substance which was starting to crumble extensively. I have asked for clarification from the manufacturers about this, and initial queries indicate that no asbestos was used after 1975. Is this the case and what might the crumbling insulating material be?

A Creda confirm that no asbestos was used in its heaters after 1975. The top, bottom and sides of storage heaters are generally lined with dense mineral-fibre insulation, and the thin insulating panels on the fronts and backs are made from a substance called opacified silica aerogel. This is allegedly the lightest solid material known to man, and hence the best insulator. It was developed for the space programme and is used in the heat-reflective tiles on space vehicle nosecones. Silica aerogel is not known to be hazardous, but if the panel is cracked or has gaps in it, then the heat from the storage bricks might start scorching the paint off the front panel – internal core temperature can reach 800°C. Creda say they can sell you a replacement panel, but because of the nature of the material this is the most expensive part of the heater, and might cost up to £100, whereas a whole new storage heater might cost only £150 (depending on size) and will probably be slimmer and more efficient than your 1984 model.

ARTEX CEILINGS

Q Most of the rooms in my house have Artex ceilings, which I would dearly like to remove. They have been in place for variable times, I think, but at least twenty years. Is there a way to remove them without getting involved with the asbestos problems?

A Artex is a brand of textured paint used to make decorative patterns on plasterboard, or to cover up cracks in old ceilings (although this is rarely successful). Other brands are Wondertex, Suretex

Artex ceilings may contain asbestos.

and Newtex, but they all tend to get referred to as 'Artex'. The big problem with these textured finishes is that they may contain asbestos. The Artex brand was still being manufactured with asbestos as recently as 1984. So textured finishes should not be drilled or dry-sanded, as the asbestos fibres could be released into the air and inhaled. The amount of asbestos included in the mix was small and *Sunday Telegraph* readers may be familiar with Christopher Booker's views that the white asbestos they contain is harmless. However, the view in the construction industry is that any asbestos product should be treated with caution, and the HSE insists that the white asbestos (chrysotile) used in textured coatings is a human carcinogen.

The 'asbestos problems' you mention probably concern the exorbitant charges being charged to local authorities by some licensed asbestos-removing firms, but as a private house-holder you are not obliged to use their services. Textured ceiling finishes can be easily removed using a steam wallpaper stripper and scraper. The scrapings should be put into plastic bin-liners whilst still damp, taped-up and labelled 'asbestos'. Your local-authority refuse department should either collect the bags free of charge or tell you which special disposal site to take them to.

If the texturing is not too thick, an easier option is probably to smooth it over with plaster. You can prime the surface with dilute PVA adhesive, and then use a standard gypsum plaster, such as British Gypsum Multi-Finish or Universal One-Coat. A specialized product called Artex Ceiling Finish is also available, which is claimed to be easy to use by DIYers [PLASTERING]. The dilemma is that the newly plastered surfaces should really be labelled, to warn future generations that asbestos lurks beneath.

ASBESTOS CEMENT SHEETING

Q The passageway between our house and garage is roofed with corrugated asbestos panels (fitted 1970) and I would like some of them to be replaced with clear panels to let in more light. Several builders who have come to quote tell me that the asbestos is dangerous and needs careful removal complying with all sorts of regulations and they are quoting unbelievable prices. Is it likely that these panels are really so dangerous to health that this is necessary? The garage is also roofed with asbestos panels which are flat but with interlocking ridges and I am being told these too should be removed as per the passage panels and replaced with a 'safe' roofing material. What I initially thought would be just a couple of hundred pounds sounds like it may cost a small fortune – maybe I should just leave them where they are and forget the whole idea as they do not leak and are not cracked?

A Asbestos-cement sheeting is made from white asbestos, also known as chrysotile, and is the least dangerous type. As long as the sheeting is in good condition, the asbestos fibres are bound-in by the cement, and should not present a health risk. Remember, the dangers of asbestos come from breathing in the air-borne fibres, so as long as asbestos-cement products are in good condition, the safest thing is to leave them undisturbed.

As regards dismantling asbestos-cement structures, this can be done by householders or non-licensed contractors, provided they conform to a plan of work (as described by the Control of Asbestos Regulations 2006) and wear suitable disposable dust masks and protective clothing, which should both be disposed of after use, along with the removed material. The sheets should be de-nailed and removed as carefully as possible, so as to avoid damage. If any cutting or breaking is inevitable, then the material should be dampened first, to minimize the possibility of fibres becoming air-borne. Contact your local-authority Environmental Health Department for advice, as many councils offer a free disposal service for asbestos cement panels for householders.

LIGHTNING PROTECTION

Q My house has a large area of flat roof comprising copper panelling on plywood decking. I am concerned about its vulnerability in a thunderstorm, since the house is high in the Pennines. Is this type of roof more prone to being struck by lightning, and should it be 'earthed' in some way or another?

A Any building can be struck by lightning, regardless of the nature of the roofing material. But most damage comes not from direct lightning hits, but from electrical discharges being conducted in via overhead telephone cables and television aerials. Protection against lightning therefore involves two processes: first, a traditional lighting conductor on the highest point of the building, to prevent lightning strikes and fire damage; and second, electronic anti-surge protectors on TV, telephone and mains electrical supplies. For details contact the National Federation of Master Steeplejacks and Lightning Conductor Engineers [HAZARDS].

RADON GAS

Q I am hoping to buy a retirement cottage in Herefordshire, but the surveyor's report states that it is in an area affected by radon gas. Is this a big problem, and how can it be dealt with? My wife is now very worried about possible harmful effects on our health, and for our visiting grandchildren.

A Radon is a natural radioactive gas that seeps out of the ground in certain areas, chiefly those with underlying granite. The radioactivity is low, and usually harmless, but if it is allowed to enter a house, then it can build up to higher levels. The main health fear is an increased risk of lung cancer from breathing the gas over long periods. Surveyors are obliged to mention the risk in a given area, but this does not mean that a particular house will have a radon problem. You should be able to get a more detailed assessment from the local-authority Environmental Health Department. In any case, preventative measures are easy. For a house with a suspended timber ground floor, the usual method is to fit an impermeable membrane below the floorboards, and ensure that the existing sub-floor ventilation is adequate. With a solid floor, a membrane is also applied, sometimes with the addition of a hollow polyethylene radon sump below floor level. This is attached to a vent pipe that disperses the radon gas above roof level. For more details contact Proctor Group Ltd [HAZARDS].

MDF

Q As a lifelong DIYer I am a relative newcomer to the use of MDF board. It cuts and routs well and cleanly. But when visiting B&Q to purchase and have a large board reduced to a manageable size I am regaled with reports of how MDF is banned in the USA as a hazard. There is also a warning on each board to wear a protective mask when using powered machinery, which is not always practicable for small operations. What are the true hazards associated with MDF?

A The hazards of MDF (medium-density fibreboard) come from the fine nature of the dust, which can cause respiratory problems, and from the 'out-gassing' of the formaldehyde-based adhesive. It is not true that MDF has been banned in the USA or anywhere else. There are regulations over its use in confined spaces such as woodworking shops where prolonged daily exposure is a factor, but occasional DIY use probably represents a threat no greater than that of, say, white spirit, i.e. take all reasonable precautions, and remember that some people will be more sensitive than others. When MDF has been stored for over three months, the adhesive is reckoned to have all 'out-gassed', and there are alternative, but more expensive, types using safer adhesives, which are used in hospitals and nurseries.

LEAD PAINT (1)

Q I am buying a house, and a surveyor's report comments on lead being present in the painted metal windows in the conservatory. Could you please advise on the best method for removal and disposal of the paint.

A Lead was widely used in paint until surprisingly recently, despite being a known health hazard. It continued in use in Britain until 1992, largely because lead compounds were valued as pigments and for the hard-wearing qualities they gave to the finished paint. Lead paint is harmful when it is ingested, and the main danger is to children under seven, whose brains and organs are still developing, and to pregnant women, who can pass the poisoning on to the foetus. The main danger to children comes from 'pica' – a habit that babies and young children have of chewing objects and surfaces. Old buildings can also have high lead-laden dust levels, so that children might be contaminated by contact with dust on floors or other surfaces.

It is important not to burn off or sand lead paintwork, as lead can be absorbed by breathing in the fumes or dust. The safest method is to use chemical paint stripper, and to sweep up and vacuum the work area thoroughly afterwards. Your local authority should advise you of how to dispose of the waste. The British Coatings Federation recommends that lead paint should not be removed at all, but sealed in by overpainting [PAINTING & DECORATING].

LEAD PAINT [2]

Q I stripped a window in my 1930s flat using a heat-gun and then saw an article about lead content in pre-1950 paintwork, and felt faint at what I read, especially with a fourteen-month-old son who gets everywhere. I'm now awaiting the result of a blood test for lead content! Why are we not made aware of the danger of this by paint retailers/DIY programmes, etc?

A Lead paint is not confined to pre-1950s decor; it was used in the UK up until 1992, although it was known as early as the 1880s that it is a dangerous neurotoxin. I think it is fairly obvious why the paint manufacturers and DIY retailers would not want to shout this from the rooftops, and TV makeover shows are interested only in 'entertainment', not public education. A better question would be why do our government departments not make more effort to warn people about this danger, and a cynical answer would be that it might expose them to huge compensation claims.

There are thousands of tonnes of lead paint on woodwork in British homes, and its removal by burning or dry-sanding represents a serious risk to young children and foetuses. Lead test kits are available from McDougall Rose decorators' suppliers and from B&Q. But the British Coatings Federation, who produce advice leaflets [PAINTING & DECORATING] do not generally encourage removal of lead paint at all. They recommend that where the paint surface is in sound condition it should be sealed in by overpainting, although they stress that the householder then has a responsibility to maintain the painted surface in good order.

I feel that this is fudging the issue. If old lead paint is sealed in by overpainting, then surely labels should be posted to warn future generations that a dangerous neurotoxin lurks beneath the surface of their skirting boards? Homes in some US states already carry such legal disclosure notices.

LEAD WATER PIPES

Q My house is over 100 years old and the mains water supply comes into the house through the original lead pipes. All the pipes inside the house have been replaced. Is this water safe to drink, or should the lead pipes be replaced?

A The amount of lead that finds its way into the drinking water depends upon several factors, including the hardness or softness of the supply. The only way to find out if your supply is safe is by asking your water supplier to test a sample taken from your kitchen tap, which they should do free of charge. Regarding replacement pipes, the service pipe which leads from the company stop valve (under the pavement) into the house is your responsibility; the 'tail' which leads from the main to the stop valve is the water company's, and you may have trouble persuading them to replace this. The European Drinking Water Directive requires lead levels to be reduced to a fifth of their current levels by 2013, but it is likely that this will be achieved mostly by phosphate dosing rather than wholesale pipe replacement. Further information is available from British Water [PLUMBING, HEATING & DRAINAGE].

GAS COOKER FUMES

Q Could you explain why it is that whilst there are strict regulations covering flues for gas heaters and boilers, it is acceptable to have four top burners, grill and oven all in use at the same time on a gas cooker in an enclosed kitchen?

A The answer to this is that gas cookers are not expected to be in constant use, nor to be left burning unattended. Also, the regulations require that a kitchen with a gas cooker must have an openable window, so if you have all the burners lit as you describe, the room would be so hot that you would be forced to open the window anyway. In addition, kitchens smaller than 10 cubic metres must have permanent ventilation. My own view is that all kitchens should also have cooker hoods, extracting direct to the outside, rather than recirculating the fumes through the filter.

TOXIC MOULD?

Q A few months ago, water penetrated the outside wall of our front bedroom. We have cured the leak but we now have mould growing on the inside wall. My wife has read that it is dangerous for your health to allow the mould to continue to grow. Is this true? If so, what is the best way of getting rid of the mould without further endangering health?

A Some people are sensitive to high concentrations of certain mould spores, and this can sometimes contribute to health problems such as asthma and other allergic reactions. Recently, however, we have had the 'toxic mould' scare stories from the USA, where landlords have been sued by tenants for alleged health problems. This would seem to owe more to the strength of the US compensation culture than to hard medical evidence. In most cases, and for most people, mould spores are harmless. Wherever you go, there are millions of mould spores in every cubic metre of air, and a patch of mould on the wall is unlikely to harm you.

As long as you are sure the leak is fixed, then things should clear up of their own accord, but if you want to hasten things along then wipe with a dilute solution of bleach in water. This is also good for black mould growth on bathroom windows, and usually keeps it away for a couple of months. Safer and considerably cheaper than proprietary mould-removing chemicals.

TIMBER TREATMENT CHEMICALS

MULTIPLE TREATMENTS

Q We have bought a barn conversion property. Our surveyor noted evidence of slight wood-boring beetle activity, and also commented that the timber had been treated before, although there is no documentation or guarantee from this treatment. We engaged a timber treatment firm, who agreed with the surveyor that infestation was not serious and confirmed that there had been prior treatment, but could not determine with what. They suggest further treatment with an inorganic boron compound in order to issue us with a guarantee. Is this a good idea?

A I follow the Building Research Establishment and Health and Safety Executive advice that if timber is dry then it will not be attacked by insects or fungi. So in a normally heated and ventilated building it is not necessary to use chemical preservatives. Old flight holes are not evidence of continuing active infestation, and will generally only be in the sapwood at the surface of the timber, so they will not necessarily have weakened timbers below their design strength.

Previous treatment can be easily identified by gas chromatography. But if the property has previously been treated then you should be asking: (a) how can there be continuing infestation (i.e. is there a continuing moisture problem allowing infestation to continue)?; and (b) what would be the health effects of introducing an additional chemical, effectively creating a chemical 'cocktail'?

Many people claim to have become ill following chemical timber treatment in their homes.

PERMETHRIN

Q I have been renovating my Victorian house myself. Where there has been evidence of wood-worm I have treated the floor with a product with permethrin in it. However, I am faced with a living-room floor with holes from woodworm. Would you repair, replace, or treat? I have installed central heating. Will this help? I'm concerned for the health of my kids.

A The central heating means that the timber will dry down to a level unable to support insect activity. Obviously any boards that have been damaged very badly should be replaced, but woodworm holes in floorboards generally only occur in the sapwood at the corners or edges of the boards, and do not affect the strength sufficiently to justify their replacement. Beyond that, the holes are only a cosmetic problem. Many people claim to have been made seriously ill by permethrin, and children are usually more susceptible, since the effects are inversely proportional to body weight.

ILLNESS CAUSED BY PERMETHRIN

Q In July 1985 we moved into a Victorian house, and had the timbers sprayed with permethrin. We moved in the day after it was done but many floorboards were still up. Shortly after our move, both my young daughter (then two and a half) and I developed myalgic encephalomyelitis (ME). I am convinced that the woodworm spraying was the cause of our illness.

We have been ill for fourteen years and there is now no hope of a full recovery for either of us. The medical profession offers little or no help. I have written to you to raise awareness of this possible result of spraying with toxins.

A There are thousands of people in your position, who have become ill following exposure to permethrin. But since it is licensed as 'safe' by the Health and Safety Executive (HSE), physicians will refuse to acknowledge that it might have injured you and your daughter. They are more likely to prescribe antibiotics, steroids and tranquillizers, before deciding that your condition is a mental problem. Pesticides victim support is currently being organized by the Pesticides Action Network [PESTICIDES].

CHEMICAL DANGERS

Q I have ME and have not been able to work for five years. I ran my own damp-proofing and timber treatment business for sixteen years, and during the early years I was actually carrying out the treatments myself. I strictly followed all health and safety procedures as detailed on the product literature and later as required by COSHH (Control of Substances Hazardous to Health Acts). The blood tests I have had show high levels of dieldrin, DDT, DDE, HCB (hexachlorobenzene), pentachlorophenol and carbaryl. I presume all of these, being persistent chemicals, will stay in my blood for many years to come. During the period that I was using these products the chemical company assured me that their products were safe. But then they were forced into changing their formulations and moving on to different products, permethrin being a good example. This they advertised as a safe, natural product, but now they have all moved on to using boron.

A As you will probably have found out by now, the industry and the Health and Safety Executive (HSE) will never believe that you followed the instructions properly. They define the chemicals as 'safe' – so they could not possibly accept that, even when used as directed, they can cause illness.

TREATED TIMBER DECKING

Q I am considering having timber decking installed in our back garden, but all the companies I have contacted want to use timber which has been pre-treated with preservatives. They say it is not possible to use untreated timber outdoors. But I am concerned about the possible dangers these chemicals may pose to our young grandchildren, who will doubtless be crawling around on the boards when they come to visit. How safe are the preservatives used on decking, and is there any alternative to chemical treatment?

The manufacturers claim that the vacuum process used to impregnate timber with insecticides and fungicides locks the chemicals into the wood, and that there is no risk of them leaching out or posing a health risk. However, I share your concerns. The chemical formulations used are generally CCA (copper/chrome/arsenic) salts, and I would not recommend allowing children to come into contact with them. You could use untreated softwood and apply an annual coat of boiled linseed oil, which is a safe and natural preservative, but the best solution would probably be to use a rot-resistant timber such as yellow cedar, which weathers naturally to a silver-grey finish and will last for twenty years or more without the need for chemical treatment.

PESTS

Wherever you live, you will be competing for living space with some kind of animals or insects. Physical exclusion is always preferable to – and usually more effective than – trapping or poisoning. And people who are worried about sharing their homes with birds or bats should be aware that these creatures are responsible for keeping the insect population in check. Get rid of them and you could find your life being made intolerable by flies!

BIRDS

Q We have just acquired a bungalow with the highest roof of the adjoining properties, and seagulls seem happy to sit and sun themselves (sometimes as many as fifteen). Could you please advise what can be done to deter them. We get a lot of mess from their droppings.

A Birds like to sit in places where they can keep an eye out for food, and you are probably quite right that they choose your roof because it is the highest. You may therefore have problems evicting them. And note that under the Wildlife and Countryside Act (1981), you are not allowed to do anything that might injure wild birds. But there are humane physical deterrents, such as anti-perch spikes. These are rows of thin stainless steel pins sticking out from a polycarbonate backing strip. They are glued in place, and cost from around £5 per linear metre. Builders and roofers can order them from builders' merchants, or they can be bought direct from Woodland Properties [PESTS].

BIRDS IN ROOF

Q I had my wooden fascia boards replaced with PVC-U recently. This was partly to reduce the maintenance aspect, but mainly to prevent birds getting in as they have been damaging the roofing felt. I was assured that the birds wouldn't get in but I now have more than ever. There are gaps between the straight edge of the board and my curved pantiles. Is there something that I can fit myself to prevent this happening, and are birds in the roof a big problem?

A I am personally not bothered about birds in the roof, unless their squawking youngsters wake me up early. Roofs in older houses would not have been built with sarking felt anyway, so damage to it should not be a problem. Obviously you want to make sure your water tanks have secure lids, so they don't contaminate them or drown themselves in them. There are a number of proprietary products which seal the spaces between fascias and pantiles, but still allow ventilation through to the roof space. They are plastic strips with flexible comb-like fingers on the top edge, which mould to the profile of the tiles. It sounds as though this is what you really needed all along, rather than the PVC-U fascias. Try a specialist roofing supplies merchants.

ULTRASONIC REPELLERS

Q We have been experiencing rats in our loft and have called in the local council's pest control officer to deal with them. I have seen advertised an 'ultrasonic rodent repeller' and am considering buying one of these to discourage any further intruders. The unit is claimed to emit an ultrasonic sound which the advert says drives away rats and mice. It has a continuously changing

ing frequency so that rodents do not become resistant to it, and covers up to 4000 square feet. My concern is, will the ultrasonic sound affect the building structure in any way?

A Whatever it says in the Old Testament about Joshua and the walls of Jericho, high-pitched sound is unlikely to cause any damage to a house. Unfortunately, it is unlikely to have any effect on rodents, either. There are a few of these devices on the market, claiming to use various combinations of electromagnetic waves and ultrasonic sound to repel rats, mice and even insects (although, curiously, to have no adverse effect on household pets). Several companies advertise these products, and claim to have independent scientific research supporting their efficacy, but when investigated by the Advertising Standards Authority, this has been found to be bogus. There are many factors that affect the presence of mice and rats, and although some readers have reported that they are sure the devices have kept vermin out of their homes, it is possible that installing the device has coincided with other changes in the local environment that have affected the animals' nesting and feeding behaviour. There is no independent scientific evidence to show that these devices have any effect whatsoever, other than to remove money from the pockets of unsuspecting customers.

MASONRY BEES

Q Every summer I notice dozens of bees emerging from gaps in the brickwork of my cottage (soft red bricks, lime mortar, built 1880), and I am worried that they are burrowing into the mortar to make nests. How can I get rid of this pest?

A Some homeowners get worried when they see bees emerging from holes in their brickwork, but so-called masonry bees, *Osmia rufa*, have simply adapted from their natural home in soft sandstone rocks, and it is rare for them to cause serious damage to brickwork. They do not sting, and they are solitary creatures that do not live in colonies or build nests, as such, but lay their eggs in holes and crevices that they find. If you have a lot of them, then it may be a sign that your brickwork has unfilled perpend joints (vertical joints), and it may be an idea to think about raking out and repointing with lime mortar.

BATS

Q My house was converted from an old timber barn, by building lightweight block walls on the inside of the timber frame. In the two summers that I have lived here, pipistrelle bats have made my life intolerable. They are creating a colony within the cavity walls, their points of entry and exit being the gaps between the wooden cladding under the eaves. I know that the bats are a protected species and I have no desire to harm them. However, the noise they create within the cavities, particularly in the small hours, is sufficient to prevent a good night's sleep, night after night, all summer long.

A Bats, which are suffering a dramatic decline in numbers, are voracious insectivores, and perform a valuable service in keeping insect numbers down. They are being deprived of roosting sites in houses by the ubiquitous plastic ventilation grilles, and by the current trend for filling cavity walls with insulation. The spraying of timber treatment chemicals in loft spaces has also taken its toll on the bat population, although the Wildlife and Countryside Act (1981) achieved a notable success in clamping down on this practice.

Bats are harmless and eat a lot of insects.

British bats are completely harmless; they do not use nesting materials and, unlike mice, they never nibble cables or wires. There is no known health risk associated with British bats or their droppings.

Most bats roost in roofs between April and June. *Pipistrellus* like to nest in cavity walls, and can be noisy for a few weeks during the breeding season. You may be able to lessen the noise nuisance by building an insulated soundproofing stud wall on the inside. But if you are determined to evict them then English Nature should put you in touch with your local bat worker. Further information is available from the Bat Conservation Trust [PESTS].

CLUSTER FLIES

Q We have been building a house surrounded by fields and dairy farms. Every autumn we have been inundated with flies nestling in enormous 'clumps' in the frames of the windows. It is no exaggeration to say that when a window is opened 100 flies are disturbed. They are fairly dozy and will eventually die on the floor or fly out through the open window. But however much fly killer I use, they keep accumulating. Neighbours have a similar experience. Do you have any solution to this problem?

A These flies are either *Pollenia rudis* or *Dasyphora cyanella*, both known as cluster flies, or *Musca autumnalis*, known as the autumn fly. They breed outside in decaying matter in farmland and are attracted to warm, south-facing walls. They get in through gaps, and once inside are then attracted to the light at the windows. Most of them die of dehydration but some hibernate over winter. They seem to prefer some houses to others, and people whose houses have been invaded by cluster flies can find it very difficult to keep them out. You can cut down the numbers entering by sealing all the gaps around the windows, and draught-proofing the opening casements, but some will always find their way in. I am personally not keen on insecticides, as I am not convinced about their safety. A reader has also suggested that painting the brickwork around the windows with Jeyes Fluid every autumn seems to act as a deterrent. Electric fly killers can be a good solution, although the large numbers of dead flies can sometimes build up in the catch tray and create a fire hazard.

If you want to use an electric fly killer to kill cluster flies in an unoccupied area such as a loft, then choose one that is open at the bottom, so that when the catch tray is removed, the dead flies fall through into a separate metal container positioned underneath. I have tried several of these fly killers, and I have to say they are of variable quality. The main point to bear in mind is that the ultra-violet (UVA) lamps need to be changed regularly. Although the lamp may appear bright to the human eye, it loses its attraction to insects quite quickly; after 5000 hours (thirty weeks of continuous use) the output will be down to only 50 per cent of the original. Also, normal UVA lamps are not as effective as more specialist insect-attractant lamps. 'Insect-o-cutor' make a special UVA-green lamp, in sizes to fit all insect killers, which they claim attracts more species of insects and is longer lasting than a normal UVA lamp [PESTS].

BIRDS' NESTS

Q Despite our removing their nests after they've gone, house martins continue to return and rebuild them. Is there a solution?

A House martins are migratory birds who return year after year to the same sites to build their nests and breed. The nests are made from mud, and are usually stuck up on the walls below overhanging eaves. Most people find house martins welcome summer guests, with their entertaining evening flights as they swoop in formation around the house. They also perform a valuable role in controlling insect populations – adult house martins catch around 600 flying insects per hour to feed their chicks. You don't say why you find them a nuisance, but if it is because of their droppings, the

House Martins.

answer is to collect these on a board fixed to the wall below the nests. This can be a DIY effort, or purpose-made droppings boards are available from Jacobi Jayne [PESTS], who also sell artificial house martin nests for people who would like to encourage these delightful birds to nest around their homes.

USEFUL CONTACTS

The following is a list of the various bodies and organizations mentioned in the book. Their inclusion does not mean that I endorse or recommend them, but they may be worth contacting for advice, or as a starting point in your investigation of a particular topic or problem.

ARCHITECTS, SURVEYORS & ENGINEERS

Readers who have read my grumbles about surveyors and architects are sometimes confused when I then recommend that you engage one to plan and supervise building work. But the fact is that, whilst there are many ignorant and incompetent building professionals, there are also some very good ones. The problem is sorting the wheat from the chaff. If you call the following bodies, they will give you a list of members in private practice in your area. It is then a matter of interrogating them until you find one suitable for the job you have in mind.

ABE – Association of Building Engineers – 0845 126 1058, www.abe.org.uk
CIOB – Chartered Institute of Building (Incorporates the Association of Architects and Surveyors – ASI) – 01344 630700, www.ciob.org.uk
RIBA – Royal Institute of British Architects – 020 7256 7222, www.ribafind.org
RICS – Royal Institution of Chartered Surveyors – 0870 333 1600, www.rics.org

BRICKWORK & MASONRY

Brick Development Association / Brick Information Service (details of brick-matching service) – 01344 885651
Prema Diamond Tools (Easy Raker mortar-removing tools) 01273 588174, www.premadiamondtools.co.uk
Stonehealth (stone cleaning) 01672 511515, www.stonehealth.com
Watco Wallseal from 01483 418418, www.watco.co.uk

BUILDING ORGANIZATIONS

Chartered Institute of Building (Chartered Building Company Scheme) – 01344 630700, www.cbcschemes.org.uk
National Federation of Builders – 020 7608 5150, www.builders.org.uk

CHIMNEYS & FIREPLACES
Chimney Balloon Company – 01252 319325
A good (American) source of advice on fireplace problems is Hearth News – www.hearth.com

CONSERVATION
Building Conservation Directory – 01747 871717, www.building conservation.com
Society for the Protection of Ancient Buildings (SPAB) 020 7377 1644, www.spab.org.uk

CONSTRUCTION LITERATURE
Building Regulations Approved Documents (£12.50 each) and the Building Regulations
    Explanatory Booklet (free) from 020 7256 7222, or they can be downloaded free from
    www.planningportal.gov.uk
Building Research Establishment publications can be ordered online from www.brebookshop.com or
    by phone from 01344 328038
Construction Industry Publications (supply the JCT Contract for the homeowner/occupier for
    £10.99 including p&p) – 0121 722 8200
Building Your Own Home, by David Snell, is published by Ebury Press

DAMPNESS
Cavity trays
Cavity Trays – 01935 474769, www.cavitytrays.com
Manthorpe Building Products – 01773 743555, www.manthorpe.co.uk
Drained-membrane systems
Platon from Triton Chemicals Ltd – 020 8310 3929
Newlath from John Newton & Co – 020 7237 1217

Dampness & timber surveyors
Abbey Independent Surveys – 01572 774398, email abbeyis@talk21.com
Dampness Diagnosis Consultancy – 020 8657 3750, www.dampnessdiagnosis.co.uk

ELECTRICS
Fire-safe downlighters – 01527 831794, www.firesafelighting.co.uk
Honda generators – 0845 2008000 or www.honda.co.uk, through which you can contact a local
    supplier
NICEIC – 020 7564 2323, www.niceic.org.uk
Tenmat (downlighter fire protectors) – 0161 872 2181, www.tenmat.com
Freestyle (loft-box downlighter covers) – 01707 662002
Trace Heating UK – 01473 280444, www.traceheatinguk.co.uk

FLOORING
Pioneer Woodfloors – 01799 541144
Victorian Wood Works – 020 8534 1000, www.victorianwoodworks.co.uk
Schluter Systems (uncoupling membrane for floor tiling) – 01530 813396, www.schluter.co.uk

GAS
CORGI – 0870 4012300, www.corgigassafety.com

HAZARDS
National Federation of Master Steeplejacks and Lightning Conductor Engineers – 0115 9558818
Proctor Group Ltd (radon gas protection) – 01250 872261

INSULATION
Celotex – 01473 822093, www.celotex.co.uk
Kingspan insulation – 0870 850 8555, www.insulation.kingspan.com
Kingspan Panels – 01352 716100, www.kingspanpanels.com
Marmox – 01634 862277, www.marmox.com

LOFT CONVERSIONS
The Loft Shop – 0870 6040404, www.loftshop.co.uk

PAINTING & DECORATING
British Coatings Federation (lead paint advice) – 01372 360660, www.coatings.org.uk
Dulux Select Decorator Service – 0840 7697668, www.duluxdecorator.co.uk
Stonehealth (paint removal) – 01672 511515, www.stonehealth.com
Strippers Paint Removers (chemical paint strippers) – 01787 371524,
        www.stripperspaintremovers.co.uk

PAVING
Geosynthetics – 01455 617139, www.geosyn.co.uk
Hauraton (grass paving blocks) – 01923 285601
Hoofmark Ltd (grass paving blocks and soakaways) – 0191 5845566

PESTICIDES
Pesticides victim support is provided by Pesticide Action Network – 020 7065 0905,
        www.pan-uk.org

PESTS
Bat Conservation Trust – 020 7627 2629, www.bats.org.uk (send SAE to 15 Cloisters House,
        8 Battersea Park Road, London SW8 4BG)
Woodland Properties (bird repellers/fly screens) – 01344 886459
Insectocutor (electric fly killers) – 0161 428 0622, www.insectocutor.co.uk
Jacobi Jayne (bird-care products) – 01227 714 314, www.birdcare.com

PLASTERING
Artex Ceiling Finish – 0115 945 6100 for stockists
British Gypsum – 0800 225225, www.britishgypsum.bpb.co.uk
Insulated Render and Cladding Association – 01428 654011, www.incaltd.org.uk
Fibrin polypropylene fibres – from Adfil, 01482 86377, www.adfil.co.uk

Lime Mortars & Plasters
The Building Limes Forum – School House, Rocks Road, Charlestown, Fife KY11 3EN; send SAE for a list of suppliers, enthusiasts and tradesmen
Tarmac Limelite – 01992 715155 for stockists

PLUMBING, HEATING & DRAINAGE
AB Sealants (coloured silicone sealant) – 01264 359984, www.absealantsltd.com
Ariston (under-sink heaters) – 01494 755600
Betz Dearborn (Sentinel central-heating additives) – 0151 4209595, www.betzdearborn.com
Brannan pipe thermometers – 01946 816600, www.brannan.co.uk
British Water publish ten free fact sheets on all aspects of domestic water treatment – www.britishwater.org or call 020 7957 4554
Cramer UK Ltd (Fugi sealant smoother) – 01934 713377
Creda (storage heaters) – 01733 456789, www.credaheating.co.uk
Ecosave (water leak detectors) – 01803 521415, www.ecosaveltd.com
Electroheat electric flow boilers – 01256 363417
Fernox Helpline – 01799 550811, www.fernox.com
Heatrae Sadia (under-sink heaters) – 01603 420111
Hoofmark (plastic soakaways) – 0191 5845566
The Institute of Plumbing – 01708 472791, www.plumbers.org.uk
Interflush (variable WC flush) – 0845 045 0276, www.interflush.co.uk
Jaeger Bath Resurfacing kit – from www.plumbworld.co.uk (click on 'Bathroom' and choose 'Bath Repairs and Resurfacing' from the drop-down menu)
Polypipe (Pacific dual-flush valve) – 01709 770990
Plumbworld (online discount plumbing and heating supplies), www.plumbworld.co.uk
Renubath (bath resurfacing) – 01285 656624, www.renubath.co.uk
RS Components (O-rings) – 01536 201201, http://rswww.com; (ask for the 'Plumbers' O-ring kit', Stock No. 4008288)
SureStop water switch – 0121 782 5777, www.surestop.co.uk

Boiler parts
Curzon Components – 0870 510 3030
FMT Ltd – 01245 357993
HRPC – 01282 834400 (parts availability can also be checked on their website www.hrpc.co.uk)
Thermagas – 01257 275080
Peter Porter Electronics Ltd – 01920 871711

Cast-iron guttering
J & JW Longbottom Ltd – 01484 682141
Saint-Gobain – 0115 930 5000, www.saint-gobain-pipelines.co.uk

RAINWATER HARVESTING/RECYCLING

Aquarius Water Engineering – 01704 878786
Tank Exchange – 01226 206157, www.thetankexchange.com

ROOFING

Flat Roofing Alliance – 01444 440027, www.fra.org.uk/home.html
National Council of Master Thatchers' Associations – 0700 0781909
National Federation of Roofing Contractors – 020 7436 0387, info@nfrc.co.uk
Ubbink (SimFix slate strap) – 01280 700211, www.ubbink.co.uk
Owens Slate Services (Jenny Twin slate fixings) – 01248 605575, www.owensslate.com

SOUNDPROOFING

Custom Audio Designs (acoustic quilt) – 01730 269572, www.customaudiodesigns.co.uk
Perko (door closers) – 0121 772 2303, www.samuelheath.com
Soundproofing leaflet available from BRE website, www.bre.co.uk (click on 'sound insulation'),
    or send an SAE to BRE Bookshop, Garston, Watford WD22 9XX

TREES

The Tree Care Company – 01234 376254, email treecare88@hotmail.com

WINDOWS & GLAZING

Crittall Windows – 01376 324106, www.crittallwindows.co.uk
Fein MultiMaster (for putty removal) – 01327 308 730
Fenestration Associates (window surveyors) – 01676 523583, www.fenestrationassociates.com
Glazpart (window vents) – 01295 264533
James Hetley (leaded-light repairs) – 020 7780 2344
Mighton (sash-window fittings, weatherproofing products – also network of independent sash-
    window restorers) – 0800 056 0471, www.mighton.co.uk
Reddiseals (dry-glazing system) – 01905 791876, www.reddiseals.co.uk
Renson (window vents) – 01622 685658
Sapa Building Systems (Monarch secondary-glazing system) – 01684 853500,
    www.sapabuildingsystems.co.uk
Selectaglaze (secondary glazing) – 01727 837271, www.selectaglaze.co.uk
Steel Window Association – 020 7637 3571, www.steel-window-association.co.uk
Window Film Company (heat-reflecting film) 01494 794477, www.windowfilm.co.uk
Window hardware suppliers are listed on the Glass & Glazing Federation website www.ggf.co.uk,
or try:
Groupco – 01733 234750, www.groupcoltd.co.uk
A1 hardware – 0870 464 0399, www.a1hardware.co.uk
Caldwell – 024 7643 7900, www.caldwell.co.uk

INDEX